EUROPEAN EMPLOYMENT
AND
INDUSTRIAL RELATIONS GLOSSARY:
FRANCE

EUROPEAN FOUNDATION
FOR THE IMPROVEMENT OF LIVING AND
WORKING CONDITIONS

EUROPEAN EMPLOYMENT
AND
INDUSTRIAL RELATIONS
GLOSSARY:
FRANCE

BY

ANTOINE LYON-CAEN

SWEET AND MAXWELL

OFFICE FOR OFFICIAL PUBLICATIONS OF
THE EUROPEAN COMMUNITIES

1993

Published in 1993 by
Sweet and Maxwell Limited of
South Quay Plaza, 183 Marsh Wall, London E14
and Office for Official Publications of the European Communities,
2 rue Mercier, L-2985 Luxembourg
Typeset by Printset and Design Ltd., Dublin
Printed and bound in Great Britain by
BPCC Hazell Books Ltd
Member of BPCC Ltd

British Cataloguing in Publication Data

A catalogue record for this book is
available from the British Library

Sweet and Maxwell, South Quay Plaza, London E14
ISBN 0421-44870-9 ✓

Office for Official Publications of the European Communities,
2 rue Mercier, L-2985 Luxembourg
ISBN 92-826-2604-0
Catalogue Number SY-70-91-005-EN-C

Publication No. EF/91/12/EN of the European Foundation for the
Improvement of Living and Working Conditions,
Loughlinstown House, Shankill, Co. Dublin, Ireland.

General Editor of the European Employment and Industrial
Relations Glossary Series

TIZIANO TREU
Professor of Labour Law
Catholic University of Milan

Revising Editor for the English language volumes

MICHAEL TERRY
Senior Lecturer in Industrial Relations
University of Warwick

Project Manager

HUBERT KRIEGER
Research Manager
European Foundation for the Improvement of Living
and Working Conditions, Dublin

The present volume is an edited translation of an original French text
prepared for the European Foundation for the Improvement of Living
and Working Conditions, Dublin

under the editorship of

ANTOINE LYON-CAEN
Professor of Labour Law
University of Paris X-Nanterre

with contributions from

ANTOINE JEAMMAUD
Professor of Labour Law
University of Saint-Etienne

MARTINE LE FRIANT
Senior Lecturer in Labour Law
University of Montpellier

MARTINA YANNAKOUROU
Researcher in Labour Law
University of Paris X-Nanterre

STRUCTURE OF THE WORK

There are companion volumes of the Glossary (both national and international editions) already published for:

Country	National Team Leader
Italy	Tiziano Treu Fondazione Regionale Pietro Seveso Milan
Spain	Antonio Valverde University of Seville
United Kingdom	Michael Terry University of Warwick
Belgium	Roger Blanpain Catholic University of Leuven
Germany	Manfred Weiss University of Frankfurt

Further volumes to appear will be:

Greece	Yota Kravaritou
Portugal	Mario Pinto
Ireland	Ferdinand von Prondzynski
Denmark	Ole Hasselbalch
Netherlands	Erik de Gier
Luxembourg	Guy Thomas

TABLE OF CONTENTS

USER'S GUIDE

This Guide is designed to help readers use the Glossary by providing an explanation of the contents and some of the conventions adopted.

This volume of the Glossary contains the following sections:

1. *List of Abbreviations*

This list comprises all the principal abbreviations used in the text.

2. *Foreword*

Written by the Director and Deputy Director of the European Foundation for the Improvement of Living and Working Conditions, the Foreword sets out the Foundation's aims in publishing this series of Glossaries.

3. *Preface*

A Preface to the series has been prepared by Professor Tiziano Treu in his capacity as Co-ordinating Editor. It serves as a background introduction to the Glossaries, explaining the origination of the material and the method of compilation and translation.

4. *List of Entries*

For cross-referencing purposes, the entries have been listed alphabetically in French and English, with their relevant number in the text.

5. *Introduction*

The introduction provides a commentary and analysis of national characteristics, and highlights particular features giving an historical perspective to the background information.

6. *Glossary*

All the main entries are numbered and appear in **BOLD** upper case. They are listed alphabetically in French with appropriate English translations.

Cross-references are indicated in the text by *e.g.* "see", "see also", etc., and also appear in **bold** upper and lower case.

Each letter of the alphabet starts on a new page. The running heads refer to the first and last main entry to appear on each double page.

7. *Tables*

A selection of tables is included showing employment trends and other statistical factors.

8. *Bibliography*

A selective Bibliography of suggested further reading and source material has been compiled by the editorial team for each volume. The titles of all references appear in French, but other details have been translated where appropriate.

9. *List of Useful Addresses*

The addresses of selected organizations and institutions are listed after the Bibliography, for easy reference.

10. *Index*

The Index comprises two parts: an alphabetical index in English, followed by an alphabetical index in French.

All Index entries refer to the numbers of the definitions in the Glossary text.

LIST OF ABBREVIATIONS

ANACT	National Agency for the Improvement of Working Conditions
ANPE	National Employment Agency
ASSEDIC	Association for Employment in Industry and Commerce (bodies responsible for managing local unemployment insurance funds)
BIT	International Labour Office (ILO)
CE	European Communities (EC)
CECA	European Coal and Steel Community (ECSC)
CEE	European Economic Community (EEC)
CES	European Trade Union Confederation (ETUC)
CFDT	French Democratic Confederation of Labour
CFTC	French Christian Workers' Confederation
CGC-CFE	General Confederation of Professional and Managerial Staff-French Confederation of Professional and Managerial Staff
CGPME	General Confederation of Small and Medium-Sized Enterprises
CGT	General Confederation of Labour
CGT-FO	General Confederation of Labour-"Force ouvrière"
CISL	International Confederation of Free Trade Unions (ICFTU)
CMT	World Confederation of Labour (WCL)
CNIL	National Commission for Information Technology and Civil Liberties
CNPF	National Council of French Employers
COTOREP	Commission technique d'orientation et de reclassement professionnel (technical commission responsible for the registration and assessment of disability)
FEN	Federated Education Union
FO	see CGT-FO
FSM	World Federation of Trade Unions (WFTU)
INSEE	National Statistical and Economic Research Institute
OIT	International Labour Organization (ILO)
ONI	National Immigration Office
OS	semi-skilled worker
OST	"scientific" work organization (*cf.* O&M, *i.e.* organization and methods)
SCOP	workers' and producers' co-operatives
SGF	statut général des fonctionnaires (service regulations for established civil servants)
SIDA	AIDS (acquired immune deficiency syndrome)
SIVP	stage d'initiation à la vie professionnelle (form of job-start scheme for young job-seekers)

SMIC	salaire minimum interprofessionnel de croissance (national minimum wage)
TUC	travail d'utilité collective (special employment scheme for young unemployed)
UIMM	Federation of Metal and Mining Industries (employers' organization)
UNEDIC	umbrella organization for all ASSEDICs *(q.v.)*
URSSAF	union de recouvrement des cotisations de sécurité sociale et d'allocations familiales (independent body in each département responsible for collecting social security and related contributions)
VRP	voyageur, représentant, placier (sales representatives with special status entitling them to the protection of labour law)

FOREWORD

The Foundation believes that social dialogue at international level should provide, for all those taking part in it, a better understanding of the different contexts — for example, legal frameworks and traditions — in which dialogue about employment and industrial relations takes place. An essential prerequisite for such improved understanding is an awareness of the precise meaning of the terms used to describe the features of industrial relations systems in each Member State of the Community. This series of glossaries sets out to provide clear explanations of terms and the context in which they are used.

The Foundation hopes that the series will be of value to a wide spectrum of users. Novices in the field of employment and industrial relations will welcome a guide to the working of the system in their own country, whilst experts will seek the distinguishing characteristics of systems operating in Member States other than their own. By providing both a national glossary for each Member State and also an "international" edition, the Foundation believes it is providing an important aid to international understanding in the complex field of employment and industrial relations.

Clive Purkiss   Eric Verborgh
Director   Deputy Director

European Foundation for the Improvement of Living and Working Conditions, Dublin.

PREFACE TO THE SERIES

The idea to write a series of glossaries dealing with the industrial relations, labour markets and employment laws of the 12 EC Member States emerged gradually, out of the experience of expert academics and practitioners aware of the need to systematize and codify experiences in this important area. The development of a social dialogue, and the ever-increasing need for debate and discussion between the Member States, employers and unions, spurred by the prospect of full European economic integration in 1992, have given a fresh impetus to the need for clarity and mutual understanding in this vital subject. But these glossaries are not intended only as resources for such formal settings. Throughout Europe there are thousands of potential users of the glossaries: national and international administrators, academics and researchers, trade unionists and managers, and specialised journalists, among others. All these groups will increasingly need to communicate across borders in different languages, about a whole range of industrial relations-related topics. For them too, the need for greater understanding and clarity has become more urgent. The glossaries should become the standard tools for persons involved in meetings, formal and informal, of a whole range of interested economic and social actors.

The European Foundation for the Improvement of Living and Working Conditions immediately recognized the importance and usefulness of the proposal to compile a series of glossaries, and provided the funding for the first three: those dealing with Italy, Spain and the United Kingdom. Later, it was to agree to provide additional funding for the remaining nine states, with Belgium, the Federal Republic of Germany and France being the next three. It was agreed that the Foundation should provide resources for the translation of all the glossaries into English, for publication as a uniform series. It is now proposed to make the glossaries also available in electronic database form, which will greatly enhance the speed and flexibility with which they may be used. The glossaries for all countries are also available in their original languages, published domestically. In some cases these "domestic" glossaries are larger and longer than the English translations, since they have been designed as domestic as well as international sources of reference, and may contain material of little immediate relevance to the foreign reader.

Professor Tiziano Treu was appointed international co-ordinator, and he, in turn, worked to set up teams of experts in the first three countries, consisting of experts in all the disciplines involved in industrial relations, each team under its own co-ordinator. These teams were under instructions to provide comparable glossaries, covering the same range of topics. The intention was to produce volumes that would provide both definitions of several hundred terms of particular importance, and an insight into their relevance to the country concerned. The combined experience of all those involved in the project (academics, practitioners and others) was that simple translations of terms were insufficient, since they fail fully to communicate the substantive importance of the institutions and processes described. The products are designed to be of direct use both to the practitioner and to the academic student of the subject, so the glossaries have to be both technically correct and informed by relevant policy debate. The glossaries are intended to serve the practical needs of a diverse readership, of varying levels of knowledge and need, and to serve as an immediate reference or translation source or a starting-point for in-depth research. The audience will be a broad and diverse one; our researches have confirmed that the glossaries will be of interest to national, European and other international readers, given the worldwide interest currently expressed in European industrial relations.

Inevitably, we have had to be selective in our choice of terms. It was not the intention to produce an encyclopedia, but rather an annotated guide to key issues and concepts. In order to achieve this we sought both a degree of commonality in the terms to be covered (in order to ensure above all that the key concepts were dealt with in all the volumes) and a degree of differentiation, reflecting the national idiosyncracies that remain important aspects of the European scene. Our descriptions have had to be less than encyclopedic; the entries do not provide all the detail with regard to specific pieces of legislation, for example. Readers who need further precision will be able to make use of the reference works cited in the concluding bibliographies.

The glossaries all share the same format. An introductory essay covers the key features of the national system: the political-economic environment, the key actors, the role of law, and the current state of labour relations. This is meant to help the average user of the glossary (it is not particularly designed for a specialist audience) and it has been written in such a way as to be understandable to an international audience, and therefore to be as clear and "candid" as possible. The main body of entries follows, and the volumes conclude with sets of tables showing trends in labour markets, collective bargaining coverage, unionisation and industrial conflict, with a brief guide to further reading. Those texts which have been translated into English also contain an additional index in the original language.

Certain conventions have been adopted in the translation. Wherever possible we have used English translations whose meaning is clear and which involve no specialised "jargon". But there are two other cases. First, where no English term in common usage exists and we have created our own translation. Here we have put the English term into double inverted commas, to indicate that it is not common English usage, but is simply an accurate translation. Second, in a few cases we have been unable to find a translation of less than a sentence for particular terms. Here we have left the term in the original language, and readers in English will need to read the entry to discover its meaning.

The process of writing and translating these glossaries has convinced the participants of the usefulness of the exercise. The European

Foundation has, in its usual way, sought the views of the social partners in the countries concerned, and their response has also been enthusiastic. The exercise has also revealed that beneath the superficial similarities of some terms there may lie significant differences of meaning and interpretation, but that, deeper still, lie important patterns of similarity and convergence and, above all, a keen interest in the consequences of an increasingly integrated and united Europe. We are confident that we have produced an instrument that will help forge a clearer understanding and, in its turn, a greater co-operation, in this vital area of social activity.

Acknowledgements

Many people have co-operated closely in the preparation of this series. This co-operation has been under the general direction of Hubert Krieger, the Foundation's manager for the project, and Tiziano Treu, the "rapporteur" who has acted as general editor.

The series is based on the dedicated efforts of the national teams, who have had the task of reducing formidable amounts of material to manageable proportions.

The task of editing the international (English-language) version has been particularly onerous. It is only fitting to acknowledge the exceptional contributions of Rita Inston, the reviser (of Cave Translations Ltd.) and of Michael Terry (Warwick University) who, in addition to having the main responsibility for the United Kingdom volume, has given invaluable advice on explanations in English of concepts peculiar to individual Member States. Professor Brian Napier (Queen Mary & Westfield College, University of London) provided many helpful suggestions in the editing of the volume for France.

With regard to general aspects of publication, the Foundation is grateful for the co-operation of the publishers and for advice from the Office for Official Publications of the European Communities, for the services of the Commission and those of Solon Consultants (UK).

Throughout the project there has been close co-operation between the research, information and translation services of the Foundation.

Professor Tiziano Treu

NUMBERED ALPHABETICAL LIST OF ENTRIES IN FRENCH

FRENCH	ENGLISH
1. absence	absence from work
2. absentéisme	absenteeism
3. accident de trajet	accident *en route*
4. accident du travail	accident at work
5. accord-cadre	framework agreement
6. accord collectif	collective agreement
7. accord de branche	industry-wide agreement
8. accord de concession	concession agreement
9. accord d'entreprise	company-level agreement
10. accord de groupe	group agreement
11. accord de méthode	framework agreement
12. accord de modulation	adjustable hours agreement
13. accord d'orientation	framework agreement
14. accord de participation	profit-sharing agreement
15. accord dérogatoire	derogation agreement
16. accord "donnant-donnant"	"give-and-take" agreement
17. accord "gagnant-gagnant"	"win-win" agreement
18. accord interprofessionnel	general multi-industry agreement
19. acompte	payment on account
20. acteurs sociaux	social actors
21. action collective	collective action/industrial action
22. action en justice	legal action
23. action sanitaire et sociale	health and social services provision
24. action syndicale en justice	institution of legal proceedings by trade unions
25. actionnariat ouvrier	employee share ownership
26. activités sociales et culturelles	company welfare and cultural facilities
27. activités syndicales	trade union activities
28. adhésion	union/employers' organization membership
29. administrateur salarié	worker member of the board
30. administration publique	public administration
31. administration du travail	labour administration
32. affichage	display of notices
33. affiliation	registered membership
34. âge	age
35. Agence nationale pour l'amélioration des conditions de travail	National Agency for the Improvement of Working Conditions
36. Agence nationale pour l'emploi	National Employment Agency
37. agent commercial	commercial agent
38. agent de maîtrise	supervisor
39. agents publics	public employees
40. agrément	approval
41. agriculture	agriculture
42. aide à l'emploi	employment support
43. aide publique	government aid
44. aide sociale	social assistance
45. alerte	notification
46. allocation de chômage	unemployment benefit
47. allocation d'insertion	work programme allowance
48. allocation de solidarité	guarantee supplementary benefit

49.	allocations familiales	family allowances
50.	alternance	combined training and work
51.	amende	fine
52.	ANACT	ANACT
53.	ancienneté	length of service
54.	annualisation (du temps de travail)	annualization of working hours
55.	ANPE	ANPE
56.	apprentissage	apprenticeship
57.	arbitrage	arbitration
58.	artisanat	self-employed craft sector
59.	artiste	performing artiste
60.	ASSEDIC	ASSEDIC
61.	assemblée (de travailleurs)	mass meeting
62.	assistance	assistance
63.	assistance sociale	public assistance
64.	assistante sociale	welfare worker
65.	association (liberté d')	freedom of association
66.	association capital-travail	philosophy of capital-labour co-operation
67.	association intermédiaire	intermediary association
68.	association professionnelle	"association professionnelle"
69.	association syndicale	syndicate
70.	assurance garantie des salaires	wage guarantee insurance
71.	assurances sociales	social insurance
72.	astreinte	stand-by
73.	audit social	personnel audit
74.	augmentation au mérite	merit pay increase
75.	augmentation de salaire	pay increase
76.	auteur	author
77.	autocommutateur	automatic telephone log
78.	autogestion	(workers') self-management
79.	automatisation	automation
80.	automatisme	automatic effect
81.	autonomie collective	collective autonomy
82.	autoréglementation	self-regulation of strike action
83.	autorisation	authorization
84.	autorisation d'embauche	authorization for hiring
85.	autorisation de licenciement	authorization for dismissal
86.	autorisation de travail	work permit
87.	auxiliaire	auxiliary public employee
88.	avance	advance
89.	avancement	promotion (at work)
90.	avantages acquis	acquired rights
91.	avantages en nature	payments in kind
92.	avantages sociaux	social rights
93.	avenant	amendment
94.	avertissement	warning
95.	badge électronique	electronic identity card
96.	base	rank and file
97.	bilan social	social balance sheet
98.	blâme	reprimand
99.	blocage (salarial)	pay freeze
100.	bonne foi	good faith
101.	bourse du travail	Labour Centre
102.	boycott	boycott
103.	branche	branch of economic activity
104.	bulletin de paie	itemized pay statement
105.	bureau de conciliation	conciliation board

106.	bureau de placement	job placement agency
107.	cadence	pace of work
108.	cadre	professional or managerial employee
109.	cadre supérieur	senior executive
110.	cadre syndical	full-time official
111.	caisse de congés payés	holiday insurance fund
112.	caisse de sécurité sociale	social security office
113.	carrière	career
114.	catégorie professionnelle	occupational category
115.	cause réelle et sérieuse	genuine and serious cause
116.	cautionnement	guarantee deposit
117.	célibat (clause de)	marriage clause
118.	centrale	central trade union organization
119.	centralisation	centralization
120.	centralisme	centralism
121.	cercle de qualité	quality circle
122.	certificat de travail	certificate of employment
123.	cessation	end of the contract of employment
124.	cession d'entreprise	change of ownership or control
125.	CFDT	CFDT
126.	CFTC	CFTC
127.	CGC-CFE	CGC-CFE
128.	CGPME	CGPME
129.	CGT	CGT
130.	CGT-FO	CGT-FO
131.	champ d'application	scope of application
132.	changement d'employeur	change of employer
133.	chantier	construction site
134.	charge du travail	workload
135.	charges sociales	employment-related costs
136.	Charte d'Amiens	Charter of Amiens
137.	chef d'entreprise	head of an enterprise
138.	chômage	unemployment
139.	chômage intempéries	bad-weather unemployment insurance scheme
140.	chômage partiel	partial unemployment
141.	chômage technique	layoff
142.	citoyenneté	retention of civil liberties in employment
143.	classification	job classification
144.	clause	clause
145.	clause d'exclusivité	sole-employment clause
146.	clause de maintien des avantages acquis	acquired rights clause
147.	clause de paix sociale	no-strike clause
148.	clause de sécurité syndicale	union membership (closed shop) clause
149.	CNPF	CNPF
150.	coalition	collective industrial organization
151.	Code du travail	Labour Code
152.	cogestion	co-determination
153.	comité d'entreprise	works council
154.	comité d'établissement	establishment-level works council
155.	comité de grève	strike committee
156.	comité de groupe	group-level works council
157.	comité d'hygiène, de sécurité et des conditions de travail	workplace health and safety committee
158.	Comité supérieur de l'emploi	Higher Committee on Employment
159.	Comité technique paritaire	Joint Technical Committee
160.	commandement	notice of compliance

317.	éducation permanente	lifelong education
318.	effectif	workforce
319.	efficacité juridique	legal force
320.	égalitarisme	egalitarianism
321.	égalité entre les femmes et les hommes	equality between men and women
322.	élection	election
323.	élections professionnelles	workplace-level elections
324.	embauche	hiring
325.	emploi	employment/job
326.	employé	white-collar worker
327.	employé de maison	domestic worker
328.	employeur	employer
329.	encadrement	professional and managerial staff
330.	enfants (travail des)	child employment
331.	enrichissement des tâches	job enrichment
332.	entrave	interference
333.	entreprise	enterprise
334.	entreprise artisanale	craft trades enterprise
335.	entreprise de tendance	ideologically oriented enterprise
336.	entreprise familiale	family enterprise
337.	entreprise intermédiaire	intermediary enterprise
338.	entreprise multinationale	multinational corporation
339.	entreprise publique	public enterprise
340.	équipe autonome	autonomous work team
341.	équipe de suppléance	relief (weekend) shift
342.	équipes successives	shifts
343.	équivalence	equivalence
344.	*erga omnes*	*erga omnes*
345.	ergonomie	ergonomics
346.	essai	test/probation
347.	établissement	establishment
348.	État minimum	minimalist state
349.	étranger	alien
350.	évaluation (du personnel)	staff appraisal
351.	expert	expert
352.	expression	expression
353.	expulsion	deportation/eviction
354.	extension	extension of collective agreements
355.	extériorisation (de l'emploi)	externalization of employment
356.	faillite	bankruptcy
357.	faute	misconduct/fault
358.	faveur pour le salarié	favourability to the employee
359.	Fédération de l'éducation nationale	Federated Education Union
360.	fédération patronale	employers' federation
361.	fédération syndicale	trade union federation
362.	femmes	women
363.	FEN	FEN
364.	fermeture d'établissement	closure of establishments
365.	fête	official holiday
366.	fidélité	loyalty
367.	filiale	subsidiary
368.	fiscalisation	tax funding of social benefits
369.	flexibilité	flexibility
370.	flexibilité du temps de travail	flexibility of working time
371.	flexibilité du travail	labour flexibility
372.	FO	FO
373.	fonction	function

374.	fonction publique	civil service
375.	fonctionnaire	established civil servant
376.	Fonds d'action sociale	Social Action Fund
377.	fonds d'assurance formation	training insurance fund
378.	Fonds national de l'emploi	National Employment Fund
379.	fonds salariaux	employee investment funds
380.	force du travail	labour power
381.	force majeure	*force majeure*
382.	Force ouvrière	"Force ouvrière"
383.	fordisme	Fordism
384.	formalisme (contractuel)	formalization of employment contracts
385.	formation professionnelle continue	further vocational training
386.	formation syndicale	training in union affairs
387.	formes d'action	forms of industrial action
388.	forme d'emploi	form of employment
389.	fraction (syndicale)	union faction
390.	fragmentation	fragmentation (of the labour market)
391.	frais professionnels	expenses
392.	franchisage	franchising
393.	fusion de sociétés	company merger
394.	fusion de syndicats	union merger/amalgamation
395.	garantie d'emploi	guarantee of employment
396.	garantie des salaires	guarantee of pay
397.	gérant	manager (of a private company)/agent
398.	gestion du personnel	management of personnel
399.	gestion prévisionnelle (des emplois et des compétences)	human resource planning
400.	gestion des ressources humaines	human resource management
401.	gratification	discretionary bonus
402.	grève	strike
403.	grève bouchon	selective strike
404.	grève d'avertissement	token strike
405.	grève du zèle	work-to-rule
406.	grève générale	general strike
407.	grève perlée	go-slow
408.	grève politique	political strike
409.	grève sauvage	unofficial strike
410.	grève thrombose	selective strike
411.	grève tournante	rotating strike
412.	grossesse	pregnancy
413.	groupe autonome	autonomous work group
414.	groupe de sociétés	group of companies
415.	groupe semi-autonome	semi-autonomous work group
416.	groupement d'employeurs	employers' pool
417.	groupement syndical	trade union group(ing)
418.	handicapé	disabled person
419.	harcèlement (sexuel)	sexual harassment
420.	heures de délégation	time-off rights
421.	heures supplémentaires	overtime
422.	hiérarchie	hierarchy
423.	horaire du travail	scheduling of working hours
424.	horaire flexible	flexible working hours
425.	horaire individualisé	individualized working hours
426.	hygiène du travail	occupational health
427.	immigration	immigration
428.	implantation syndicale	union presence in the enterprise
429.	inaptitude physique	physical unfitness

430.	inaptitude professionnelle	incompetence
431.	incitation	incentive
432.	indemnité	compensation
433.	indemnité de chômage	unemployment benefit
434.	indemnité de clientèle	goodwill indemnity
435.	indemnité de licenciement	compensation for dismissal/severance pay
436.	indemnité de maladie	sick pay
437.	indemnité de préavis	compensation in lieu of notice
438.	indemnités de rupture	entitlements payable on termination of the employment contract
439.	indépendant	self-employed person
440.	indérogabilité	''inderogability''
441.	indexation	index-linking/indexation
442.	indice du coût de la vie	cost-of-living index
443.	individualisation	individualization
444.	industrie	industry
445.	information	information
446.	information nominative	personal data
447.	information syndicale	union information
448.	informatique	information technology
449.	informel	informal
450.	infraction	offence/infringement
451.	ingénieur	engineer
452.	insaisissabilité	immunity from seizure/immunity from attachment
453.	insertion professionnelle	absorption into employment
454.	inspecteur du travail	labour inspector
455.	inspection du travail	Labour Inspectorate
456.	intempéries	bad weather
457.	intéressement	pay related to company performance
458.	intérêt collectif (de la profession)	collective interest (of an occupational group)
459.	intérim	temporary-employment agency work
460.	intermédiaire	intermediary
461.	invalidité	disability
462.	invention (de salarié)	inventions by employees
463.	jeune travailleur	young worker
464.	journée	working day
465.	jours fériés	public holidays
466.	juridification	juridification
467.	jurisprudence	case law
468.	label syndical	trade union label
469.	législation industrielle	industrial legislation
470.	législation promotionnelle	legislative promotion of collective bargaining
471.	législation sociale	social legislation
472.	légitimité	legitimacy
473.	liberté des salaires	freedom to negotiate pay
474.	liberté du travail	freedom of labour
475.	liberté individuelle	freedom of the individual
476.	liberté syndicale	freedom of collective industrial organization
477.	licenciement	dismissal
478.	licenciement pour motif économique	redundancy
479.	licenciement pour motif individuel	dismissal for reasons relating to the individual
480.	limite d'âge	age limit

481.	liquidation	settlement/liquidation
482.	litige du travail	labour dispute at law
483.	livre de paie	paybook
484.	local syndical	union room
485.	lock-out	lock-out
486.	logement du salarié	housing for employees
487.	logiciel	software
488.	loi	law/statute
489.	loyauté	loyalty
490.	maladie	illness
491.	maladie professionnelle	occupational illness
492.	manifestation	demonstration
493.	marchandage	labour-only subcontracting
494.	marché du travail	labour market
495.	mariage	marriage
496.	marin	seafarer
497.	marque syndicale	trade union mark
498.	maternité	maternity
499.	médecine du travail	company medical service
500.	médiation	mediation
501.	mensualisation	monthly pay system
502.	métier	occupation
503.	microconflictualité	"microconflict" (level of)
504.	militaire	military
505.	mineur	minor
506.	mines	mines
507.	minimum garanti	guaranteed minimum wage
508.	Ministère du travail	Ministry of Labour
509.	mise à disposition	provision of labour
510.	mise à l'index	blacklisting
511.	mixité	equality in employment
512.	mobilité du travail	labour mobility
513.	modération salariale	pay restraint
514.	modernisation	modernization
515.	modification	variation of the contract of employment
516.	mouvement ouvrier	labour movement
517.	mouvement syndical	trade union movement
518.	mutation	job move
519.	mutilés	disabled ex-servicemen
520.	mutualité	mutual insurance
521.	nationalisation	nationalization
522.	négociation articulée	articulated bargaining
523.	négociation collective	collective bargaining
524.	négociation de concession	concession bargaining
525.	négociation décentralisée	decentralized bargaining
526.	négociation d'entreprise	company-level bargaining
527.	négociation distributive	distributive bargaining/zero-sum bargaining
528.	négociation intégrative	integrative bargaining/positive-sum bargaining
529.	négociation interprofessionnelle	national multi-industry bargaining
530.	néocorporatisme	neo-corporatism
531.	néolibéralisme	neo-liberalism
532.	niveau de négociation	bargaining level
533.	niveau des salaires	wage level
534.	nomenclature	nomenclature
535.	non-concurrence	restraint on competition

536.	non-titulaire	non-established public employee
537.	note de service	service memorandum
538.	nullité	nullity
539.	obligation de négocier	duty to bargain
540.	obstruction	obstruction
541.	occupation des lieux de travail	sit-in/occupation of the workplace
542.	oeuvres sociales	company welfare facilities
543.	Office des migrations internationales	International Migration Office
544.	offre d'emploi	job vacancy
545.	opposition (droit d')	right of objection
546.	ordonnance	ordinance/order
547.	ordre public	public policy/law and order
548.	organigramme	organization chart
549.	organisation d'employeurs	employers' organization
550.	organisation du travail	work organization
551.	organisation patronale	employers' organization
552.	organisation syndicale	trade union organization
553.	orientation professionnelle	vocational guidance
554.	OS	OS
555.	ouvrier	manual worker
556.	ouvrier agricole	agricultural worker
557.	ouvrier professionnel	skilled worker
558.	ouvrier qualifié	skilled worker
559.	ouvrier spécialisé	semi-skilled worker
560.	paie	payment
561.	panier	meals allowance
562.	paritarisme	parity principle
563.	parité (des armes)	balance of bargaining power
564.	partage de l'emloi	work sharing
565.	partenaires sociaux	social partners
566.	participation	participation/workers' participation/shareholding
567.	participation au capital	shareholding (by employees)
568.	participation aux organes	participation in company organs
569.	participation aux résultats	profit-sharing
570.	paternalisme	paternalism
571.	patron	"patron"
572.	patronage	sponsorship/patronage
573.	patronat	"patronat"
574.	pause	break
575.	pension	pension
576.	période d'essai	probationary period
577.	permanent syndical	union employee
578.	personnalité juridique	legal personality
579.	personnel	personnel/staff
580.	piquet de grève	picket
581.	placement	job placement
582.	plafond	ceiling/limit
583.	plan d'entreprise	business plan
584.	plan d'épargne d'entreprise	company savings scheme
585.	plan de formation	training plan
586.	plan social	redundancy programme
587.	plate-forme	"platform"
588.	pluralisme normatif	multiplicity of sources of law
589.	pluralisme syndical	trade union pluralism
590.	politique dans l'entreprise	politics within the enterprise
591.	politique de l'emploi	employment policy

592.	poste	post/job
593.	pourboire	tip/gratuity
594.	pouvoir de direction	employer's managerial authority
595.	pouvoir disciplinaire	disciplinary power
596.	pouvoir du chef d'entreprise	managerial prerogative
597.	pouvoir syndical	union power
598.	préavis	notice
599.	préavis (grève)	notice of strike
600.	précarité	precariousness
601.	préposé	agent and servant
602.	préretraite	early retirement
603.	prérogatives patronales	managerial prerogative
604.	prescription	limitation of actions
605.	prestation de services	provision of services
606.	prestation sociale	social benefit
607.	prêt de main-d'oeuvre	hiring-out of labour
608.	preuve	proof
609.	prévention (des conflits)	dispute prevention
610.	prévoyance sociale	social welfare
611.	prime	bonus
612.	prime anti-grève	anti-strike bonus
613.	principe	principle
614.	principe constitutionnel	constitutional principle
615.	privatisation	privatization
616.	privilège	preferential claim
617.	procédure	procedure
618.	procédure d'alerte	notification procedure
619.	procédure de négociation	bargaining procedure
620.	procès-verbal de conciliation	minute of conciliation
621.	procès-verbal de désaccord	minute of failure to agree
622.	procès-verbal de fin de conflit	minute of dispute settlement
623.	productivité	productivity
624.	profession	profession/occupation
625.	professionnalité	professional competence and status
626.	programmation	programming
627.	projet d'entreprise	enterprise plan
628.	promotion	promotion
629.	prorata	*pro rata*
630.	protection sociale	social protection
631.	protocole (d'accord)	protocol of agreement
632.	prud'homme	Industrial Tribunal member
633.	qualification	skill/skill level/qualification
634.	qualité	quality
635.	qualité de la vie	quality of life
636.	questionnaire	questionnaire/application form
637.	quota	quota
638.	rapport (officiel)	official report
639.	rapport de travail	employment relationship
640.	ratification	ratification
641.	recherche d'emploi	job-searching
642.	réclamation	grievance
643.	reclassement	redeployment
644.	recommandation (médiation)	mediation recommendation
645.	recommandation salariale	pay recommendation
646.	reconduction	renewal (of contract)
647.	reconversion	re-training
648.	recours	appeal/remedy

649.	recrutement	recruitment/hiring
650.	reçu pour solde de tout compte	receipt acknowledging full settlement
651.	récupération	make-up
652.	redressement judiciaire	compulsory administration
653.	réduction (durée du travail)	reduction of working hours
654.	référé	procedure in chambers
655.	référendum	ballot
656.	régime complémentaire (de retraite)	supplementary pension scheme
657.	régime de solidarité	guarantee supplementary scheme
658.	règlement	Regulation
659.	règlement des conflits	dispute settlement
660.	règlement intérieur	works rules
661.	réglementation	regulation(s)
662.	régulation	regulation
663.	réintégration	reinstatement
664.	relation(s) de travail	employment relationship/labour relations
665.	relations humaines	human relations
666.	relations industrielles	industrial relations
667.	relations professionnelles	labour relations
668.	relations sociales	social relations (industrial relations)
669.	renonciation	waiver
670.	répartition	distribution
671.	répartition (du temps de travail)	pattern of working time
672.	repos	rest
673.	repos compensateur	time off in lieu
674.	repos dominical	Sunday rest
675.	repos hebdomadaire	weekly rest day
676.	représentant de commerce	sales representative
677.	représentants du personnel	employee representatives
678.	représentant syndical	union representative on the works council
679.	représentation du personnel	employee representation
680.	représentativité	representativeness
681.	répression des comportements anti-syndicaux	repression of anti-union behaviour
682.	répression syndicale	union repression
683.	réprimande	reprimand
684.	réquisition	requisition/conscription for public services
685.	réserve de participation	profit-sharing reserve
686.	résiliation	termination (by the parties)
687.	résolution (contrat)	voidance of contract (for non-performance)
688.	résolution (vie syndicale)	resolution (in union affairs)
689.	responsabilité de l'employeur	employer liability
690.	responsabilité du salarié	employee liability
691.	responsabilité en cas de grève	liability in the event of a strike
692.	restructuration	restructuring
693.	retenue (sur salaire)	deduction from pay
694.	retrait	withholding of labour
695.	retraite	retirement
696.	réunion syndicale	union meeting
697.	revendication	claim/demand
698.	revenu minimum	minimum income
699.	révision (contrat)	revision (of the contract of employment)
700.	révision (convention collective)	revision (of collective agreements)
701.	risque de l'entreprise	entrepreneurial risk
702.	risque professionnel	occupational risk/occupational hazard
703.	robotique (industriel)	industrial robotics
704.	rotation	labour turnover

705.	roulement	rotation
706.	rupture (contrat)	termination of the contract of employment
707.	rupture (négociation collective)	breaking-off of negotiations
708.	rythme	work rate
709.	sabotage	sabotage
710.	sage	specialist
711.	saisie	seizure/attachment
712.	salaire	pay/wage
713.	salaire de substitution	"substitute pay"
714.	salaire direct et indirect	direct and indirect pay
715.	salaire garanti	minimum wage (guaranteed)
716.	salaire monétaire ou en nature	pay in money or in kind
717.	salarié	employee
718.	sanction	sanction/penalty/remedy
719.	sanction civile	civil sanction
720.	sanction disciplinaire	disciplinary sanction
721.	sanction pénale	penal sanction
722.	scrutin	poll/voting
723.	secrétaire (comité d'entreprise)	secretary of the works council
724.	secteur économique	economic sector
725.	secteur public	public sector
726.	section syndicale	workplace branch
727.	sécurité du travail	safety at work
728.	sécurité sociale	social security
729.	segmentation	segmentation (of the labour market)
730.	semaine comprimée	compressed working week
731.	sentence	award
732.	séquestration	false imprisonment
733.	service fait	service rendered
734.	service minimum	minimum service
735.	service national	national service
736.	service public	public service
737.	seuil	threshold
738.	SIDA	AIDS
739.	SMIC	SMIC
740.	sociologie du travail	sociology of work
741.	solidarité	solidarity
742.	sous-entreprise	subcontract (external)
743.	sous-traitance	subcontract (internal)
744.	stabilité de l'emploi	job security
745.	stage	training scheme/period of training
746.	stagiaire	trainee
747.	statut	service regulations/standing rules
748.	statut (des syndicats)	union rules
749.	structure conventionnelle	bargaining structure
750.	structure des salaires	pay/wage structure
751.	structure syndicale	union structure
752.	subordination	"subordination"
753.	sujets collectifs	social actors
754.	suspension (contrat)	suspension of the contract of employment
755.	syndicalisation	unionization
756.	syndicat	trade union/collective industrial organization/employers' organization
757.	syndicat autonome	autonomous union
758.	syndicat d'entreprise	company union
759.	syndicat d'entreprises	employers' organization
760.	syndicat horizontal	horizontal union

761.	syndicat indépendant	independent union
762.	syndicat national	national union
763.	syndicat régional	regional union
764.	syndicat territorial	territorial union
765.	syndicat vertical	vertical union
766.	tarif	tariff/collectively agreed wage
767.	taux de syndicalisation	union density
768.	taxe	levy/tax
769.	taylorisme	Taylorism
770.	technologie	technology
771.	télétravail	telework
772.	temporaire	temporary public employee
773.	terme	expiry date
774.	tolérance	tolerance
775.	tract (syndical)	union pamphlet
776.	traitement (égalité de)	equal treatment
777.	transaction	settlement by compromise
778.	transfert d'entreprise	transfer of undertaking
779.	transfert de salarié	change of employer through legal transfer
780.	travail	work/labour/employment
781.	travail à distance	remote working
782.	travail à domicile	homeworking
783.	travail à temps partiel	part-time work
784.	travail autonome	self-employment
785.	travail clandestin	clandestine employment
786.	travail de nuit	night work
787.	travail d'intérêt général	community service
788.	travail d'utilité collective	youth employment scheme
789.	travail en équipes successives	shiftwork
790.	travail en groupe	group work/team-based work
791.	travail familial	work performed within the family
792.	travail féminin	female employment/employment of women
793.	travail intellectuel	"intellectual work"/non-manual work
794.	travail intermittent	intermittent work
795.	travail manuel	manual work
796.	travail noir (travail au noir)	undeclared employment
797.	travail occasionnel	casual work
798.	travail posté	shiftwork
799.	travail précaire	precarious employment
800.	travail saisonnier	seasonal work
801.	travail subordonné	work under an employment contract
802.	travail temporaire	temporary-employment agency work
803.	travailleur étranger	foreign worker
804.	tripartisme	tripartism
805.	tutelle	guardianship/supervision/protection
806.	UNEDIC	UNEDIC
807.	union	area union/area employers' organization
808.	unité de production	work/production unit
809.	unité économique et sociale	unit of economic and employee interest
810.	unité syndicale	union unity
811.	urgence	emergency/urgency
812.	usage	custom
813.	vacataire	temporary public employee
814.	veto	veto
815.	vie privée	private life of the employee
816.	vieillesse	old age
817.	visite médicale	medical examination

818.	voie de fait	blatantly unlawful conduct
819.	vol	theft
820.	vote	vote/voting

NUMBERED ALPHABETICAL LIST OF ENTRIES IN ENGLISH

ENGLISH		FRENCH
absence from work	1.	absence
absenteeism	2.	absentéisme
absorption into employment	453.	insertion professionnelle
accident at work	4.	accident du travail
accident *en route*	3.	accident de trajet
acquired rights	90.	avantages acquis
acquired rights	310.	droits acquis
acquired rights clause	146.	clause de maintien des avantages acquis
adjustable hours agreement	12.	accord de modulation
administrative law	301.	droit administratif
adoption leave	186.	congé d'adoption
advance	88.	avance
age	34.	âge
age limit	480.	limite d'âge
agent and servant	601.	préposé
agricultural worker	556.	ouvrier agricole
agriculture	41.	agriculture
AIDS	738.	SIDA
alien	349.	étranger
amendment	93.	avenant
ANACT	52.	ANACT
annual holiday	201.	congés payés
annualization of working hours	54.	annualisation (du temps de travail)
ANPE	55.	ANPE
anti-strike bonus	612.	prime anti-grève
anti-union behaviour	169.	comportement antisyndical
appeal/remedy	648.	recours
apprenticeship	56.	apprentissage
approval	40.	agrément
arbitration	57.	arbitrage
area union/area employers' organization	807.	union
articulated bargaining	522.	négociation articulée
ASSEDIC	60.	ASSEDIC
assistance	62.	assistance
"association professionnelle"	68.	association professionnelle
author	76.	auteur
authorization	83.	autorisation
authorization for dismissal	85.	autorisation de licenciement
authorization for hiring	84.	autorisation d'embauche
automatic effect	80.	automatisme
automatic telephone log	77.	autocommutateur
automation	79.	automatisation
autonomous union	757.	syndicat autonome
autonomous work group	413.	groupe autonome
autonomous work team	340.	équipe autonome
auxiliary public employee	87.	auxiliaire
award	731.	sentence
bad weather	456.	intempéries
bad-weather unemployment insurance scheme	139.	chômage intempéries

xl

xlii

1

lii

INTRODUCTION

1.   The context

1.1   Certain ways of thinking and forms of functioning still current
in France today are closely linked to the economic and social
regulation which was a salient feature of the period 1945-1970.
A brief outline of its characteristics is therefore necessary.

1.2   Despite substantial disparities in pay, the period was marked
by a practical indexation of nominal rates of pay to the consumer
price index and an increase in purchasing power more or less
in step with gains in productivity. These trends were due both
to the pattern of growth in the economy and to the combined
effect of rules on pay determination and the calculation of social
benefits. In particular, the introduction of a national minimum
wage (the "salaire minimum interprofessionnel garanti" or
SMIG, replaced in 1970 by the SMIC formula), the
predominance of industry-wide agreements and the drive for
standard conditions pursued by the trade union confederations
meant that a share in the benefits of economic progress was
widely distributed.

1.3   Although not exclusive, a model of employment became widely
established which is nowadays referred to as the conventional
or typical model. Full-time employment under a contract of
indefinite duration with a single employer, providing employee
and family with their main income, became the typical pattern.
Certainly, it was in reference to this model that the rules on
social protection were formulated, that the collective bargaining
system was conceived and that the unions established their
structures and strategies. In short, French trade unionism was,
it has been said, centred around the semi-skilled worker in
manufacturing and processing industry.

1.4   Lastly, the feature to be emphasized is the cardinal role of the
State. In regulating and stimulating economic activity through
budget policy, monetary policy and policy on change, and
shaping pay policy through the choices made in the civil service
and public sector, the national minimum wage mechanism and
the social protection system, the State was the prime mover of
regulation in the post-war period. This essential role went hand
in hand with the historical importance of statutory regulation
of employment relations extending back to the end of the
nineteenth century.

1.5   These features, together with the relative autonomy of the
French economy, its specialization in mass consumption goods,
the centralization of monetary control and inflation, are usually
seen as the reasons for the strong, steady growth of the French
economy from 1945 until the start of the 1970s. This, at all

1

events, was the system which underwent sweeping changes from the 1970s onwards.

1.6 There have been two critical symptoms of these changes. The first was a decline in the growth rate, at least until 1987: thus, from 1984 to 1987 the real growth in output was just under 2 per cent. per year, with more than half of it attributable to gains in productivity. There was, it is true, the discernible start of a recovery from the spring of 1987: the growth rate was 3.4 per cent. in 1988 and slightly higher in 1989, reaching close on 4 per cent. But the recovery slowed again from 1990, even before the Gulf crisis. The French economy became set on a course of very slow growth, with a rate of 2.3 per cent. in 1990, 0.7 per cent. in 1991 and a figure for 1992 unlikely to exceed 2 per cent. And although a strong increase in investment in industry was discernible in 1989 and early 1990 (23 per cent. in value and 9 per cent. in volume in 1989), the trend has since been downward.

1.7 The second symptom has been a rise in unemployment and, since 1988, the persistence of a high unemployment rate. At the end of 1991, close on 10 per cent. of the working population were affected by unemployment (9.8 per cent. according to ILO figures). Behind this figure, a number of even more worrying trends emerge: net job losses in industry (2.4 per cent. decrease in employment in manufacturing industries in 1991), rising unemployment among those who have never had a job (*i.e.* young people) as well as among workers in general, and a longer average duration of unemployment. These disparities appear to have become established as long-term factors: one of the most striking features of recent years is an upsurge in job creation initiatives (albeit slowing since 1990) coupled with a persistently high level of general unemployment. The coexistence of these two trends is reflected, in particular, in the difficulty experienced by industry in finding appropriately skilled personnel.

1.8 Above and beyond these quantitative developments, a number of structural developments emerge. The physiognomy of the labour market has changed, in particular with an increased proportion of non-market services, which will undoubtedly lead to a growth and diversification of forms of employment.

1.9 Production structures have undergone changes, creating more complex links of interdependence between enterprises. Corporate strategies are giving higher priority to qualitative adjustment. All these elements are having their effect on the forms of economic and social integration which supported post-war growth.

1.10 At the heart of these trends, the effects are making themselves felt on social and occupational identities.

2. The institutional framework

2.1 Even today, the French system for the regulation of employment relationships and labour relations still owes much to the events of the late nineteenth century. This was the period that initiated the evolvement of a body of statutory regulations on work under a contract of employment as distinct from self-employment. Unquestionably, the central role given to statutory regulation was the outcome at least as much of a political compromise as of the needs of the economy and the workers' aspirations for greater protection. And although this political compromise has lost its topicality, it has firmly moulded French industrial culture to an extent that makes it difficult to envisage, short of major upheaval, any questioning of the State's role. This comment, so brief that it verges on the simplistic, at least has the merit of helping to explain why moves towards "deregulation" have been modest in France or, rather, why it is that in such areas as the State has relinquished control its manner of organizing this has been to impose new rules.

2.2 These statutory rules are not confined to work itself (working hours, terms and conditions of employment and working conditions, etc.). They also govern the collective organization and interest representation of the protagonists of employment and labour relations. For example, trade union activities within the enterprise, collective bargaining, the conclusion and application of collective agreements and employee representation within the enterprise are all covered by statutory rules, often very detailed. In other words, the French legislation is not purely protective; it actually embodies a law of labour relations.

2.3 The importance of statutory law does not mean that it is the sole regulatory source. Collective agreements are a major source of regulations and their role is growing, certainly if the actual number of agreements concluded is taken as a true indication. Custom and the employer's unilateral regulatory prerogatives are also regarded as sources of law.

2.4 Nonetheless, statutory law is still the determining influence, not only by virtue of its scope but also because of the order it introduces between the various sources. What it does, in fact, is to control the production of non-statutory rules through the regulations it establishes for them (*e.g.* the definition by law of collective bargaining conditions and the applicability of collective agreements), the recognition it grants to certain sources (*e.g.* referral by law to custom) or, in some cases, the stipulation of compulsory non-statutory rules (*e.g.* legal obligation to draw up works rules within the individual enterprise).

2.5 The majority of statutory rules are collected together in a Labour Code which carries symbolic value, although it is simply a compilation of texts and an incomplete one at that.

2.6   The past few years have seen a certain distancing of legislative intervention which, as will be seen below, takes the form not of fewer statutory rules but of a change in their nature. This shift is particularly evident in the regulation of forms of employment, where statutory law has exhibited a partial change of stance. Instead of supporting the (relative) standardization of employment relationships, it has switched towards fostering diversity to the point of incorporating this in its mechanisms. Three main routes have been used, indicating the dynamics of the alternative sources. First, a limitation (of legislative origin) of the predominance of labour law: this is reflected in policies for the "social treatment" of unemployment based on formulas for training within the enterprise which are largely outside the scope of labour law. Secondly, statutory regulation of diversified types of employment contract (temporary-employment agency work, fixed-term contracts, part-time contracts, intermittent employment contracts). In these cases statutory regulation, although becoming more closely detailed, is changing direction in that it makes various options available, while controlling their use. Lastly, the law now allows the diversification of patterns of working time to be organized by collective agreement (subject to conditions which it defines), by way of the contracting-out procedure offered by derogation agreements. If the word "flexibility" is appropriate at all, flexibility French-style means, in the first place, a greater abundance of statutory rules. Thus, the idea of the pre-eminent role of the law remains very strong; it may now foster rather than impede diversity, but it controls this development.

3.   The actors of industrial relations

3.1   Convenient though it may be to refer to the almost classic triad, distinguishing between employers' organizations, employees' organizations and government organizations, in the case of France a number of explanatory comments need to be added.

3.2   On the employers' side, there are not only the employers' organizations to be considered. Individual entrepreneurs are, indisputably, actors in the regulatory process in France. They are involved both as legitimate and actual agents of collective bargaining and, by virtue of the recognition accorded by the State to the employer's prerogative rights, as sources of regulation. On the employees' side, it is unreservedly a matter of organizations. French history has witnessed the emergence of a multiplicity of actors here, *i.e.* forms of collective employee organization, with the "coalition", surviving in the modern-day form of the strike committee or co-ordinating committee formed in the event of disputes, the "syndicat" (trade union), the works council (historical alternative to the trade union), workforce and workplace delegates (individual elected representatives), union workplace branches and trade union delegates. Lastly, government organizations encompass a range of complex realities: complex in their structures and, above all, complex because the State is at one and the same time an employer and an administrative authority invested with public powers, a bargaining agent and a bargaining issue.

Organization and structure

3.3 Individual enterprises belong to groupings, either geographical or based on form of activity, which in turn are mostly united in two national organizations: the Conseil national du patronat français (National Council of French Employers) and the Confédération générale des petites et moyennes entreprises (General Confederation of Small and Medium-Sized Enterprises). The authority of these national organizations has increased, although the relative autonomy of the constituent groupings has not disappeared.

3.4 The picture is a far more complicated one in the case of employees' trade unionism. One of its principal features is its diversity. At national level there are five confederations; one (CGC-CFE) is occupation-based and covers only "cadres", *i.e.* professional and managerial staff, while the other four (CGT, CGT-FO, CFDT, CFTC)cover all occupational categories. But some trade unions and federations, particularly in the public sector, are not affiliated to any of these confederations, although they may still exert considerable influence. Along with diversity, another characteristic is the relatively low level of membership. According to various surveys, union density is now somewhere between 9 and 15 per cent. This degree of unionization is undoubtedly the lowest since the end of the Second World War. It is, of course, true that the French tradition is one of a trade unionism of activists ("militants"), that membership offers no special advantages and that the low level of membership does not prevent the confederated unions from winning strong support in elections both within enterprises and outside them (elections of labour judges and the management committees of social security offices).

Role and functions

3.5 The functions of trade union organizations need to be considered in terms of their relations both with employees and with the State. In their relations with employees the French unions, without ceasing to be the channel for the handling of claims, have increasingly assumed a kind of "public agency" role. In their function of handling claims they possess no special prerogative rights conferred by law. Except in the public sector, the unions are not invested with any legal powers as regards the organization of disputes; they play a certain part in it, but this is outside the context of any conferment of special rights or any demand for such on their part. On the other hand, in their public agency function they are invested by law with extensive prerogative rights, ranging from a recognized monopoly of the negotiation of generally applicable *(erga omnes)* collective agreements to legislative promotion of their activities within the enterprise, and including the right to participate in numerous specialist institutions (Economic and Social Council), consultative bodies (national, regional and local commissions), regulatory bodies (administrative organs of the social protection system) and bodies responsible for dispute settlement ("conseils de prud'hommes" or Industrial Tribunals, which are first-instance labour courts with strictly joint, *i.e.* parity, composition).

3.6   As regards their relations with the State, the situation of the French unions is both simple and complex. Viewed in terms of the regulation of employment and working conditions, their role would appear to be confined to negotiating improvements on the standards and rules fixed by the State, standards and rules which, in the French tradition, form a closely meshed network. In reality, the connection with the State is more complex and this complexity manifests itself in at least two ways. First, the trade union organizations have the benefit of strong promotion of their activities by the State. The prerogative rights granted to them by law in their public agency function are a clear example of this support. Secondly, the past 20 years or more have seen the development of a strong system of centralized bargaining which, depending on its purpose, may best be termed institutional bargaining or "law-making" bargaining. The first type includes, for example, the bargaining which created and later transformed the unemployment insurance scheme. The second type is exemplified by what has occurred in the areas of vocational training, dismissal, working hours and precarious employment in some instances, areas in which a national collective agreement paved the way for legal reform, which in essence echoed the outcome of negotiation.

3.7   The underlying trend is towards a strong growth in the representative and regulatory functions of the major unions. They have become veritable industrial relations authorities, if not actually semi-public authorities, which is something of a paradox since the extension of their functions and corresponding prerogative rights has taken place over a period when their real representational strength has in fact been on the decline.

3.8   This expansion of the unions' role should not, however, be overstated. In France, centralized bargaining is still confined almost exclusively to the management of the labour market and the establishment of employment and working conditions. State fiscal policy, monetary policy and health policy remain largely beyond its scope. Anti-inflationary measures, at all events in terms of their definition, are dictated by government decisions over which the unions have little influence.

3.9 What has been said about the unions is also true of the employers' organizations, at least as regards the strong growth in their representative and regulatory functions.

The concept of representative status

3.10 The concept of representativeness is central to the French system of labour relations. Among the prerogative rights mentioned, the main ones are reserved by law for unions recognized as possessing representative status. Representativeness is therefore both a capacity to respond to the aspirations of occupational groups and express their interests and a condition of eligibility for participation in official bodies in society. But if the concept is a key one, this is as understood in a sense encompassing both social history and possible developments. Thus, in a history marked by trade union fragmentation, representativeness French-style is a pluralist and not majority-based attribute; and in a context of trade union pluralism and numerically low unionization, representativeness is understood in a relative and proportional sense rather than an absolute one. This explanation should not engender too great an illusion of flexibility in the French conception of representativeness: its attribution is predominantly historically based.

3.11 At national level, five trade union confederations are recognized as possessing representative status, four of them (CGT, CGT-FO, CFTC and CFDT) covering all occupational categories and one (CGC-CFE) covering a single occupational category. Exclusive rights of national scope are reserved for these five confederations. However, a rule has progressively become established which gives historically based representativeness its full meaning: at all levels below national level (industry-wide, regional, département or district, individual enterprise), affiliation to one of the five nationally representative confederations automatically confers attribution of a presumed representative status for the purposes of exercising exclusive rights as important as the conclusion of collective agreements, negotiation in preparation for elections within the enterprise and submission of a list of candidates for the first ballot, and access to facilities for union activity within the enterprise. Thus, representativeness deriving from affiliation to a confederation is by no means always founded on real strength or influence at the level concerned; it also constitutes a channel for the support of confederated trade unionism.

3.12   This system does not exclude the possibility of other trade union organizations acquiring representative status at the various levels. Independent or non-confederated unions possess such status, for example, in the civil service.

4.   Collective bargaining and collective agreements

4.1   A special feature of the French system is that collective agreements are the subject of a legal framework. Before being a source of law, they are the subject of statutory regulation. The law invests collective agreements with an exceptional effective force, but this effective force is conditional upon the observance of certain legal canons, the first of them being that only representative unions possess the capacity to negotiate and conclude agreements carrying such effective force. In practice, a considerable volume of bargaining activity is carried on at enterprise level with elected representatives of the workforce (works council and workforce delegates) who are not empowered by law to negotiate agreements invested with the effective force of agreements concluded by the unions ("accords syndicaux").

4.2   Although the law establishes rules on collective agreements, it leaves the matter of fixing bargaining levels to collective autonomy. There are in fact three main bargaining levels: industry level (with bargaining on a département, regional or national basis), a subdivision largely ensuing from the structural composition of the employers' organizations; multi-industry level; and enterprise (and establishment) level.

4.3   The major bargaining level is the industry level. This is explained by a number of factors, both structural and strategic: the historical composition of the employers' organizations and trade union federations, the interest for the employers in establishing conditions of minimum competition between enterprises, the interest for the unions in establishing contexts of solidarity, etc. In the 1970s, in fact, commentators predicted a decline in industry-level bargaining, which, it was asserted, would be overtaken by centralized multi-industry bargaining and bargaining at enterprise or company level. But this decline has not taken place. The volume of bargaining activity at industry level has been sustained. In parallel with this there has been a quantitative increase in company-level bargaining, although it has slowed recently. And multi-industry bargaining continues to occupy a position of some importance, in particular with the conclusion in 1988 and 1989 of framework agreements intended to lay down guidelines for industry-level and company-level bargaining, and the conclusion in 1990 and 1991 of agreements on precarious employment and vocational training. The rule is that relations between agreements concluded at these different levels are governed by the principle of favourability to the employee.

4.4 Dynamic relations between the different levels are not dictated by law and all issues may in principle be covered at any level. Each level is autonomous. The levels are not, however, really in competition with each other, and a certain distribution of coverage operates between them. This distribution relates primarily to the nature of bargaining issues; the creation and development of labour market institutions (unemployment insurance scheme, re-training of employees, etc.) are covered by centralized bargaining, with some delegation to industry level. The distribution is mainly shaped by the strategies of the employers' organizations. The reason why the role of industry-level bargaining has not declined is that it allows a degree of control over bargaining at company level. Also, the wish to develop certain new bargaining issues prompts the employers' organizations to attempt to guide bargaining practices and content.

5. Disputes

5.1 Despite the fact that in France the strike still has strong symbolic value, that the memory of past events (1936, 1968) is still very much alive and that the right to strike is recognized as a fundamental principle, there are certain developments which must be highlighted.

5.2 As its revolutionary perspective has dissipated, so the strike has lost some of its symbolic power. Following the same pattern as in other countries, it has assumed more the nature of a tactic. At the same time, however, other ways exist for workers to make themselves heard, and this realization is prompting some unions to reflect on the place of the strike in collective action. Nevertheless, for those who are unable to make themselves heard direct action, with mass stoppages and demonstrations, is still the means of affirming their collective identity and voicing their demands.

5.3 These brief observations help to explain the trend in strike practices. After falling drastically between 1977 and 1986, the number of strikes began to rise again before once more declining from 1990 onwards. The particularly evident feature is the proportion of strikes which occur in the civil service and the public enterprises in a monopoly situation. And strikes are by no means always organized at the initiative of the unions. This distancing from union control occurs because they are aimed at the protection or recognition of occupational identities.

5.4 In general, the law has very little influence over the outbreak, progress and settlement of industrial disputes. The rules applied to strike action are, essentially, decided by the courts. And although the law organizes procedures for the settlement of disputes, these procedures are voluntary. In practice, enterprises (even in the public sector) seek to prevent disputes by way of consultation mechanisms and employee communication procedures and, in the event of a strike, negotiation is the predominant means of settlement.

6.   Conclusion

6.1   Compared with others, the French industrial relations system is characterized by a high degree of juridification (except as regards collective disputes). This strong level of regulation finds approval with the actors concerned.

6.2   How deeply founded is confidence in the collective bargaining system? In the space of 20 years this system has evolved considerably. But trade union pluralism and rivalry, the unions' weak mobilizing capacity, the influence exerted by the State in centralized bargaining and the disparity in the range of issues covered by industry-level and company-level bargaining constitute seeds of fragility.

A

1. **ABSENCE — ABSENCE FROM WORK**: Employees are deemed to be absent when they perform no work. The term also implies that they remain away from their place of work. Absence from work therefore amounts to a suspension of performance of the contract of employment.

   The rules governing absence from work mainly depend on its cause. If it represents the proper exercise of a right or is caused by an event that entitles the employee to abstain from work, it is deemed to be justified and should not in principle give rise to any penalty imposed by the employer. Otherwise, it is unjustified and the employer may impose a sanction including, where appropriate, **dismissal**. Absence from work represents the exercise of a right in all cases where employees are carrying out their functions as **employee representatives** or taking time off to which they are duly entitled (see **leave of absence**). The same applies in the case of **annual holidays**. Absence from work as a result of illness (see **sick leave**) is classed as being caused by an event that entitles the employee to abstain from work. This second category of justified absence must be distinguished from the first, since it does not entirely prevent employers from exercising their prerogative rights (see **illness**).

   Since absent employees are not working, the employer is in principle not required to pay them remuneration. This principle, which rests on the reciprocity of contractual obligations, is, however, waived in many cases by statute law, by collective agreements or by the contract of employment. It is, for instance, waived in the case of annual holidays.

2. **ABSENTÉISME — ABSENTEEISM**: In principle, this term is used only in the case of unjustified **absences from work** or with reference to a particular tendency to be absent from work. Any measurement of absenteeism thus requires an analysis of the frequency and duration of absences from work and, in addition, an attempt to identify the causes.

   The average rate of absence from work is calculated from the relationship between the volume of work "lost" and the potential volume of work. Its breakdown is shown by comparing the rates obtained for categories defined according to age, sex, work/production unit (workshop, establishment, sector, etc.) and employee group. Studies also cover the distribution of absences by cause or duration.

   Absenteeism is still a major focus of management policy: improvement of working conditions, organization of pay structures to discourage absence from work, etc. For example, one widely used incentive is the attendance bonus ("prime d'assiduité''), introduced either unilaterally or by collective agreement, whose payment and amount are based on constant or regular attendance at work. Because such bonuses are difficult to reconcile with exercise of the **right to strike**, they are often popularly dubbed "**anti-strike bonuses**".

3. **ACCIDENT DE TRAJET — ACCIDENT *EN ROUTE*:** Accident suffered by an employee in the course of their normal journey between the workplace and their home (or the place where they customarily have their meals). It is a concept which gives rise to numerous legal disputes, since not all the rules applicable in the case of **accidents at work** apply to accidents *en route*: in particular, the specific provision of protection against dismissal is strictly confined to accidents at work. For accidents *en route*, the implications regarding the contract of employment are the same as for **illness**. Social security protection, on the other hand, is the same for the victim irrespective of whether the accident is classed as an accident at work or an accident *en route*.

4. **ACCIDENT DU TRAVAIL — ACCIDENT AT WORK:** The first regulations governing compensation for accidents at work (1898) marked the birth of modern law on employment relationships, which draws two of its major principles from those regulations: the liability of the enterprise irrespective of the concept of fault; and legal recognition of the contract of employment as governing a relationship based on personal "subordination". Nowadays, accidents at work are covered by a special set of regulations governing compensation, as contained in the Social Security Code (Article L. 411-1 *et seq.*) Accidents at work have given rise to a wide-ranging prevention policy consisting of rules governing organization of the workplace and conditions of production, generally referred to as health and safety regulations (see **occupational health, safety at work**), the activities of various bodies within and outside the enterprise (see **workplace health and safety committee, Labour Inspectorate**), and mechanisms governing liabilities and penalties. The effects of accidents at work on contracts of employment are also governed by law (Articles L. 122-32.1 to L. 122-32.9 of the Labour Code).

The concept of an accident at work is defined under social security law (Article L. 411-1 of the Social Security Code). It implies an accident, *i.e.* a sudden physical injury, and application of the regulations concerned presumes a link with work. Establishment of this link, which need not be strictly direct, nonetheless requires that the accident takes place when the employee is effectively in a position of personal subordination. This is presumed when the accident occurs during working hours and at the place of work.

Classification of an accident as an accident at work entitles the victim to social security benefits, in some cases supplemented by the employer to maintain the employee's income. Employees are always entitled to such supplements if they are covered by a **monthly pay system**.

The contract of employment is suspended for as long as an employee has to be absent as a result of an accident at work. Except in cases of serious misconduct or the impossibility of maintaining the contract of employment for reasons unconnected with the accident, the employer cannot lawfully dismiss such employees. Once they are fit to return to work they are entitled to do so, possibly with adapted functions if the accident has left them incapable of performing their previous job. French law makes provision for the payment of special compensation in the case of dismissal, *a fortiori* if such dismissal is unjustified and the employee has not been reinstated.

5. **ACCORD-CADRE — FRAMEWORK AGREEMENT**: A type of **collective agreement** whose name reflects its function: a framework agreement sets the aims, methods and subjects of future collective bargaining, both between the parties who have negotiated the agreement and for other, lower, levels of collective bargaining. In France, such agreements are typically reached both at the level of the overall economy and at individual sectoral levels. The terms "accord d'orientation" and "accord de méthode" are used with the same meaning.

The first framework agreements emerged in the 1970s in connection with the wish to encourage collective bargaining and to organize and co-ordinate the various bargaining levels. Recent years have therefore seen a growth of framework agreements in areas in which collective bargaining is felt to be insufficient or inadequate: technological change, duration and organization of working time, and vocational training.

6. **ACCORD COLLECTIF — COLLECTIVE AGREEMENT**: This term has two meanings. In a generic sense, it refers to any agreement between two parties where at least one of them is a collective group or that group's representatives (*i.e.* employees or their representatives). It could also be defined as necessarily having an aim that is itself collective, because its subject must concern the future of the collective group involved. Under French law, therefore, a "convention collective" as meaning a collective agreement is a type of "accord collectif" in this generic sense.

In a technical sense, conversely, an "accord collectif" is a specific example of a **"convention collective"**. According to its legal definition (Article L. 132-1 of the Labour Code), the purpose of a collective agreement in the sense of a "convention collective" is to cover all the terms and conditions of employment, working conditions and social guarantees affecting a group of employees, whereas a collective agreement in the sense of an "accord collectif" covers just "one or more particular elements of this whole". A collective agreement in the sense of an "accord collectif" is, therefore, a collective agreement with limited scope. This distinction is of little practical value, since the formulation and application of both types of collective agreement are governed by the same regulations. One of these regulations is worth noting, since it clearly illustrates the difference between the generic and technical meanings of the term "accord collectif": French law governing collective agreements in the technical sense grants a monopoly of their negotiation and conclusion to the representative trade union organizations (see **representativeness**).

7. **ACCORD DE BRANCHE — INDUSTRY-WIDE AGREEMENT**: The traditional level of collective bargaining in France, coming between multi-industry level (see **general multi-industry agreement**) and enterprise level (see **company-level agreement**). The term "branche" as used here defies precise definition (see **branch of activity**) because, whether it is used to refer to one economic activity or to a group of economic activities (often simply called an "industry" in English), its coverage owes much to history and little to any recognizable logic.

The significance of this bargaining level can be explained by various factors. French trade unions chose at a very early stage to group themselves by industry rather than on a craft basis. Demarcation by industry enables collective bargaining to establish harmonization between enterprises within the industry concerned. State intervention has also often taken the "sector" (a term that virtually coincides with an "industry" in this broad sense) as its point of reference.

Industry-wide agreements, which may be concluded at national, regional or département level (there are some 250 national industry-wide agreements in existence), cover **job classification** (thus also determining the minimum wage for each occupational category) and minimum terms and conditions of employment and working conditions. Also, since 1982 the industry-wide level has been a level of compulsory collective bargaining: every year in the case of pay and every five years for the review of job classifications (Article L. 132-12 of the Labour Code).

8. **ACCORD DE CONCESSION — CONCESSION AGREEMENT**: See **concession bargaining**.

9. **ACCORD D'ENTREPRISE — COMPANY-LEVEL AGREEMENT**: A **collective agreement** whose scope is confined to an individual enterprise.

The law governing all collective agreements is applicable, and there is no legal obstacle limiting bargaining at enterprise level. In fact, French law has since 1982 recognized the enterprise as a level at which bargaining should be encouraged: hence the introduction of a legal obligation to bargain at enterprise level (see **company-level bargaining, duty to bargain**).

Whereas 20 years ago there were few company-level agreements in existence, the situation has now been reversed: some 6,750 company-level or establishment-level agreements were signed in 1991, and this figure includes only agreements formally signed with the representative unions (which in principle possess sole authority to conclude them on the employees' side) and deposited with the labour, employment and vocational training authorities (see **labour inspector, Labour Inspectorate**). The great majority of these agreements (close on 60 per cent.) were signed in industrial enterprises, with 20 per cent. in the service sector, 8 per cent. in the commercial sector and 3 per cent. in the building and public works sector. They mainly cover pay and also working time in the broad sense, but a significant number of such agreements now also relate to employment, vocational training and job classification.

10. **ACCORD DE GROUPE — GROUP AGREEMENT**: A collective agreement applicable in some or all of the companies that make up a group. By contrast with an industry, an enterprise or an establishment, a **group of companies** is not recognized by law as a bargaining unit. This has two consequences. Firstly, the group is deemed to be a relevant framework for collective bargaining only if management and trade unions agree to treat it as such. In practice, some groups have encouraged bargaining at this level to give the group an identity in its own right. The subjects covered by such agreements mainly relate to employee representation and the right to organize collectively. Secondly, the boundaries of the group are defined by the bargaining itself.

11. **ACCORD DE MÉTHODE — FRAMEWORK AGREEMENT**: Synonym of **accord-cadre**.

12. **ACCORD DE MODULATION — ADJUSTABLE HOURS AGREEMENT**: See **annualization of working hours**.

13. **ACCORD D'ORIENTATION — FRAMEWORK AGREEMENT**: Synonym of **accord-cadre**.

15

14. **ACCORD DE PARTICIPATION — PROFIT-SHARING AGREEMENT**: An agreement with the specific purpose of guaranteeing employees a share in the profits made by the enterprise for which they work, in the form of pecuniary benefits whose amount depends on the financial situation of the enterprise. A profit-sharing agreement thus provides employees with income that does not derive from the contract of employment.

The special nature of these agreements derives essentially from the regulations governing the way they are concluded. Three possible procedures are provided for under the law: the conclusion of a collective agreement with the representative trade union organizations in the enterprise; the adoption of an agreement within the **works council**, *i.e.* with the majority of the members elected by the workforce to sit on this body; or the ratification of a draft agreement by a two thirds majority of the workforce. The law thus removes the monopoly of the representative trade unions and opens up the way for bargaining with elected representatives and for decision by ballot, elsewhere ignored by positive law.

The benefits deriving from a profit-sharing agreement are paid in addition to remuneration, which they may not replace. Strong encouragement is given to enterprises to set up such agreements, by way of tax concessions and exemption from social security contributions.

15. **ACCORD DÉROGATOIRE — DEROGATION AGREEMENT**: Concept which exists by virtue of the hierarchy that the law establishes between the various sources of law (see **hierarchy, public policy**).

Usually, under French law (Article L. 132-4 of the Labour Code), the purpose of collective agreements is solely to improve upon statutory regulations to the benefit of employees. Since 1982, however, the law has in some cases allowed collective agreements to lay down regulations that are not necessarily more favourable than the provisions laid down by law: such an agreement is called a "derogation" agreement.

At present, the scope of derogation agreements is limited to those areas in which express provision is made for them: the duration and scheduling of working time. Their conclusion is sometimes subject to certain conditions. In some cases, for example, the law permits a derogation only under an industry-wide agreement extended by ministerial decree (see **extension of collective agreements**). Non-signatory representative trade unions always possess a recognized **right of objection**, provided they have obtained a majority vote at the most recent elections of the works council (see **workplace-level elections**). Valid exercise of this right of objection deprives a derogation agreement of all legal effect.

16. **ACCORD "DONNANT-DONNANT" — "GIVE-AND-TAKE" AGREEMENT**: See **concession bargaining**.

17. **ACCORD "GAGNANT-GAGNANT" — "WIN-WIN" AGREEMENT**: See **concession bargaining**.

18. **ACCORD INTERPROFESSIONNEL — GENERAL MULTI-INDUSTRY AGREEMENT**: A collective agreement, usually concluded at national level, which covers all or most occupational categories. Its breadth of scope derives from the nature of its signatories. It is an agreement made between confederal structures, *i.e.* on the employees' side the five **trade union confederations** whose representativeness has been recognized, and on the employers' side the **National Council of French Employers** and the **General Confederation of Small and Medium-Sized Enterprises**. This means that multi-industry bargaining could also be called inter-confederation bargaining.

This level of bargaining has been extremely active in France for more than 20 years; the unemployment insurance scheme, for instance, was set up under a general multi-industry agreement in 1958. In practice, it is a form of bargaining that tends to concentrate on specific issues, its purpose being to manage the labour market (unemployment insurance, **partial unemployment** or **short-time working, re-training**); sometimes it acts as the vehicle for the generalization of experience (*e.g.* the introduction of the **monthly pay system**); in recent years, it has also been aimed at organizing collective bargaining through **framework agreements**.

From another viewpoint, recent practice appears to indicate that general multi-industry agreements reflect a change in relations between the State and the trade-union and employers' organizations, to whom the State is delegating responsibility for drafting or amending laws (two recent examples are the Law of December 30, 1986 on **redundancy**, whose content is drawn from an agreement of October 1986; and the Law of July 12, 1990 on **fixed-term contracts** and **temporary-employment agency work**, which confirms an agreement of April 1990). In this way, the State achieves a certain consensus in return for restricting its own intervention.

19. **ACOMPTE — PAYMENT ON ACCOUNT**: Proportion of pay paid by the employer before the normal date of payment. It is thus a payment in advance of part of the employee's pay and is

deducted in full when the rest is paid. In principle, payments on account must be provided for by a collective agreement in the case of monthly paid workers (see **monthly pay system**).

20. **ACTEURS SOCIAUX — SOCIAL ACTORS**: The protagonists of **industrial relations**. Although widely used, or perhaps because of this, the term "actors" is rather vague. At macrosocial level, it usually refers to three parties, *i.e.* the State, the employers and the trade unions, as opposed to the two parties (employers and unions) implied by the term **social partners**; at enterprise level, it refers to management and those unions that have a presence within the enterprise. But other levels are also possible: European Community, sector, region, group of companies, etc. The imprecision of the term is mainly due to the fact that the broad concepts of the State, the employers and the unions embrace a multitude of different realities. It is, therefore, only in very general terms that the unions can be viewed as constituting a single social actor.

21. **ACTION COLLECTIVE — COLLECTIVE ACTION/ INDUSTRIAL ACTION**: In its most general sense, joint action with the purpose of achieving shared aims. In French law, particular attention is paid to forms of joint action taken by or on behalf of employees, *i.e.* industrial action. In the days when even the right to unite in groups was prohibited or restricted by the law, analysis of collective action bore as much on the institutions of representation (trade union, workforce delegate, etc.) as on the more concrete processes of expression and the exertion of pressure (demonstrations, boycotts, strikes, etc.). Nowadays, studies tend to concentrate on the significance, diversity and legal status of these processes. The emergence of new forms of collective action has, for instance, been observed: the occupation of workplaces; instances of employees continuing production and sales despite the fact that the enterprise concerned has ceased formal operation (work-in); negotiation with the creditors of an enterprise in financial difficulty; the issue of press releases, etc. There is within the French trade union movement some debate on the current appropriateness of strike action and the possible use of other forms of collective action.

Sociologists and economists, for their part, are more interested in the causes and conditions underlying collective action.

22. **ACTION EN JUSTICE — LEGAL ACTION**: The right to apply to the courts to obtain observance of one's rights or legitimate interests. In the French context, a separate concept both from the substantive right and from the actual pleadings.

23. **ACTION SANITAIRE ET SOCIALE — HEALTH AND SOCIAL SERVICES PROVISION:**
    1. Name given to the external branches of the Ministry of Social Affairs which are responsible for health and social welfare. The regional directorates of health and social affairs are essentially responsible for co-ordination, while the département directorates are responsible for administration (of benefits) and supervision (of establishments providing state health and social services).
    2. Activities of the social security offices (now largely regulated) intended to improve the structures, level and forms of social protection, independently of the payment of statutory social security benefits.

    In a general sense, the French term refers to all measures which are taken outside the framework of social security policy but have the same aims.

24. **ACTION SYNDICALE EN JUSTICE — INSTITUTION OF LEGAL PROCEEDINGS BY TRADE UNIONS:** The capacity of the unions to intervene in proceedings before the courts, which may take various forms. Firstly, as a legal person, a union is entitled to take legal action to defend its own interests. It can also defend the individual interests of its members, provided that it has special authority to this effect. French law, however, now exempts unions from the need to possess special authority when they are acting before an **Industrial Tribunal** on behalf of a foreign worker, a temporary worker (supplied by an agency), a homeworker (as concerns the application of a collective agreement) or an employee who has been made redundant, or, lastly, in order to enforce observance of the principle of equality between men and women at work. In all these cases, the union must give the employee concerned advance notice of its intention to take legal action, so that the employee has an opportunity to object to the action or to take part in the proceedings.

    It should be stressed, in particular, that in France the unions possess the right to take legal action against any threat to the collective interest of the occupational groups they represent (see **collective interest of an occupational group**).

25. **ACTIONNARIAT OUVRIER — EMPLOYEE SHARE OWNERSHIP:** Employee access to the share capital of the company that employs them. In France, there is a distinction between employee share ownership and popular share ownership, whose aim is to ensure the broader distribution of the securities issued by companies to represent their capital. Numerous obstacles stand in the way of employee share ownership. One

19

problem, which can be overcome, is that caused by many employees' limited ability to save. Various measures have been taken to transfer all or part of the cost of purchase to other shareholders or to the general community: the issue of free shares, as in the case of public enterprises (Régie Renault, national banks and insurance companies, etc.); the grant of incentives to employees who subscribe to or purchase shares (*e.g.* mechanisms for purchase or subscription options provided for by the Laws of 1970, 1973, 1984 and 1987); the introduction of a preferential taxation system for companies formed by members of the workforce with a view to ensuring the continuing existence of an enterprise by purchasing a proportion of its share capital ("reprise d'une entreprise", *i.e.* buy-out or takeover by an enterprise's own employees); assistance for an employee in starting up a business, etc.

All these measures form the skeleton of a policy whose achievements have been somewhat limited. As things stand, employee share ownership, where it exists, does not enable workers to exercise any real influence over the running of companies.

26. **ACTIVITÉS SOCIALES ET CULTURELLES — COMPANY WELFARE AND CULTURAL FACILITIES**: Responsibility for the management of services and facilities set up within an enterprise for the benefit of its employees (canteens, supplementary welfare schemes, etc.) was transferred to **works councils** when they were introduced in 1945. Such company welfare and cultural benefits (referred to as "oeuvres sociales" prior to 1982) are an area in which a form of self-management operates. This is why it is so important that they be clearly defined. According to case law, they are services and facilities quite separate from the payment of remuneration which are set up without any legal obligation for the benefit of employees and their families, with a view to improving collective working and living conditions. These services and facilities may not be of a political or trade union nature, but the reference to "culture" permits the organization of meetings and debates. When they involve the payment of monetary benefits (relief funds, contingency funds, subsidies for leisure activities), allocation must be completely non-discriminatory, although this does not preclude adjustment according to resources and needs.

Although, in practice, employers contribute to the financing of such services and facilities, this is stipulated by law only in the case of enterprises in which they already existed prior to the creation of the works council.

Various forms of management are possible under the law: direct management by the works council (often adopted in the case of canteens and facilities connected with holidays and leisure activities); joint management with an institution made responsible for the service or facility concerned (mutual-benefit societies, consumer co-operatives, sports associations); or mere supervision of their management (institutions made responsible for providing housing for employees, etc.). Some services, such as the **company medical service**, are governed by special rules.

In practice, works councils often have substantial financial resources at their disposal to spend on these welfare and cultural benefits. The employer's contribution to their financing ranges, according to different sources, between 0.5 per cent. and 4 per cent. of the total wage bill. It should nonetheless be emphasized that there are disparities between enterprises and so also between employees: the employees of small and medium-sized enterprises enjoy few or no such benefits.

27. **ACTIVITÉS SYNDICALES — TRADE UNION ACTIVITIES**: All initiatives relating to union activity. The term may therefore be used with reference either to the union or to an employee.

1. French law defines the purpose of a union and thereby also specifies the scope of union activities. They concern the study and protection of the interests (both material and non-material, collective and individual) of the persons alluded to in the union's standing rules. Union activity is justified not only by the interests of its existing members but also by those of prospective members. Also, the introduction in 1982 of the reference to material and non-material interests, instead of occupational interests, is intended to make the purpose of a union more flexible and up-to-date. Given that they do not call the fundamental principles of the State into question, it is difficult nowadays to set limits to the activities of the unions.

2. With respect to employees, the trade union freedom they are granted by law covers not only their right to join a union but also their right to take part in union activities. The issue of primary importance to employees is the protection they are guaranteed when performing union activities. French law provides dual protection: employers are deemed to be in breach of criminal law if they allow the fact of union activity to influence their decisions on hiring, dismissal, promotion, etc., and under civil law discriminatory treatment by employers is automatically void.

28. **ADHÉSION — UNION/EMPLOYERS' ORGANIZATION MEMBERSHIP**: The concept of union membership, given that in France a union ("syndicat") can denote both trade unions and employers' organizations, is an act whereby an individual employee (or an individual enterprise in the case of an employers' organization) becomes a member of a union or a union becomes a member of a regional union or of a federation. In principle, a union is in control of its own recruitment, which means that it can make membership subject to certain conditions, including approval of a body. In practice, particularly extensive checks are carried out when a union joins a regional union or a federation.

Membership obliges the member concerned to respect the union's standing rules and, in particular, to pay a subscription. Subscriptions provide a measure of the degree of unionization (see **union density**). On the other hand, membership does not confer any advantages, since discrimination (by the employer or any other party) based on union membership is unlawful.

A distinction that has been introduced for the study of political parties, as between sympathizers, members and activists ("militants"), is frequently also used to analyse this. Any value as such of the distinction, in the case of France, is that it highlights the fact that membership has not been the main driving force behind trade unionism. A further distinction is made between "occupational" members ("l'adhérent catégoriel"), who are defined by their occupational status and forced into membership by their environment; "ideological" members ("l'adhérent idéologique"), who support the values of the organization concerned; and "opportunist" members ("l'adhérent utilitariste"), whose motives for joining are wholly selfish.

29. **ADMINISTRATEUR SALARIÉ — WORKER MEMBER OF THE BOARD**: Employees who are appointed as members of a company's board of directors or (in the new two-tier structure modelled on German company law) supervisory board. Although French law provides for the compulsory attendance by two members of the works council at meetings of a company's board of directors or supervisory board, these delegates are not worker members of the board: they do not possess their powers or responsibilities and can act only in an advisory capacity.

In public sector enterprises, which are fewer in number since the privatization wave of 1986-87, representatives elected by the workforce sit on the board of directors or supervisory board, usually accounting for one third of the members. In the private sector, French law leaves it to shareholders to decide whether or not worker members of the board should be appointed. Only a handful of examples exists, although admittedly this form of employee participation is not favoured either by the employers or by the trade unions, with the exception of some Christian factions and bodies representing professional and managerial staff ("cadres").

30. **ADMINISTRATION PUBLIQUE — PUBLIC ADMINISTRATION**: All the bodies and institutions responsible for managing public affairs. Many of them intervene in employment and labour issues in France: some have general powers (as in the case of the Prime Minister and, at local level, Prefects and mayors; also certain advisory bodies, such as the Economic and Social Council); others have specific powers concerning employment and labour (see **labour administration**).

Recent attempts to decentralize administrative powers have had little impact on the spheres of labour and employment, where power is still concentrated in the hands of the State and its agents. There is, however, a trend whereby municipal, département and regional authorities (the three main levels of public administration in France) are developing services in these spheres, *e.g.* various forms of aid for starting and relaunching enterprises, assistance for job-seekers, etc.

31. **ADMINISTRATION DU TRAVAIL — LABOUR ADMINISTRATION**: The set of state bodies with specific powers and responsibilities concerning labour and employment issues.

The Ministry of Labour was first set up in France in the early twentieth century (1906) but, depending on circumstances and on government policy, has been either grouped with or separate from other ministerial offices responsible for social security and health.

For employers, employees and the trade unions, labour administration (also referred to in English as "employment administration") is most apparent in the guise of the **Labour Inspectorate**, the name given to the Ministry's external services. See **labour inspector**.

32. **AFFICHAGE — DISPLAY OF NOTICES**: The posting-up of notices to provide the workforce with information. The various representative institutions in an enterprise (*i.e.* trade unions, workforce delegates, works council) possess a legally recognized right to display notices, in accordance with procedures which are defined by collective agreement. Union notices must be transmitted to the employer, but the latter possesses no direct authority to object to their being displayed.

33. **AFFILIATION — REGISTERED MEMBERSHIP**: In the context of the law on social protection, general term denoting a person's membership of a social security scheme. Under the French system, it is compulsory for employees (*i.e.* those working under a contract of employment) to belong to what is known as the general social security scheme. The term "immatriculation" indicates the actual administrative operation whereby a person is registered on the list of beneficiaries of the benefits provided under a social security scheme. Since membership constitutes a legal relationship, registration involves various formalities for which the employer bears responsibility in cases where membership is compulsory.

34. **ÂGE — AGE**: With the exception of the rules setting a minimum age for entry into employment (currently 16 in France) or imposing restrictions on the performance of work by young people under the age of 18, any discrimination on the basis of age is, theoretically, a violation of the **freedom of labour** which is a recognized universal right.

   Nevertheless, the public employment policies which have emerged in response to growing unemployment and demographic change are to a large extent "ageist", *i.e.* measures which are either introduced or applied with a particular age group in mind. Numerous policy measures in France are aimed at fostering the employment of young people (the target age is sometimes 18, sometimes 25 and sometimes 26), more particularly by reducing the costs involved in hiring them. Other measures provide incentives for older workers to leave employment; in particular, these include schemes for **early retirement** or the lowering of the age at which a worker is entitled to start drawing a retirement pension, and in 1987 a special scheme was introduced whereby contracts of employment can be terminated when workers attain entitlement to a full pension.

   The effects of such measures are not always positive. In the context of a society in which youth is idealized, they make the situation of older workers even more precarious. There is now a reaction against this, with the aim of ensuring better protection for older employees.

35. **AGENCE NATIONALE POUR L'AMÉLIORATION DES CONDITIONS DE TRAVAIL — NATIONAL AGENCY FOR THE IMPROVEMENT OF WORKING CONDITIONS**: Public agency (referred to as ANACT) which comes under the Minister for Labour and is responsible for promoting research, experiments and practical measures to improve working conditions.

Founded in 1973, ANACT concentrates its activities especially on information and expertise. It covers a very broad field, including all aspects of working life.

36. **AGENCE NATIONALE POUR L'EMPLOI — NATIONAL EMPLOYMENT AGENCY**: Public agency (referred to as ANPE) which comes under the Minister for Labour and is responsible for helping individuals who are seeking employment, training or career guidance in changing their occupation or achieving advancement in their existing occupation, and for helping employers in the hiring or re-training of employees.

Although ANPE formerly had a monopoly as a public service for the placement of **job-seekers**, this has ceased to be the case since a reform of 1986 (see **job placement**).

Any worker who is seeking employment must apply to the local ANPE office for registration on its list of job-seekers. These lists are used to compile unemployment statistics.

37. **AGENT COMMERCIAL — COMMERCIAL AGENT**: An individual responsible for purchases, sales and related activities who works on behalf of an enterprise without being bound by a **contract of employment**. French law establishes a special status for commercial agents, defined as individuals who, as their habitual occupation on a self-employed basis and without being bound by a contract of employment, negotiate and possibly conclude purchases, sales, leases or the provision of services in the name of and on behalf of producers, industrialists or traders.

38. **AGENT DE MAÎTRISE — SUPERVISOR**: Category of employees recognized by statistical nomenclatures and collective agreements. This category traditionally comes between production workers and managerial staff. (In English, the traditionally equivalent term "foreman/forewoman" is increasingly regarded as outdated.)

39. **AGENTS PUBLICS — PUBLIC EMPLOYEES**: All those persons who work for the State, public authorities or public institutions. The term is, however, sometimes reserved for persons who fall within this category but are not classed as **established civil servants**. It is worth describing their legal position in more detail.

Public sector employees in industry and commerce are covered by a contract of employment governed by labour law (with the exception of departmental managers ("dirigeants") and financial comptrollers ("agents comptables")).

Other public sector employees (who are classed in one of three categories: "auxiliaires", "contractuels", and "vacataires" or "agents temporaires"), are either covered by labour law or deemed to be employed under a contract governed by public law: these are employees who participate directly in the provision of public services or whose contract of employment includes clauses extending beyond the scope of ordinary law. A contract of employment governed by public law observes specific rules and regulations which may differ from one sector to another. The tendency is, however, to deem any public sector employee employed under a contract governed by public law as being entitled to rights which are at least equivalent to those enjoyed by law by all employees. This tendency is reflected in the confirmation in court decisions of the general principles of labour law (minimum wage, protection for pregnant employees, etc.).

40. **AGRÉMENT — APPROVAL**: Process of administrative intervention whereby the exercise of an activity by a person or the legal validity of a document is made subject to a decision by the administrative authorities, or whereby the scope of application of a document is modified by such a decision. In the former case, it is a person who receives official authorization; in other cases, it is a document. Agreements bearing on certain matters (unemployment, retirement and welfare benefits) or concerning certain sectors (non-profit-making health and social welfare sector, social security bodies) must be so approved by the relevant Ministry if they are to be valid in law. An example of the latter type of approval is where the Minister for Labour may follow a procedure for the **extension of collective agreements** in order to render an agreement applicable to all enterprises in a particular industry.

41. **AGRICULTURE — AGRICULTURE**: French statutory labour law applies to the agricultural sector without any significant exemptions or adjustments. This sector has its own unique industrial relations system, owing to the history of agricultural trade unionism.

42. **AIDE À L'EMPLOI — EMPLOYMENT SUPPORT**: Transfer of employment costs from one or more enterprises to the State, with a view to preserving or creating jobs. In principle, the term should apply only to formal decisions made to this effect, where the transfer of costs is then clearly connected with a specific initiative. There is nonetheless a tendency to use it to refer to any general and automatically applicable measure which is expected to have a positive effect on employment, even if its results cannot be verified.

There are various means of transferring employment costs: the grant of a subsidy or low-interest loan, exemption from social security contributions, tax relief and, sometimes, even the waiver of a labour law regulation that entails a certain level of expenditure.

43. **AIDE PUBLIQUE — GOVERNMENT AID**: Transfer of costs from one or more individuals, or from one or more enterprises, to the State (see **employment support**).

44. **AIDE SOCIALE — SOCIAL ASSISTANCE**: All benefits and services provided by the authorities to persons in difficulty. The assistance is intended to meet a situation of need. Although the distinction has become rather blurred, social assistance is deemed to complement **social security**.

   In principle, social assistance is the responsibility of the authorities at département level, but central government still has some residual responsibility in the matter.

45. **ALERTE — NOTIFICATION**: Term used, for example, in the following three contexts:
   1. The expression "droit d'alerte" (right to notify) refers to the legally recognized right of employees to alert their employer to some condition at work which they have good reason to believe poses a serious and immediate threat to their life or health.
   2. The expression "procédure d'alerte" (notification procedure) refers to a statutory procedure whereby members of the **workplace health and safety committee** may notify the employer of a serious and **imminent danger**, whether or not pointed out by an employee, and whereby, without themselves possessing the authority to alter the organization of work, they are entitled to investigate appropriate ways of eliminating the risk.
   3. The expression "procédure d'alerte" is also used to refer to a statutory procedure whereby the **works council** may request the employer to clarify facts that may have a detrimental effect on the enterprise's economic situation and, without itself possessing the authority to ask the courts to intervene in the management of the enterprise, is entitled to investigate appropriate ways of remedying the situation.

46. **ALLOCATION DE CHÔMAGE — UNEMPLOYMENT BENEFIT**: France has a dual system for the provision of unemployment benefits.

There is an unemployment insurance scheme whose principles, operation (see **ASSEDIC, UNEDIC**) and provision of benefits are laid down by a national collective agreement, although it is also subject to close supervision by the State. The scheme is financed from contributions, and unemployed individuals are entitled to receive benefits provided they are members of the scheme, have lost their job through no fault of their own and are seeking a new job. It dispenses benefits whose initial provision and duration of payment depend on the length of time for which the individual concerned has been a member of the scheme. There are two successive levels of benefit: basic benefit ("allocation de base") and post-entitlement benefit ("allocation de fin de droit").

Alongside this, a guarantee supplementary scheme ("régime de solidarité") was set up in 1984, funded by the State and with the purpose of providing benefits for young people, widowed or divorced women and other disadvantaged job-seekers who are not members of the insurance scheme because they have not paid in the appropriate contributions. It also covers the long-term unemployed who no longer qualify for entitlements under the insurance scheme. Some receive a work programme allowance ("allocation d'insertion") and others a guarantee supplementary benefit ("allocation de solidarité").

47. **ALLOCATION D'INSERTION — WORK PROGRAMME ALLOWANCE**: See **absorption into employment, unemployment benefit**.

48. **ALLOCATION DE SOLIDARITÉ — GUARANTEE SUPPLEMENTARY BENEFIT**: See **unemployment benefit**.

49. **ALLOCATIONS FAMILIALES — FAMILY ALLOWANCES**: In a general sense, the term is synonymous with "prestations familiales" (family benefits), *i.e.* benefits provided under the **social security** system to guarantee that families enjoy a certain standard of living.

   In the more technical sense of social security law, family allowances are child benefits, a category of family benefits whose purpose is to help families meet the cost of bringing up their children. Payment is not conditional upon employment (of either the father or the mother) and the amount is not subject to means testing.

50. **ALTERNANCE — COMBINED TRAINING AND WORK**: Combination of training, provided in the form of general, vocational and technological instruction imparted during working hours, and work in an enterprise. (In some cases, such as when

28

this takes place at two different places, the meaning is equivalent to the English term ''sandwich course''.) This combination is at the centre of French policy on initial vocational training. It has given rise to many different formulas for employment; some involve contracts of employment governed by special rules (special types of employment contract: see **apprenticeship, employment and training contract**), while others take the form of **training scheme** arrangements not involving a contract of employment. This latter formula has been the subject of so much criticism that its use is on the decline.

51. **AMENDE — FINE**: In a general sense, a sanction or penalty imposed on a person at fault, consisting in the payment of a sum of money. The definition also applies in labour law, except that in this context it takes the form of a deduction from pay. The imposition of fines by employers is expressly prohibited under French labour law.

52. **ANACT**: See **National Agency for the Improvement of Working Conditions** (Agence nationale pour l'amélioration des conditions de travail).

53. **ANCIENNETÉ — LENGTH OF SERVICE**: The length of time that has elapsed since an employee commenced employment, usually calculated as within the same enterprise but sometimes as within the same occupation. Also referred to in English as ''seniority''.

   Length of continuous service is a fundamental concept in labour law, since it provides the basis of a career path and of job security; it also fosters commitment and loyalty.

   There are many rights and benefits for which basic eligibility as well as their magnitude depend on length of continuous service: period of notice, compensation for dismissal, the right to vote and to stand as a candidate in workplace-level elections, etc. It is mainly collective agreements that have linked rising skill grades and pay to increasing length of service; in particular, agreements very often include provision for length-of-service bonuses, which are nowadays criticized by some employers who would prefer to see a link between pay and company results.

54. **ANNUALISATION (DU TEMPS DE TRAVAIL) — ANNUALIZATION OF WORKING HOURS**: Since statutory **working hours** are calculated with reference to the period of one week, an operating rhythm which includes peak periods (even if predictable) during which employees work for more than 39 hours per week entails the application of enhanced rates of pay

for **overtime**. Since 1982, and in particular since 1986, it has been possible to avoid this: hours of work can be adjusted over the year (or over a shorter period of, say, three or six months), provided that average working time does not exceed 39 hours per week. This adjustment, provided for by law, requires either an extended industry-wide agreement (see **extension of collective agreements**) or a company-level agreement, and is always subject to consultation of the works council. It is also conditional upon employees receiving a counter-consideration, whether financial or otherwise. Given these conditions, hours worked over and above the statutory 39 hours do not attract entitlement to overtime pay.

In practice, such adjustable hours agreements are rare. Where they have been reached, employees are often granted a **reduction of working hours** in exchange.

55. **ANPE**: See **National Employment Agency** (Agence nationale pour l'emploi).

56. **APPRENTISSAGE — APPRENTICESHIP**: Form of **combined training and work** provided for by law. Its purpose is to give young people (nowadays classed as being between the ages of 16 and 25) who have completed their compulsory schooling a general, theoretical and practical training to enable them to acquire vocational skills certified by an official diploma or other evidence of a formal qualification recognized by the State.

Apprenticeship gives rise to the conclusion of a special contract of employment which is governed by the rules of labour law subject to some special provisions. The contract must make arrangements for training within the enterprise and training at a training establishment.

The formula is a traditional one which, although common in small enterprises, does not have the importance in France that it has, for example, in Germany.

57. **ARBITRAGE — ARBITRATION**: Process for settling a conflict or dispute at law whose distinctive feature lies in the agreed appointment of a third party (arbitrator) to deliver judgment on the claims of the parties, in accordance with the relevant rules of law in the case of a dispute of rights and in accordance with "equity" in other cases.

In the case of individual disputes, *i.e.* disputes arising from a contract of employment, arbitration may be used only if the parties jointly decide to do so once·the dispute has arisen. A unilaterally inserted arbitration clause in a contract of employment is therefore null and void.

In the case of collective disputes, the law makes provision for an arbitration procedure which nowadays is always voluntary, unless the relevant collective agreement stipulates otherwise. In practice, arbitration is very rare.

58. **ARTISANAT — SELF-EMPLOYED CRAFT SECTOR**: French law does not in principle make any distinction between small and large enterprises, all of which are subject to the same legal system. The sole exception, under labour law, is the application of **thresholds**. One category of small enterprises does, however, escape the general rules: small-scale craft enterprises. These consist of self-employed workers who make a living primarily from the product of their own manual labour and that of their family and a small number of apprentices (see **apprenticeship**) or employees. United in strong organizations, they have succeeded in securing numerous regulatory advantages in terms of taxation, social protection (protection against unemployment, retirement scheme, health insurance, maternity protection, etc.) and industrial relations. Chambers of Craft Trades ("chambres des métiers"), which they control, have significant powers. The definition of these self-employed workers ("artisans") varies somewhat according to the particular regulation concerned, but always includes a criterion relating to size of enterprise, expressed in terms of the number of apprentices or employees.

59. **ARTISTE — PERFORMING ARTISTE**: Any person whose gainful employment, whether as an individual or as a member of a group, involves using bodily, vocal or musical expression to communicate a work of the imagination to public audiences. France has no legislative text that gives a definition of the concept, although special provisions relating to performing artistes have been adopted. Some of these provisions regulate their relationship with the enterprises that collaborate with them; in particular, this relationship is deemed to constitute a contract of employment. Other provisions determine their rights over their performance. The uncertainty which is characteristic of their occupation has also been invoked as grounds for the introduction of special rules, from various sources, to regulate their annual holidays (creation of a holiday fund for performing artistes, "caisse des congés-spectacle") and to protect them, especially, against the risk of unemployment.

60. **ASSEDIC**: Abbreviation denoting the Associations for Employment in Industry and Commerce (Associations pour l'emploi dans l'industrie et le commerce), bodies which are

responsible for managing the local unemployment insurance funds (see **unemployment**). The fact that unemployment insurance is based on collective agreement means that they are administered in accordance with the principle of joint management.

Enterprises are members of the ASSEDICs, which collect contributions and pay out benefits. The State has also made them responsible for paying out the benefits provided by central government under the guarantee supplementary scheme known as the "régime de solidarité".

61. **ASSEMBLÉE (DE TRAVAILLEURS) — MASS MEETING**: There is no legal provision in France which treats all the employees of an enterprise or establishment as a collective body or subject, empowered to make decisions and governed by a principle of majority voting. Nor does the law confer on representative trade unions within an enterprise the right to convene meetings of all the employees at the workplace.

The only relevant provision is the new **right of expression** granted to employees by the Law of August 4, 1982 (individual right of direct participation, exercised collectively within what are termed "expression groups"); this allows for the formation of small units within which employees are able to voice their opinion on working conditions and terms and conditions of employment. In practice, the holding of mass meetings is not prohibited by law and may take place during strike action.

62. **ASSISTANCE — ASSISTANCE**: (Equivalent in meaning to the now outdated English term "relief".) Intervention by public or private bodies in favour of the needy, on a voluntary and consequently discretionary basis. It was in reaction against this mode of intervention that the system of social insurance was instituted.

63. **ASSISTANCE SOCIALE — PUBLIC ASSISTANCE**: See **health and social services provision, social assistance.**

64. **ASSISTANTE SOCIALE — WELFARE WORKER**: The functions associated with providing social services (see **health and social services provision**) and **social assistance** are entrusted to social workers ("travailleurs sociaux") who may be established civil servants (within the département or municipal authorities), other public employees or employees of private sector bodies. Among these social workers, the welfare worker is a traditional figure encompassing several categories. The main category consists of those whose task is to identify people with social problems ("cas sociaux", *i.e.* "cases"), bring them to the

attention of the authorities, provide them with information and advice and seek ways of resolving their problems.

65. **ASSOCIATION (LIBERTÉ D') — FREEDOM OF ASSOCIATION**: As the keystone of democracy, freedom of association (formally, the freedom of individuals to unite to defend their rights, propagate their ideas and jointly pursue a collective objective) is, according to an elegantly worded formula, "a freedom whereby the individual reshapes society". We can see that the formula still holds good if we look at the proliferation of associations, the social integration and apprenticeship in collective living that they provide, and the role they perform as mediators in relations between individuals and the governing authorities.

Freedom of association was not recognized in France until 1901 (although it had briefly been so following the revolution of 1848), *i.e.* later than **freedom of collective industrial organization** or the right to form and belong to a "**syndicat**". This means that, although there is no essential difference between the two, a distinction is made between a formal association and a "syndicat" (trade union or employers' organization).

Nowadays, it is one of the fundamental freedoms guaranteed by the Constitution and has several facets: the formation and functioning of an association, and the option to join or not to join. There are, however, some anomalies: membership is sometimes compulsory (see **ASSEDIC**).

An association does not acquire full legal capacity until it has lodged a declaration with the public authorities (this is not subject to any vetting other than as to its form). Undeclared associations therefore exist, with only modest legal capacity.

66. **ASSOCIATION CAPITAL-TRAVAIL — PHILOSOPHY OF CAPITAL-LABOUR CO-OPERATION**: Term capturing a philosophy developed by the Gaullist movement during the period while de Gaulle was not in power (1946-58), and later readopted under the name of "participation". This latter term is not interpreted as stipulating a formal presence for employees in the organs responsible for managing a company. Rather, it is a philosophy of co-operation: conflicts of interest between capital and labour are seen as obstacles to the smooth running and successful performance of enterprises.

In concrete terms, this philosophy proposes that profits and risks should in some measure be shared between capital providers and employees. It served as the underlying principle of the special legal rules reserved for agreements arranging forms of **profit-sharing** or **pay related to company performance** for the benefit of employees. It has not, however, had any further real influence on the legal policy of French governments since 1958.

67. **ASSOCIATION INTERMÉDIAIRE — INTERMEDIARY ASSOCIATION**: See **intermediary enterprise**.

68. **"ASSOCIATION PROFESSIONNELLE"**: Name given to employees' and employers'organizations by the 1884 Law establishing freedom of collective industrial organization (also referred to more loosely as trade union freedom). At the time, freedom of association had not yet been recognized in law. Since 1901 it has been so, and associations have a legal form which is not strictly the same as that of the "syndicats", *i.e.* collective industrial organizations encompassing both employers' associations and trade unions (the former "associations professionnelles"). Consequently, an "association professionnelle" is nowadays distinguished from a "syndicat" proper by a formal criterion: the former possesses the legal form of an association, while the latter does not.

69. **ASSOCIATION SYNDICALE — SYNDICATE**: Term used by various groups whose members do not practise an identical or similar occupation but are linked simply by the fact that they have shared interests to defend. It is also used by groups of co-owners of a single building (*e.g.* a householders' association) or of ground landlords who join forces to carry out works to the benefit of all their properties.

The French term is misleading (since "syndicale" nowadays suggests a connection with trade unions), and is attributable to historical circumstances: the 1884 Law establishing trade union freedom referred to unions (now "syndicats") under the name of **"associations professionnelles"**; also, the concept of a "syndicat" as an organization of persons with shared interests to defend is a very old-established one.

70. **ASSURANCE GARANTIE DES SALAIRES — WAGE GUARANTEE INSURANCE**: Mechanism introduced in France in 1973 which operates like an insurance to protect employees' interests in the event of default on the part of their employer. It came into being as a result of the proven inadequacy of traditional protection mechanisms based on **preferential claims**, which gave priority to certain claims over others.

The insurance is funded from compulsory contributions paid by enterprises. It comes into play only in cases where an enterprise is the subject of compulsory administration or of compulsory liquidation by the court, procedures which have replaced that of bankruptcy, and enables employees to receive a proportion of the payment provided for in the event of dismissal, especially for example compensation for dismissal, and of entitlements payable on termination of the contract of employment. The insurance body concerned is subrogated to the employees' rights.

Depending on the conditions and scope of the insurance, it contributes to varying degrees to the financing of enterprises in difficulty.

71. ASSURANCES SOCIALES — SOCIAL INSURANCE: Use of insurance techniques to provide certain workers with protection against various forms of financial insecurity.

Leaving aside the compulsory old age insurance scheme for employees set up in 1910, the creation of a comprehensive system of social insurance in France dates back to 1928-30. These various insurances formed the foundation of the present social security system, which was instituted in 1945-46.

72. ASTREINTE — STAND-BY: This term, which has originated in the practice of certain occupations and has no general recognition in law, denotes the period of time during which employees are required to keep themselves at their employer's disposal, outside their normal working hours and usually at their home, so that they can be called upon in the event of emergency or necessity.

The obligation to perform stand-by duty derives either from the individual contract of employment or from custom and practice. Some collective agreements have organized stand-by systems (chemical industry, electricity industry, radio and television, security staff, etc.).

Stand-by duty must not involve any obligations other than that of being available for work. Subject to this condition, it is not deemed to constitute actual working time. It does, however, usually attract remuneration, although on a flat-rate basis.

73. AUDIT SOCIAL — PERSONNEL AUDIT: The audit, as a set of procedures for the review and examination of accounting and management, is nowadays applied relatively widely to personnel or human resource management. It involves assessing terms and conditions of employment with respect to the regulations laid down by law, collective agreement or the company's own works rules, and devising and applying ways of measuring methods of labour utilization.

74. **AUGMENTATION AU MÉRITE — MERIT PAY INCREASE**: Provided their discretionary powers are not restricted by the individual contract of employment, custom and practice or collective agreement, employers may fix differential pay increases according to the merits of particular employees. If, however, they withhold a general pay increase from one or more employees when no real difference in conduct or ability exists, this is deemed to be discriminatory treatment.

In order to avoid being accused of discrimination in the awarding of unfair pay increases and to establish acceptance of the principle of differential pay increases, a number of enterprises have introduced methods of measuring or defining merit. This trend is accompanied by a growing use of appraisal interviews and target or performance clauses (see **individualization**).

75. **AUGMENTATION DE SALAIRE — PAY INCREASE**: Alteration to the contract of employment involving raising the rate of pay (per hour, per week, per month, etc.) or introducing or increasing a bonus.

General pay increases are still often the result of a change in minimum wage rates, as fixed by an industry-wide agreement, which has an impact on actual rates of pay within an enterprise. They may also take the form of new bonuses for certain categories, which avoids altering the pay structure laid down in the **job classification** for the industry concerned.

The past few years have seen the emergence of two major trends. Firstly, general pay increases are no longer linked, in advance, to movements in prices; breaking this linkage is referred to as "de-indexation". Secondly, they are small, in order to leave more scope for differential or personalized increases.

76. **AUTEUR — AUTHOR**: The creator of a work protected by the right of literary or artistic property, sometimes an employee. In principle, if the work has been created in the course of an employee's normal duties, any rights of a pecuniary nature are deemed to have been ceded to the employer, with the employee retaining a moral right. Special rules have, however, been laid down by law to cover cases where the work is collective or the product of collaboration.

77. **AUTOCOMMUTATEUR — AUTOMATIC TELEPHONE LOG**: Dedicated computer used to handle telephone calls and store in its memory all the numbers dialled; it makes it possible to monitor not only telephone costs but also employees' activities. The **National Commission for Information Technology and Civil Liberties** has defined the guarantees that must be observed when such systems are installed.

78. **AUTOGESTION — (WORKERS') SELF-MANAGEMENT**: In the literal sense, self-management means the management of an enterprise by those who work in it. In a less precise sense, however, the term is also used in debates on socialism; in this case, it refers to the opposite of a centralized, bureaucratic form of organization, *i.e.* a self-organized form of structure in which the dynamism of those who perform the production function is not blocked.

79. **AUTOMISATION — AUTOMATION**: A term applicable wherever automatic equipment is capable of triggering the movement of a machine. Nowadays, however, it tends to be used only with reference to devices driven by electronic signals.
   Since the early 1960s there has been widespread debate on the impact of automation on skills and, ultimately, on employment.

80. **AUTOMATISME — AUTOMATIC EFFECT**: Routine event or, more accurately, adjustment which does not require a fresh act of will. The term "automatisme salarial" is used to describe a situation where pay increases are automatic, *i.e.* predetermined because fixed in accordance with a rule. Promotion is also described as automatic (as opposed to selective) when advancement from one post to another or from one grade to another in the **job classification** is dictated by a rule not involving any appraisal by the employer.

81. **AUTONOMIE COLLECTIVE — COLLECTIVE AUTONOMY**: Determination of rules through negotiation between the particular parties whom they are to govern, or their representatives. Collective bargaining is one example of the phenomenon. More generally, however, the term is used in the context of examining what role is or should be played by the autonomous determination of rules as against their "heteronomous" (*i.e.* external) determination by a constitutionally competent authority.

82. **AUTORÉGLEMENTATION — SELF-REGULATION OF STRIKE ACTION**: Little used in France because the associated practices are very uncommon, this term refers to the issuing by the trade unions themselves of rules applicable in the event of a strike (relating to the duration of strikes, procedures for conducting strikes, the organization of emergency services, ways of meeting the needs of customers or users, etc.).

83. **AUTORISATION — AUTHORIZATION**: Administrative act which entitles a (private) individual to do something that may

not be done without such authorization. In the sphere of labour law, it is with regard to employment that most requirements for authorization have been imposed, enabling the State to keep a check on the movement of labour.

Autorisation d'embauche — Authorization for hiring: This mechanism, introduced in 1945, soon fell into disuse. It now survives only in the context of agreements concluded between an enterprise and the **National Employment Fund** for the organization of **early retirement**.

Autorisation de licenciement — Authorization for dismissal: In practice, the only remaining instance nowadays in which dismissal is subject to prior authorization by the administrative authorities is for the dismissal of **employee representatives**. Between 1975 and 1986, such authorization was required for redundancies.

Autorisation de travail — Work permit: The employment of a foreign worker who is a national of a non-EC country is subject to authorization. Failure to obtain a work permit means that the contract of employment is null and void and the employer incurs penal and administrative sanctions.

84. **AUTORISATION D'EMBAUCHE — AUTHORIZATION FOR HIRING**: See **authorization**.

85. **AUTORISATION DE LICENCIEMENT — AUTHORIZATION FOR DISMISSAL**: See **authorization**.

86. **AUTORISATION DE TRAVAIL — WORK PERMIT**: See **authorization**.

87. **AUXILIAIRE — AUXILIARY PUBLIC EMPLOYEE**: One of the three categories of **public employees** who do not possess **established civil servant** status. A major example is the "maître auxiliaire", *i.e.* a supply teacher who is called in to replace an absent teacher in secondary schools.

88. **AVANCE — ADVANCE**: Sum paid by the employer which has no connection with the normal timing of the payment of pay. Unlike **payments on account**, advances are in principle repayable; they constitute loans. In practice, they are deducted from pay, *i.e.* repaid by means of set-off, but within limits stipulated by law.

89. **AVANCEMENT — PROMOTION (AT WORK)**: Advancement to a higher level in the enterprise's hierarchy. Independently of a simple pay increase, it represents a change to the contract of employment.

Promotion may be left to the employer's discretion, in which case it is said to be selective. It is sometimes the subject of rules in collective agreements which apply without involving any appraisal on the part of the employer; in this case it is said to be automatic (*e.g.* compulsory progression to a higher grade on the basis of length of continuous service).

90. **AVANTAGES ACQUIS — ACQUIRED RIGHTS**: One of the most equivocal concepts of French law. The unions have traditionally attributed great significance to them, in order to debar any initiative that might reduce the rights or advantages of any or all employees. This approach has not, however, been upheld by the courts. In practice, the concept is at the centre of discussions that arise when a collective agreement expires or when one agreement is replaced by another following a **notice of termination of a collective agreement** or company restructuring. If a new agreement is concluded or becomes applicable, it automatically replaces the old one, with the result that all the rights established under that earlier agreement disappear. If no new agreement is concluded within a specified period, the rights established under the old agreement disappear in this case also.

Since 1982, however, the law has made provision (expressed in very brief terms) for the maintenance of individual acquired rights when the old agreement is not replaced within a specified period. But what are these individual acquired rights? Are they all the rights which, at the time when the collective agreement disappeared, the employee was able to count on? This broad interpretation, frequently advocated, has not won acceptance by the courts. They insist that, for a right to be deemed an acquired right, the employee must have already benefited from it before the disappearance of the collective agreement, *i.e.* the fact giving rise to the right must predate it.

91. **AVANTAGES EN NATURE — PAYMENTS IN KIND**: Non-monetary remuneration (food, clothing, accommodation, heating, lighting) which is common in some occupations such as agriculture, the hotel and catering trade and domestic service. It is deemed to be part of total pay and is governed by the same legal provisions.

Payments in kind are taken into account in the calculation of the national minimum wage (**SMIC,** *i.e.* "salaire minimum interprofessionnel de croissance") and allowances of all types, and in the basis of assessment for calculating social security contributions and income tax, although only standard valuations are applied.

92. **AVANTAGES SOCIAUX — SOCIAL RIGHTS**: A loosely interpreted term relating to the network of social and customary rights and positions within and outside employment which are available to citizens and residents. Reference is frequently made to such rights suffering attack ("atteinte") or setback ("recul").

93. **AVENANT — AMENDMENT**: Change made to an individual contract of employment or to a collective agreement. The term refers in particular to the actual document or schedule setting out the change; such a document (appended) is essential in the case of a collective agreement, which is valid only if it is in written form.

   Amendments to collective agreements are the outcome of their **revision**.

94. **AVERTISSEMENT — WARNING**: Disciplinary sanction usually provided for in **works rules**. It constitutes an instruction to remedy the situation which has occasioned it, as well as a reprimand. It does not affect the employee's employment or duties.

   In practice, a distinction is often made between a warning and a reprimand ("blâme"), although their meanings are very similar.

B

95. **BADGE ÉLECTRONIQUE — ELECTRONIC IDENTITY CARD**: "Smart" card incorporating magnetic stripes or a memory which allows remote identification of the wearer. The **National Commission for Information Technology and Civil Liberties** has made efforts to restrict the ways in which these cards may be used, in the name of the freedom of movement guaranteed to **employee representatives** and of due respect for individual privacy.

96. **BASE — RANK AND FILE**: Activists or members of a trade union (or political party) who do not hold any form of office within it.

97. **BILAN SOCIAL — SOCIAL BALANCE SHEET**: Document which has been compulsory since 1977 in enterprises with 300 or more employees, drawn up by the head of the enterprise and submitted to the works council for its opinion. It must contain the main numerical data needed to assess the work and employment situation within the enterprise, record activities and evaluate changes over the past year and the two preceding years.

98. **BLÂME — REPRIMAND**: Synonym of **réprimande**.

99. **BLOCAGE (SALARIAL) — PAY FREEZE**: Prohibition of pay increases. French law incorporates the possibility of freezing pay levels as a means of fighting inflation. The last occasion was in 1982.

100. **BONNE FOI — GOOD FAITH**: Criterion governing the conduct of a person engaged in a bargaining or contractual relationship. It is an extremely fluid concept; it may impose an obligation to prove that such conduct is reasonable or does not cause unjustified damage to the protagonist.

    As a matter of principle, any contract must be performed in good faith. For the employee, this requirement rests on a duty of **loyalty**. Good faith in collective bargaining is a more difficult matter. The outline of the **bargaining procedure** which is given by the law enshrines the idea that the employers' side must act in good faith, without clarifying what this entails.

101. **BOURSE DU TRAVAIL — LABOUR CENTRE**: Form taken in the nineteenth century by workers' first attempt at collective activity and organization at multi-industry level. A Labour Centre was usually organized on the basis of a municipality ("commune"), France's smallest unit of administration.

At the end of the nineteenth century the Labour Centres formed themselves into a federation, with a wide variety of ambitions: to structure and educate the labour movement, organize mutual assistance in the event of unemployment or accidents at work, manage the administration of strike funds, provide legal assistance, etc. This federation became the basis of the present **General Confederation of Labour**. Their narrow coverage, the emergence of institutions which took over responsibility for their objectives and the formation of area trade unions at département level all contributed to the decline of the Labour Centres.

They still exist today, but essentially as premises for trade unions and so as the municipal centres of trade union life. Their status varies; the Paris Bourse du travail is governed by special regulations.

102. **BOYCOTT — BOYCOTT**: Old-established method of defending labour interests, whereby a group or trade union impedes the gainful activity of an enterprise or its products and services by calling on other people, or exerting pressure on other people, to reject or break off employment or business relations with the enterprise in question. The term "mise à l'index" (blacklisting) is also used.

It is in principle unlawful and is tolerated only within narrow limits.

103. **BRANCHE — BRANCH OF ECONOMIC ACTIVITY**: May also simply be called an "industry" in English. It serves not only as a collective bargaining level (see **industry-wide agreement**) but also as a statistical category for the analysis of economic activity and as a framework for the definition of government policy (Steel Plan, Textiles Plan, etc.).

There are complex links between these three forms of demarcation. Essentially, they are determined on the one hand by the structures of the employers' and trade union organizations and on the other by the reasoning that underlies state intervention. This means that some branches or industries are enormous (metal) while others are very small (china and porcelain).

104. **BULLETIN DE PAIE — ITEMIZED PAY STATEMENT**: Document which the employer is obliged by law to issue to employees each time they receive their pay. It serves simply to indicate payment of the sums detailed therein.

105. **BUREAU DE CONCILIATION — CONCILIATION BOARD**: See **conciliation, Industrial Tribunal**.

106. **BUREAU DE PLACEMENT — JOB PLACEMENT AGENCY**: See **job placement**. (May also be referred to as an "employment agency" in English.)

C

107. **CADENCE — PACE OF WORK**: Rhythm of work and of production. The term is mainly used with reference to jobs that involve repetitive movements, where an attempt is made to measure the pace of work, fix preset times for it, etc.

108. **CADRE — PROFESSIONAL OR MANAGERIAL EMPLOYEE**: Term which has acquired official recognition in France only since 1945, with the introduction of special regulations for this category of employees, and in particular a retirement scheme. Its definition nonetheless remains uncertain, since it requires the combination of two elements which are themselves uncertain. The first is professional worth, which may be assessed either in terms of training and formal qualifications (in which case an individual is described as a ''cadre par titre''), or on the basis of accumulated experience. This dual criterion explains, to a large extent, why the category is so widely established. The second element is the possession of authority over subordinates, exercised by delegation from the employer; the threshold that must be crossed in order to gain classification in the category may be set at numerous different levels.

A body of special rules for such professional and managerial staff has gradually been instituted. For instance, they are entitled to a period of at least three months' notice in the event of dismissal and to a higher level of severance pay. They are liable for any infringements committed in the department over which they exercise delegated powers of authority. Their contracts of employment often contain special clauses: long **probationary period**, covenant in restraint of competition. Collective agreements usually devote a special annex to professional and managerial staff. In workplace-level elections, they constitute a separate electoral body and elect their own delegates. They also elect members of Industrial Tribunals, who, together with the members elected by employers, form part of the staffing within the system of first-instance labour courts. They have their own unions, which are affiliated either to the general trade union confederations or to a special confederation (see **CGC-CFE**).

109. **CADRE SUPÉRIEUR — SENIOR EXECUTIVE**: See **executive manager**.

110. **CADRE SYNDICAL — FULL-TIME OFFICIAL**: Full-time employed officials of the national trade union federations, area unions at département level or large area unions at local level, whose organization and activities have not yet been fully analysed.

111. **CAISSE DE CONGÉS PAYÉS — HOLIDAY INSURANCE FUND**: To cover occupations in which employment is occasional or irregular, or where there is no continuity of employment, French law has created, following the model of **social insurance** administered by a fund, a system of compulsory contributions to be paid by employers to ensure that such workers enjoy the equivalent of the annual holidays with pay granted to other employees.

     Such funds exist for workers in the building and public works sector, workers in maintenance and transport services, performing artistes and dock workers.

112. **CAISSE DE SÉCURITÉ SOCIALE — SOCIAL SECURITY OFFICE**: Body responsible for administering a social security scheme. For the general scheme in France, there are three types of office: health insurance offices, which deal with illness, maternity, disability, death, and accidents at work and occupational illnesses (at three levels, *i.e.* national, regional and local); the national old-age insurance office; and the national family allowances office. Contributions are collected by independent bodies called "unions de recouvrement des cotisations de sécurité sociale et d'allocations familiales" (URSSAF), *i.e.* Associations for the Collection of Social Security and Family Allowances Contributions, and there are also co-ordinating bodies which are responsible for administering health and social assistance and, within the social security system itself, managing finances and personnel.

     At present, the management committees of these offices have a tripartite composition with a minority of government representatives. Both this composition and the method of appointing the members are the subject of continuing debate.

113. **CARRIÈRE — CAREER**: Evolvement of the status, role and responsibilities associated with working life.

     To make a career in an occupation or enterprise is to succeed in it. And success, as it is most widely perceived, is marked by an advancement in functions, financial resources and honours. Two concepts are associated with it: **length of service** and **promotion (at work)**.

114. **CATÉGORIE PROFESSIONNELLE — OCCUPATIONAL CATEGORY**: Term used with two different meanings:
     1. Groups exhibiting a certain social homogeneity into which statistics divide the working population. The major statistical nomenclatures use socio-occupational categories; these reflect,

44

at any given time, society's perception of itself. The categories currently used conform to a logic of social stratification.

2. The job classifications in industry-wide or company-level agreements also group employees into occupational categories, which in this case codify a division of occupations, a hierarchy of abilities and a scale of pay levels.

115. **CAUSE RÉELLE ET SÉRIEUSE — GENUINE AND SERIOUS CAUSE**: Any **dismissal** (with the exception of dismissal during the **probationary period**) may be subjected to verification that it satisfies this criterion. Verification is carried out by the courts responsible for dealing with individual labour disputes, which at first-instance level are the **Industrial Tribunals**. All dismissals must, therefore, be justified. If not, the employees concerned are entitled to compensation for any damage caused to them, which in certain cases has a minimum evaluation laid down by law. The requirement for genuine and serious cause is merely a guide for the courts. There is, however, agreement that it should be interpreted as a need to establish that the circumstances invoked, which must be proven, constitute a real obstacle to continuing performance of the contract of employment. The employer may simply invoke reasons; the initiative lies with the judges to investigate, by questioning the parties, whether these reasons constitute genuine and serious cause. Only when their investigation is completed are judges obliged, by law, to give the employee the benefit of any doubt that remains.

The concept of rendering dismissal null and void is only slowly entering French law, which at present incorporates it, with shades of interpretation, only in the case of unlawful reason, *i.e.* infringement of a fundamental freedom or right.

116. **CAUTIONNEMENT — GUARANTEE DEPOSIT**: It was at one time common practice in various sectors (hotels, cafés, restaurants, theatres, music halls, casinos, transport enterprises, etc.) for employers to demand from employees, at the commencement of their employment, the deposit of a certain sum of money (referred to variously as "retenue de garantie", "dépôt", "cautionnement") which enabled the enterprise to recover, immediately as and when it occurred, the cost of any damage caused by the employee.

This practice is now strictly prohibited.

117. **CÉLIBAT (CLAUSE DE) — MARRIAGE CLAUSE**: Notorious clause in contracts of employment in the civil aviation industry, whereby female employees undertook not to marry

45

during the lifetime of their contracts. The criticism levelled in the 1960s at this contractual restriction of the freedom to marry marked the emergence of a movement for retention of the fundamental freedoms in employment.

Such restriction is found in an attenuated form in denominational teaching establishments, where sometimes all employees are forbidden to marry a divorced person.

118. **CENTRALE — CENTRAL TRADE UNION ORGANIZA-TION**: See **trade union confederation**.

119. **CENTRALISATION — CENTRALIZATION**: Action directed at concentrating power within a system or organization; see **decentralization (of bargaining)**.

120. **CENTRALISME — CENTRALISM**: System which produces centralization, or feature of a system in which power is concentrated in the hands of a single controlling body, often called the centre or head. A trade union system is centralized if power is principally sited in the governing bodies of the **trade union confederations**. This tends to be the case with the French system. A system of administration is centralized if power is concentrated in the hands of the national State and its representatives. Despite the recent introduction (since 1982) of significant legislation, the French system of public administration is described, compared with others, as highly centralized.

121. **CERCLE DE QUALITÉ — QUALITY CIRCLE**: Small group of people belonging to the same work unit who, usually on a voluntary basis, meet regularly to identify, analyse and resolve problems encountered in their work.

When they were first introduced in France in the late 1970s, the original purpose of quality circles (QCs) was seen as that of countering the excessive division of labour and improving the quality of production and hence of work, by combining the drive for productivity with concern for acceptable working methods. Later, this approach was partly replaced by that of total quality management, which gives priority to the prevention of defects in production. In this approach, quality circles have become no more than one element of the structure on which it is based.

Quality circles have flourished in France, first in the industrial sector and later in the service sector and the public administration (proponents claim that in 1987 there were 30,000 in existence). They are regarded with considerable scepticism by the trade unions, and sometimes also by managerial staff.

122. **CERTIFICAT DE TRAVAIL — CERTIFICATE OF EMPLOYMENT**: Document which employers are obliged, on request, to issue to any employee whose contract of employment comes to an end. In principle, it need mention only objective facts relating to the post occupied.

123. **CESSATION — END OF THE CONTRACT OF EMPLOYMENT**: Term indicating the various ways in which the contract of employment can come to an end, depending on whether it is a **fixed-term contract** or a contract of indeterminate length (see **resignation, dismissal**). *Cf.* **termination of the contract of employment**.

124. **CESSION D'ENTREPRISE — CHANGE OF OWNERSHIP OR CONTROL**: Transfer of the ownership of the assembled means of production which make up an enterprise. This transfer may take place in various ways: total or partial transfer of assets, sale of goodwill, etc. A change of ownership or control must, by law, be accompanied by the transfer of the contracts of employment to the new employer (see **change of employer**). The works council must also be informed and consulted in advance. In terms of the council's powers, transfer of the majority shareholding in a company is equated with a change of ownership or control: although it may not involve a transfer of actual ownership of the means of production, this too must be submitted to the works council for its opinion.

     French law on the compulsory administration and liquidation of enterprises by the courts (see **bankruptcy**) lays down special rules on the total or partial change of ownership or control.

125. **CFDT**: Abbreviation of French Democratic Confederation of Labour (Confédération française démocratique du travail). See **trade union confederation**.

126. **CFTC**: Abbreviation of French Christian Workers' Confederation (Confédération française des travailleurs chrétiens). See **trade union confederation**.

127. **CGC-CFE**: Abbreviation of General Confederation of Professional and Managerial Staff-French Confederation of Professional and Managerial Staff (Confédération générale des cadres-Confédération française de l'encadrement). See **trade union confederation**.

128. **CGPME**: See **General Confederation of Small and Medium-Sized Enterprises** (Confédération générale des petites et moyennes entreprises).

129. **CGT**: Abbreviation of General Confederation of Labour (Confédération générale du travail). See **trade union confederation**.

130. **CGT-FO**: Abbreviation of General Confederation of Labour-"Force ouvrière" (Confédération générale du travail-Force ouvrière). Also known simply as FO. See **trade union confederation**.

131. **CHAMP D'APPLICATION — SCOPE OF APPLICATION**: Category of relationships to which a rule of law is intended to apply. It is usually defined on the basis of the nature of the persons concerned and the content and location of their relationships.

132. **CHANGEMENT D'EMPLOYEUR — CHANGE OF EMPLOYER**: Where an enterprise continues to operate under a new owner, the contracts of employment are transferred from the former employer to the new one. This rule, which has been established under French law since 1928, attests to the fact that the contract of employment does not simply represent a relationship between people. Its aim, as stated, is to ensure job security in the face of changes of circumstance that may affect the legal organization of the enterprise. It has, nevertheless, caused numerous difficulties of interpretation. At present, the courts deem it applicable in all cases of the "transfer of an economic entity which retains its identity and whose activity is either continued or resumed". The rule does not prohibit dismissals, but nor does it authorize them on the sole ground of transfer of ownership. See **change of ownership or control, transfer of undertaking**.

133. **CHANTIER — CONSTRUCTION SITE**: Term denoting the place where workers in the building and public works sector perform their work. They work on a "chantier". By extension, the French term also denotes actual works whose execution will necessarily last for only a limited period: such works always come to an end.

Because of this second meaning, there are special regulations on dismissal which are termed as applying to "fin de chantier", *i.e.* when such works come to an end; dismissals in this case are not treated as **redundancies**. In its first meaning, the "chantier" or construction site is mentioned as the subject of special arrangements to ensure that the employees who work there are able to participate fully in workplace-level elections.

134. **CHARGE DU TRAVAIL — WORKLOAD**: Burden borne by workers in performing their job. Loads and burdens may be understood in two different senses. The first is confined to the physical effort demanded of the worker. The fact that a mental activity requires no physical activity leads quickly on to the second meaning. In this case, it is the work activity itself that has to be measured. Nowadays, the measurement of work involves distinguishing its various components: physical (muscular exertion), sensory (use of eyes, ears, etc.), mental (processing of sensory information), social (structure of relations with other workers, supervisory staff), etc. The study of workload is therefore increasingly concerned with analysing the work activity and the characteristics of the workers themselves together with the situation (work areas, technical system, general surroundings, etc.) affecting it.

135. **CHARGES SOCIALES — EMPLOYMENT-RELATED COSTS**: Cost of employment to the enterprise. Such costs therefore include not only actual pay but all the expenses incurred as a result of employing the employee (social security contributions, unemployment insurance contributions, annual holidays with pay, etc.). The expressions "social charges" and "social costs" are also used.

The term is sometimes used to refer to the cost of employment exclusive of actual pay or, in an even narrower sense, to refer to sums paid by the enterprise to finance social protection (social security and social welfare).

136. **CHARTE D'AMIENS — CHARTER OF AMIENS**: Document adopted in 1906 at the Congress of the **General Confederation of Labour**, which expounded the Confederation's doctrine. It has had a profound effect on the trade union movement in France through its extolling of direct action by labour, furthering the education of the workers, its rejection of all links with political parties and its criticism of the State. It was a treatise on anarcho-syndicalism. Abandoned in 1914 when the CGT rallied to the united cause against Germany, this doctrine has nonetheless left deep marks that are still visible today: weakness of discipline, high regard for militancy and dedicated conviction, together with the creation of a workers' élite that this allows, distrust of parliamentary action, etc.

137. **CHEF D'ENTREPRISE — HEAD OF AN ENTERPRISE**: Whereas the employer is a party to the contract of employment and as such may be either a natural person (individual entrepreneur) or a legal person (company), the head of an enterprise is the natural person who exercises managerial prerogatives. In this capacity the head of an enterprise is liable for any infringements of labour legislation (in so far as the criminal liability of legal persons has not yet been adopted as a principle) and, above all, is the opposite number of the collective body of employees for the purposes of dialogue (by chairing the works council, for example).

The status of head of enterprise is in principle attributed to the *de jure* managers of the legal person (general manager, chairperson of the management board), but it is common for powers to be delegated (see **delegation of authority**).

138. **CHÔMAGE — UNEMPLOYMENT**: Within the meaning of current statistical categories, the situation of a person who is without a job, available for work and seeking such work. This definition, the elements of which are sometimes subject to debate, necessarily entails an arbitrary distinction between employment in the sense of a contract and economic inactivity in the sense of not seeking to enter into employment under a contract.

As a concept, unemployment exists only by virtue of the fact that most employment takes the form of wage-earning, and the consequent conviction that employment under a contract of employment is the normal route to economic activity and an income. Its definition also flows from the policies aimed at reducing it or, by granting assistance, alleviating the consequences of involuntary economic inactivity. Although the definition as given is well established, there is general acceptance nowadays that unemployment takes various different forms, that its boundaries are blurred and that the status of unemployed persons varies.

139. **CHÔMAGE INTEMPÉRIES — BAD-WEATHER UNEMPLOYMENT INSURANCE SCHEME**: See **bad weather**.

140. **CHÔMAGE PARTIEL — PARTIAL UNEMPLOYMENT**: Situation of employees who, in the event of the temporary closure of an enterprise (or establishment) or a temporary reduction of working hours, are in receipt of partial maintenanceof their pay via a compensatory mechanism set up by general multi-industry agreement, possibly with assistance from the State. The purpose of the mechanism is to pay compensation for partial unemployment.

By extension, and through confusion, the term is also used to refer to the situation of exclusion from work suffered as a result of temporary closure. It also applies to situations where short-time working is temporarily introduced for economic reasons. These situations, which should properly be referred to as "chômage technique" (layoff), do not exempt employers from paying wages in full unless they succeed in arranging payment of the compensatory allowances for partial unemployment.

Use of the mechanism is limited by the need to obtain authorization (for payment) from the authorities and by the fact that compensation is payable for only a fixed quota of hours.

141. **CHÔMAGE TECHNIQUE — LAYOFF**: See **partial unemployment, reduction of working hours**. (Must not be confused with the English term "technological unemployment", *i.e.* unemployment deriving from the replacement of human workers by machines as a result of technological change.)

142. **CITOYENNETÉ — RETENTION OF CIVIL LIBERTIES IN EMPLOYMENT**: Employees should be citizens within the enterprise: such was the formula that guided the reforms of labour law introduced in France in 1982.

It is a formula open to two interpretations. According to the first, employees must retain, within the enterprise, the rights and freedoms which, like everyone, they enjoy outside the enterprise. For instance, they are entitled to respect for their individual privacy within the enterprise, or may exercise their freedom of expression there. This interpretation means, therefore, setting limits to the employer's managerial prerogatives and ensuring that the enterprise is not an island where fundamental freedoms and rights are excluded. The alternative interpretation is that employees must become citizens of the enterprise itself, that is, participate in the exercise of the authority which is exercised over them and determines the fate of the enterprise. The word "citoyenneté" is, in this case, nothing other than a different name for what has been termed, outside France, industrial or economic democracy.

The 1982 formula, which met with opposition from some employers, has, through force of circumstance, lost some of its innovative qualities. Nowadays it is a philosophy encouraged by certain enterprises in the interests of mobilizing human resources.

143. **CLASSIFICATION — JOB CLASSIFICATION**: In the sense most commonly attributed to it for decades, this term refers to a list of all the job titles in an enterprise, an occupational sector or an industry.

It has long been the practice to set out these job classifications in **industry-wide agreements**, mainly with a view to fixing minimum wages. But the construction of job classifications, with their hierarchical ranking, divisions into categories and, in some cases, definitions of functions, also expresses a view of the career of employees and of the organization of work.

Under the influence of the model set by the iron and steel industry and the decrees passed after 1945 to fix wages, job classifications were based on the traditional concept of crafts, involving a simple list of job titles. In fact, the systems used vary: sometimes the tasks corresponding to jobs are described, sometimes formal qualifications and training feature more prominently, and sometimes generally applicable evaluation criteria are used. By tradition, separate lists are constructed for manual workers, technicians and supervisors, and professional and managerial staff. But there are also instances where a single-scale system is used, with the same classification criteria applied to all employees.

French law encourages collective bargaining on job classifications, mainly by making it compulsory for industries in which they are used to review such classifications at least every five years.

144. **CLAUSE — CLAUSE**: Specific provision of a legal document. A contractual clause is a provision which establishes and specifies an obligation incumbent on one of the parties to the contract. Contracts of employment may, for example, include clauses constituting a covenant in restraint of competition or clauses specifying the period of notice to be observed in the event of dismissal.

145. **CLAUSE D'EXCLUSIVITÉ — SOLE-EMPLOYMENT CLAUSE**: See **multiple jobholding**.

146. **CLAUSE DE MAINTIEN DES AVANTAGES ACQUIS — ACQUIRED RIGHTS CLAUSE**: Clause inserted in a collective agreement which replaces another agreement, concluded between the same parties and having the same occupational and territorial scope, stipulating that the new agreement may not give rise to any restriction of the entitlements acquired prior to its signature. Failure to specify in detail the entitlements whose maintenance is sought renders such clauses inoperative, owing to the restrictive interpretation given by the courts to the concept of **acquired rights**.

147. **CLAUSE DE PAIX SOCIALE — NO-STRIKE CLAUSE**: Undertaking by the signatories to a collective agreement to refrain, for the duration of the agreement, from engaging in any collective industrial action in connection with the matters regulated in it.

    Under the French system, the existence of a collective agreement does not, according to prevailing legal opinion, imply a peace obligation, and the scope of any explicit obligation is controversial. The strike is not made subject to the principle of *ultima ratio*; furthermore, the holder of the right to strike is the individual employee, a fact which makes it inconceivable for strike action to be conditional upon the absence or failure of collective bargaining.

    The law does nevertheless establish a principle of loyal performance of the collective agreement, although its implications are uncertain.

148. **CLAUSE DE SÉCURITÉ SYNDICALE — UNION MEMBERSHIP (CLOSED SHOP) CLAUSE**: Clause in a collective agreement whereby membership of the signatory trade union is rendered necessary *de jure* or *de facto*. Except in certain sectors, such clauses are very rare. Studies of their various forms usually have to draw on examples from other countries.

    Since 1946 all union membership clauses have been prohibited by French law, although this has not prevented the unions from continuing to exert a monopoly over hiring in some instances.

149. **CNPF**: See **National Council of French Employers** (Conseil national du patronat français).

150. **COALITION — COLLECTIVE INDUSTRIAL ORGANIZATION**: Obsolete term denoting any form of grouping of workers or entrepreneurs motivated by a commonality of occupational interests. The Revolution, anxious to eliminate any intermediary grouping between the individual, as citizen and producer, and the assembled nation, prohibited all such "coalitions" or collective organizations. The corresponding offence disappeared in 1864.

151. **CODE DU TRAVAIL — LABOUR CODE**: Most (though not all) French legislative and regulatory texts concerning employment as an employee and the relationships which are established in connection with it have been collected together and classified in a document called the Labour Code.

    This classification is purely administrative and is a compilation or consolidation, rather than a codification in the historical sense of the word.

The first Labour Code was promulgated between 1920 and 1927; the current one dates from 1973 but is continuously updated, by decree.

152. **COGESTION — CO-DETERMINATION**: Joint management of an enterprise by the capital providers (or their representatives) and the employees (or their representatives). In practice, co-determination means that major decisions may only be taken jointly.

French law does not recognize any form of co-determination. At most, it attempts to promote employee participation in management. Representation of employees in the management or supervisory organs of a company may be organized (see **worker member of the board**). Otherwise, participation resides in two elements: the consultation functions of the works council, and the stipulation of a **duty to bargain** on particular matters within the enterprise.

153. **COMITÉ D'ENTREPRISE — WORKS COUNCIL**: (Term sometimes misleadingly translated as "enterprise committee".) Institution of employee representation, compulsory since 1945 in enterprises with more than 50 employees. Possessing legal personality, the works council in France is a collegiate body composed not only of employee members elected by the workforce but also of the head of the enterprise (who chairs the council and takes part in certain votes) and of representatives appointed by the trade unions (who act in a purely consultative capacity).

Its position in the enterprise is singular: it has charge of **company welfare and cultural facilities**; the law invests it with only consultative powers in regard to employer initiatives concerning the organization and management of the enterprise; and other than in the case of **profit-sharing agreements**, it possesses no formal bargaining power. In practice, the dividing line between consultation, which is the prerogative of the works council, and collective bargaining, which is the prerogative of the representative trade unions, is a very fine one. Numerous agreements, formal or otherwise, are concluded between the head of an enterprise and the works council, and the courts accord these a certain legal force, at the least as unilateral undertakings on the part of the employer.

The institution is a complex one. It is a counterweight to managerial prerogatives, yet also enables their exercise to be rationalized. It is a complement to union power, yet is also virtually its competitor.

154. **COMITÉ D'ÉTABLISSEMENT — ESTABLISHMENT-LEVEL WORKS COUNCIL**: Body representing the workforce of an **establishment**, with a similar structure to that of the **works council** at enterprise level, and parallel powers and functions. These powers and functions are, however, restricted to the context of those conferred on the head of an establishment.

155. **COMITÉ DE GRÈVE — STRIKE COMMITTEE**: Informal group set up in the event of a strike, composed of employees of the enterprise concerned who may or may not be invested with elective functions or trade union office, which presents itself *de facto* as the employer's opposite number for the purposes of dialogue. If, as sometimes happens, the strike committee signs an agreement to end the dispute, this does not have the legal force of a **collective agreement**.

156. **COMITÉ DE GROUPE — GROUP-LEVEL WORKS COUNCIL**: Institution of employee representation whose formation has been compulsory in groups of companies since 1982. It is a body derived from the works councils of the various individual companies in the group. In law, it is empowered merely to receive retrospective and prospective economic information and to discuss it.

157. **COMITÉ D'HYGIÈNE, DE SÉCURITÉ ET DES CONDITIONS DE TRAVAIL — WORKPLACE HEALTH AND SAFETY COMMITTEE**: Body representing the workforce of an enterprise.

    Prior to 1982 it formed part of the works council; since 1982 it has been a separately constituted body, with the purpose of helping to protect employees' health and safety at work and to improve working conditions. Compulsory in enterprises with more than 50 employees, it is composed of the head of the enterprise and employee members appointed by a special body comprising elected representatives of the workforce (see **works council, workforce delegate**). It has special means of access to information, may take certain initiatives (such as the right to issue a **notification** of danger) without, however, possessing the authority to halt production, and performs a major consultative role.

158. **COMITÉ SUPÉRIEUR DE L'EMPLOI — HIGHER COMMITTEE ON EMPLOYMENT**: Tripartite body chaired by the Minister for Labour and responsible for advising on the direction and implementation of employment policy. Its role is a modest one, but the same cannot be said of its standing commission, which, in particular, examines the activities of the **National Employment Fund**.

159. **COMITÉ TECHNIQUE PARITAIRE — JOINT TECHNICAL COMMITTEE**: Joint body with strict parity of representation for the employer's and employees' sides which, in the **civil service**, must compulsorily be consulted on major issues concerning the organization and functioning of the public administration and its various branches.

160. **COMMANDEMENT — NOTICE OF COMPLIANCE**: In civil procedure, official document issued after a court judgment or in settlement of a debt, served by a bailiff in order to enforce execution of a judgment or settlement.

    In labour law, this remedy is used by employees to enforce payment in the event of non-payment of remuneration, or by employers to enforce eviction in the event of unlawful occupation of the workplace by employees.

161. **COMMISSION DE CONCILIATION — CONCILIATION COMMITTEE**: See **minute of conciliation**.

162. **COMMISSION EXÉCUTIVE — EXECUTIVE COMMITTEE**: In **trade union confederations** which follow the organizational model of the General Confederation of Labour, an expanded management body that performs the functions of a board of directors or supervisory board; day-to-day management is the responsibility of the confederal or national office. The French Democratic Confederation of Labour has chosen to reverse these roles: its executive committee is its governing body and the office serves as a board of directors.

163. **COMMISSION MIXTE — JOINT COMMITTEE**: Name given to a specific form of joint committee which is actually a forum where the representative trade union organizations and employers' associations meet in the presence of a representative of the Minister for Labour, who is there in an advisory capacity. (The presence of the Minister's representative is therefore the feature distinguishing a joint body described as "mixte" from a strictly joint (social partners) body defined as "paritaire".) This is the normal procedure followed for negotiations on a collective agreement that qualifies for extension (see **extension of collective agreements**).

    In practice, extensions of collective agreements may be agreed without this procedure, provided that the conditions of extension are otherwise met.

164. **COMMISSION NATIONALE DE L'INFORMATIQUE ET DES LIBERTÉS — NATIONAL COMMISSION FOR INFORMATION TECHNOLOGY AND CIVIL LIBERTIES**: Independent administrative authority (referred to as CNIL) created by the Law of January 4, 1978 which, in regard to the threats posed by information technology, grants new rights to the individual and regulates the computerized processing of **personal data**.

    The Commission is responsible for enforcing observance of the rules laid down by this Law and for updating them as new practices and problems arise.

165. **COMMISSION NATIONALE DE LA NÉGOCIATION COLLECTIVE — NATIONAL COLLECTIVE BARGAINING COMMISSION**: Tripartite body which must be consulted before a collective agreement is extended (see **extension of collective agreements**) or before the SMIC (see **minimum wage**) is raised. It also has general responsibilities of review and recommendation with respect to collective bargaining.

166. **COMMISSION PARITAIRE — JOINT COLLECTIVE AGREEMENT COMMITTEE**: Title of the body set up under a collective agreement to interpret the provisions of the agreement, monitor its application and, sometimes, arrange for its revision. It is the body that administers the collective agreement.

167. **COMMUNICATION DANS L'ENTREPRISE — EMPLOYEE COMMUNICATIONS**: The more that trust and commitment on the part of employees are seen as means of securing the economic success of an enterprise, the more important internal information and communication become.

    Organizing seminars, distributing information bulletins, defining objectives for each individual department or establishment and giving film shows are all examples of the methods used to disseminate information and ensure communication. Directed primarily at professional and managerial staff, they are also targeted at technical and production workers. The aim is to change the face of personnel management and present managers as leaders and advisers within the individual departments of the enterprise. This trend, whose feasibility is sometimes challenged, has not met with general hostility from the unions. It nonetheless raises the difficult question of the relationship between direct communication with employees and the more institutionalized machinery of discussion with their representatives.

168. **COMMUNICATION SYNDICALE — UNION COM-MUNICATIONS**: French law provides for only two methods by which trade unions can communicate information to employees within an enterprise: the display of notices and the distribution of printed material. The first method is open to all unions (see **display of notices**), whereas only members of representative unions are guaranteed the right to use the second.

The content of the information communicated is decided by the unions themselves without any restrictions.

169. **COMPORTEMENT ANTISYNDICAL — ANTI-UNION BEHAVIOUR**: See **interference**.

170. **COMPRESSION D'EFFECTIFS — STAFF REDUCTION**: A cut in the number of employees employed by an enterprise for reasons of an economic, financial or technical nature. The term "sur-effectifs" (overstaffing) is much used nowadays. French law treats staff reduction as an instance of dismissal for economic reasons. See **redundancy**.

171. **CONCERTATION — CONCERTED CONSULTATION**: Policy whereby the parties concerned confer to ensure that their respective interests are taken into account in the decision-making process.

At the macrosocial level of industrial relations, the term is used in the sense of "social concertation", less common in France than in other countries because there is no permanent forum for interaction between the **social actors**. Negotiation on the law has, nevertheless, been a relatively active phenomenon for the past 20 years (the regulation of working hours and redundancy have been prime examples of these negotiated laws).

At the level of the individual enterprise, establishment and department, the concerted attempt to reach an active consensus is often referred to as "concertation" in order to create a sense of distance from the formal powers of consultation conferred by law on the various institutions of employee representation. The term serves as a euphemism for denoting forms of co-operative consultation with the works council and negotiation with the unions. In practice, it is characterized by debate rather than concrete outcomes.

These processes are frequently referred to as "social dialogue".

172. **CONCESSIONAIRE — CONCESSIONAIRE**: An individual or firm that undertakes, for a certain period, to purchase an enterprise's products from it in order to resell them, while the enterprise providing the concession undertakes to grant the

concessionaire exclusive rights (of varying extent) for the resale of its products. When it is an individual, the unusual characteristic of a concessionaire lies in neither being an employee of the enterprise providing the concession nor (in contrast to a **commercial agent**) enjoying any special status. The concessionaire may, however, also be another company.

173. **CONCILIATION — CONCILIATION**: Method of settling a conflict or a dispute at law whose distinctive feature is agreement between the parties. The term therefore refers sometimes to the procedure and sometimes to its outcome.

In the case of individual disputes, French law stipulates a conciliation phase in the proceedings before **Industrial Tribunals**, prior to the judgment phase and compulsory in principle, during which two judges (members of the Industrial Tribunal) attempt to bring the parties to agreement. These two judges form the Tribunal's conciliation board. The conciliation rate varies from one Tribunal to another.

In the case of collective disputes, the law makes provision for a conciliation procedure which is voluntary, unless the relevant collective agreement stipulates otherwise. In practice, little use is made of this procedure.

174. **CONDITIONS DE TRAVAIL — TERMS AND CONDITIONS OF EMPLOYMENT/WORKING CONDITIONS**: Expression which has several meanings:
1. In a broad sense, it encompasses all the elements which may have an effect on the life and work of the employee. Thus, the study of "conditions de travail" and the deliberations which this engenders include the organization of working time, health and safety at work, payment systems and rules on training and promotion.
2. In a narrower sense, the expression indicates the physical performance of work and involves analysis of the work context and the work environment (*i.e.* the physical conditions usually meant by the term "working conditions" in English), work organization and command procedures.
3. In a legal sense, which is little used, the expression applies to the formal elements of the contract of employment (in English, specifically called "terms and conditions of employment").
4. Two further considerations should be mentioned. Firstly, the expression appears as the title of one of the subdivisions of the **Labour Code**; grouped under this are the provisions relating to the minimum age for entry into employment, working hours and night work, but not the rules on leave and

rest periods, nor those relating to health and safety at work. This formal demarcation is, of course, of no consequence. Secondly, during the past 30 years the subject of improvement of "conditions de travail" has evolved very considerably in France. In its present form, it exists as a keynote of public policy termed "changer le travail" (changing work). Essentially, it amounts to emphasizing the advantages, both economic (in terms of productivity and profitability) and social (better protection of personal safety and health in general, self-fulfilment, etc.), to be gained from effecting changes in the organization of work to improve risk prevention, allow employees a voice in job definition, reduce the fragmentation of work and systematize opportunities of improving skills.

175. **CONFÉDÉRATION — TRADE UNION CONFEDERA-TION**: National trade union body, in most cases multi-industry, serving as an umbrella organization for individual national trade unions, area unions at département and regional level, and occupational or industrial federations.

Five such confederations have been recognized as representative (see **representativeness**) at national level, and they have a major role to play. Not only do they ensure that labour interests are protected, but they also regulate the functioning of the confederated organizations attached to them. And they participate in the formulation of the rules of labour and social security law. In practice, a considerable amount of power is concentrated in their hands.

The five confederations possessing representative status are as follows:

CFDT: Confédération française démocratique du travail (French Democratic Confederation of Labour). This trade union confederation is a continuation of the French Christian Workers' Confederation, which changed its name in 1964 in order to mark the wish of the majority of its members to eliminate any religious connotation.

Purely in terms of the results of **workplace-level elections**, *i.e.* the votes won by the candidates standing in its name, it occupies second place among the confederations.

CFTC: Confédération française des travailleurs chrétiens (French Christian Workers' Confederation). Trade union confederation originally formed in 1919, whose name has been preserved by the minority of its members who were opposed to the elimination of the religious connotation which took place in 1964 (see **CFDT**, French Democratic Confederation of Labour, above) and broke away in order to maintain its traditional image.

CGC-CFE: Confédération générale des cadres-Confédération française de l'encadrement (General Confederation of Professional and Managerial Staff-French Confederation of Professional and Managerial Staff). Trade union confederation which was originally formed in 1946 and then known simply as the CGC. It is the only one of the five confederations possessing recognized representative status at national level which is intended for a single occupational category. The other four do, however, have professional and managerial employees among their members. Consequently, the CGC-CFE does not possess monopoly representation of this category, whose definition is in any case uncertain (see **professional or managerial employee**).

CGT: Confédération générale du travail (General Confederation of Labour). As the oldest of the five representative trade union confederations, this confederation was created in two stages, in 1895 and 1906. It has left its mark on the entire labour movement and still occupies first place among the confederations in terms of the number of votes won in workplace-level elections and, undoubtedly, the number of its members, although it has lost the pre-eminent position it occupied until as recently as 30 years ago. The links between some of its senior officials (and in particular its General Secretary) and the Communist Party have frequently been the subject of much emphasis and comment. But it has to be remembered that the transformation of society is one of the objectives of the French trade union movement as it exists today.

CGT-FO: Confédération générale du travail-Force ouvrière (General Confederation of Labour-"Force ouvrière"). This trade union confederation (also known simply as FO), was formed in 1947 in the climate of the start of the "cold war", by some of the CGT's officials and member unions. It was therefore born in the name of "trade union independence", which, in the early years, mainly signified hostility towards the CGT because of its links with the Communist Party, and nowadays embodies the total rejection of all ties with political parties, the active promotion of collective bargaining (particularly at multi-industry and industry level) and a certain reluctance towards any form of integration within the enterprise. The confederation, whose member unions embrace widely diverse ideological persuasions, claims to be the true heir of a trade unionism whose heritage is free and unfettered collective bargaining.

176. CONFÉDÉRATION FRANÇAISE DÉMOCRATIQUE DU TRAVAIL — FRENCH DEMOCRATIC CONFEDERATION OF LABOUR: See **trade union confederation**.

177. **CONFÉDÉRATION FRANÇAISE DES TRAVAILLEURS CHRÉTIENS — FRENCH CHRISTIAN WORKERS' CONFEDERATION**: See **trade union confederation**.

178. **CONFÉDÉRATION GÉNÉRALE DES CADRES-CONFÉDÉRATION FRANÇAISE DE L'ENCADREMENT — GENERAL CONFEDERATION OF PROFESSIONAL AND MANAGERIAL STAFF-FRENCH CONFEDERATION OF PROFESSIONAL AND MANAGERIAL STAFF**: See **trade union confederation**.

179. **CONFÉDÉRATION GÉNÉRALE DES PETITES ET MOYENNES ENTREPRISES — GENERAL CONFEDERATION OF SMALL AND MEDIUM-SIZED ENTERPRISES**: Employers' confederation (referred to as the CGPME) which serves as an umbrella organization formed by enterprises with fewer than 500 employees. A founder member of the **National Council of French Employers**, it broke away in the mid-1950s to concentrate on promoting the special interests of small enterprises.

180. **CONFÉDÉRATION GÉNÉRALE DU TRAVAIL — GENERAL CONFEDERATION OF LABOUR**: See **trade union confederation**.

181. **CONFÉDÉRATION GÉNÉRALE DU TRAVAIL-FORCE OUVRIÈRE — GENERAL CONFEDERATION OF LABOUR-"FORCE OUVRIÈRE"**: See **trade union confederation**.

182. **CONFIANCE — TRUST**: Trust, understood as the firm belief that the other party will do what is expected of them, is the condition for the conclusion of a contract of employment. That is why a contract of employment is always classed as a contract concluded *intuitu personae* (in respect of the person). There is, however, some question as to whether trust has a role in the strictly legal sense within the contract: whether, for example, employers can expect more of employees than strict performance of their contractual obligations. The practical issue at stake here is the legitimacy of dismissal on the ground of loss of trust. For certain employees (professional and managerial staff, and employees of small enterprises) the courts tend to uphold this as justifying dismissal (see **dismissal for reasons relating to the individual**) provided that specific evidence is produced to support it.

183. **CONFLICTUALITÉ — LEVEL OF INDUSTRIAL CONFLICT**: Frequency of **industrial disputes**. For the purposes of official statistics in France, the level of industrial conflict is in practice synonymous with the number of strikes. The statistics show a relative increase in public sector strikes and hence in what are termed generalized, as opposed to localized, disputes, and a diversity of reasons for strikes, with claims relating to employment featuring alongside pay claims. Pay claims sometimes disguise what is actually a reaction relating to sense of identity, characteristic of categories of employees who resent the hierarchical ranking and organization of work reflected in **job classifications**, and the lack of recognition of their abilities.

184. **CONFLIT DU TRAVAIL — INDUSTRIAL CONFLICT**: Situation in which relations between employers and employees are marked by opposing viewpoints or claims, accompanied by events and action which may or may not include the use of coercive measures.

There are widely varying attitudes to industrial conflicts and, more generally, to social conflicts, that is, declared collective rivalries concerning general issues. Some see them as integral to the very nature of the social relationships of production, while others consider their dominant issue to be control (and not ownership) of the means of production, and their explanation to be the unequal distribution of authority. In the functionalists' view social conflicts are, rather, a sign of dysfunctional regulatory systems. And lastly, conflict is sometimes argued to be a rational process of social change. These debates are important for labour law itself, whose development is generally agreed to be strongly influenced by conflicts.

Although technically incorrect, rather than in this sense of industrial conflict as a social situation the term "conflit du travail" is sometimes used for "litige du travail" (*i.e.* labour dispute), which, strictly, denotes a specific legal (procedural) situation created simply by the fact that the parties present opposing claims to the court. In some contexts it may also best be translated as referring to a specific industrial dispute

185. **CONGÉ — LEAVE (OF ABSENCE)**: Term which has two different meanings:
1. Legitimate absence from work which is justified either by law or by an agreement between employer and employee. It is used, for example, in the expressions "congé de maladie" (sick leave) and "congés payés" (annual holiday with pay). In this sense, the term has come to denote the period of absence itself.

2. In a second sense, now rather fallen into disuse, it denotes the act by which one party informs the other of their intention not to continue the contract. Here, it is part of the terminology relating to hiring agreements ("bail"), one of which was the former contract for services that became the present-day contract of employment. Hence, the expression "délai de congé" was used to denote the period of notice (now "délai de préavis").

186. **CONGÉ D'ADOPTION — ADOPTION LEAVE:** Period of parental leave intended to enable an employee who adopts a child to organize arrangements for the child's arrival. The law treats it in accordance with the model of maternity leave but does not restrict it to women.

187. **CONGÉ DE CONVERSION — RE-TRAINING LEAVE:** Innovation introduced by a Law of 1985 which lost much of its relevance when **re-training agreements** were instituted.

It relates to the organization, with the aid of government funds, of training arrangements intended to help employees about to be faced with **redundancy** to find new employment. Their contract of employment is therefore suspended for the duration of the leave.

188. **CONGÉ D'ÉDUCATION OUVRIÈRE — WORKERS' EDUCATIONAL LEAVE:** Obsolete term, nowadays replaced by the term **leave for education in economic, social and union affairs.**

189. **CONGÉ DE FORMATION — EDUCATIONAL LEAVE:** Allows employees, on their own initiative and in accordance with their own choice, to attend courses of vocational, cultural or industrial-relations training. It is an individual right enjoyed by every employee, and the conditions and formalities of its exercise are laid down by law.

Departure on such leave implies suspension of performance of the contract of employment. Employees do not receive their pay during the period of leave, unless the employer has agreed to continue paying all or part of it or it is paid by a **training insurance fund**.

190. **CONGÉ DE FORMATION ÉCONOMIQUE, SOCIALE ET SYNDICALE — LEAVE FOR EDUCATION IN ECONOMIC, SOCIAL AND UNION AFFAIRS:** As provided for by law, such leave of absence allows employees to attend training courses organized by centres run by the trade union bodies that possess representative status at national level, or specialized establishments.

Members of **works councils** and **workplace health and safety committees** have the benefit of special preferential rules in regard to such leave.

191. **CONGÉ DE MALADIE — SICK LEAVE**: Legitimate period of absence from work, treated as a suspension of the contract of employment, necessitated by the employee's **illness**. The employee receives social security benefits (called "indemnités journalières", *i.e.* daily allowances), often supplemented by a complementary sum payable by the employer (see **sick pay**).

192. **CONGÉ DE MATERNITÉ — MATERNITY LEAVE**: Legitimate period of absence from work, treated as a suspension of the contract of employment, due to pregnancy and childbirth.

     Under French law, maternity leave commences six weeks before the expected date of the employee's confinement (eight weeks if she already has two or more children), and ends ten weeks after the confinement (sixteen weeks from the third child onwards). It is extended in the event of a pathological condition or of multiple births, and is adjusted if the birth is premature.

     This leave is deemed, in principle, to be a period of effective employment. It constitutes a period during which protection against dismissal is specially increased (see **maternity**), with the guaranteed right to return to the same job.

193. **CONGÉ PARENTAL D'ÉDUCATION — PARENTAL CHILDCARE LEAVE**: Entitlement available to employees as a direct continuation of either **maternity leave** or **adoption leave** (*i.e.* not restricted to women), intended to enable them to bring up a child until its third birthday (or until the third anniversary of the child's arrival in the home in the case of adoption).

     In such a case the contract of employment is terminated, but there is an obligation on the employer to give the employee preference for re-hiring for available jobs.

194. **CONGÉ POUR CONVENANCES PERSONNELLES — SPECIAL PERSONAL LEAVE**: Some collective agreements make provision for an entitlement whereby employees may suspend performance of their contract of employment without needing to invoke any particular grounds that prevent them from working.

195. **CONGÉ POUR CRÉATION D'ENTREPRISE — ENTERPRISE CREATION LEAVE**: One year's leave of absence, unpaid and renewable, for which the law grants entitlement to employees intending to establish or take over an

enterprise provided that they are to be responsible for its management. See **enterprise creation, job creation**.

196. **CONGÉ POUR ÉVÉNEMENTS FAMILIAUX — SPECIAL FAMILY LEAVE**: Certain occasions (such as an employee's marriage, the death of their spouse or child, the death of their mother or father, etc.) entitle employees to time off from work without loss of pay. (Some instances are also referred to in English as "compassionate leave".)

The period of time off allowed is fixed by law and collective agreement. In some cases no particular length of continuous service is required, while in others it constitutes a condition of eligibility.

197. **CONGÉ POUR L'EXERCICE DE FONCTIONS PUBLIQUES OU PROFESSIONNELLES — RELEASE FOR PUBLIC DUTIES**: For the purposes of performing certain public offices and duties (Deputy or Senator in the two parliamentary chambers, local government councillor, member of an Industrial Tribunal, jury service in the Courts of Assize) or employment-related functions (member of the management committee of a social security office, etc.), employees are entitled by law to periods of time off from work of varying duration and subject to varying conditions. Performance of the contract of employment is suspended during the period of release.

198. **CONGÉ SABBATIQUE — SABBATICAL LEAVE**: Unpaid leave of absence of between six and 12 months to which employees are entitled, subject to certain conditions laid down by law, for the purposes of pursuing an activity of their own choosing.

199. **CONGÉ SANS SOLDE — UNPAID LEAVE**: See **special personal leave**.

200. **CONGÉDIEMENT — DISMISSAL**: Term coined from the old terminology of the word **congé**, and synonymous with **licenciement**.

201. **CONGÉS PAYÉS — ANNUAL HOLIDAY**: The right of every employee to abstain from working for a certain period during the year, while still receiving pay, was established by law in 1936. Its introduction was a milestone in the history of French labour law.

In 1982 this paid holiday entitlement, originally set at two weeks in 1936, was increased to two and a half working days for each month worked, with the reference period running from June 1 to May 31. It is no longer necessarily taken in one continuous block and in the summer; the law, in fact, encourages the staggered timing of holidays.

202. **CONSEIL D'ADMINISTRATION — BOARD OF DIRECTORS**: Traditional company organ of a public limited company ("société anonyme", or SA), whose members are appointed by the shareholders' meeting and whose powers are partly exclusive and partly shared with its chairperson.

Directors must be shareholders; their powers and responsibilities may be determined by the shareholders in accordance with special conditions, and they may be removed from the board on a discretionary basis.

The law has made provision for the appointment of **worker members of the board**, but little use is made of this option.

203. **CONSEIL D'ATELIER ET DE BUREAU — SHOP-FLOOR AND DEPARTMENTAL COMMITTEE**: Term sometimes used to refer to the context within which employees are able to exercise their **right of expression**.

204. **CONSEIL CONSTITUTIONNEL — CONSTITUTIONAL COURT**: Body created under the 1958 Constitution. Although originally political in nature by virtue of its composition and its general task of supervising Parliament, the "Council" has become, in effect, a constitutional court.

Its main function is to ensure that the laws passed by Parliament do not contravene the Constitution. In particular, it ensures observance of the fundamental individual and collective freedoms (right to strike, freedom of association, etc.). For the time being, recourse to its authority is still limited: firstly in terms of time, since a law may be referred to the Constitutional Court only after it has been passed but before it has been promulgated; and secondly by the fact that the power to refer laws to it is restricted to the President of the Republic, the Prime Minister, the Presidents of the National Assembly and the Senate, and any group of 60 Deputies or 60 Senators. Its rulings have, nevertheless, acquired considerable significance in labour law.

205. **CONSEIL D'ÉTAT — SUPREME ADMINISTRATIVE COURT**: Both an administrative court of the highest instance and a consultative organ of the Government in legal and administrative matters. (Often misleadingly translated as "Council of State".) As an administrative court, it judges upon the legality of administrative acts. In this capacity, it deals with disputed matters in labour relations between the State and the public

authorities on the one hand and their established civil servants and public employees on the other.

As a consultative body of experts, it is required to issue an opinion on all draft legislation proposed by the Government. The latter also entrusts the Court with numerous studies.

206. **CONSEIL DE PRUD'HOMMES — INDUSTRIAL TRIBUNAL**: First-instance labour court, of long-established tradition, whose unique feature is its strictly joint composition, with half of its members (judges) elected by employees and half by employers. It has exclusive competence for dealing with individual disputes arising from the contract of employment.

The way in which the Industrial Tribunals function follows rules which justify their composition. All disputes must, as a matter of principle, be the subject of an initial conciliation stage (before a joint conciliation board). In this stage the procedure is oral; the parties need not necessarily be assisted or represented by a lawyer, but they must appear in person.

But the Tribunals are courts in the true sense. Their members ("prud'hommes") possess a status which protects them against the risk of pressure or sanction. Appeals against their rulings may be brought before the **Courts of Appeal** and before the **Supreme Court**.

Although frequently criticized, the Industrial Tribunals are strongly supported both by many employers and by the trade unions.

207. **CONSEIL DE SURVEILLANCE — SUPERVISORY BOARD**: Supervisory body which, together with the body responsible for day-to-day management (management board), constitutes an alternative two-tier structure for a public limited company (as opposed to the traditional structure with a single **board of directors**). This new two-tier structure, modelled on German company law, was made an option for shareholders in France in 1966 to enable non-shareholding senior executives to be invested with managerial authority, their activities being supervised by a body composed of shareholders. The concept has met with little success, since less than 1 per cent. of public limited companies have adopted the two-tier structure.

208. **CONSEIL NATIONAL DU PATRONAT FRANÇAIS — NATIONAL COUNCIL OF FRENCH EMPLOYERS**: The major employers' organization in France, known as the CNPF. It takes the form of an umbrella association uniting two types of constituent groupings: "horizontal" regional groupings of employers, and the activity-based groupings or industrial

federations which are the essential "vertical" structures of the employers' side in industrial relations.

Since 1968 the CNPF has acquired increased authority and, except in the matter of pay, may sign collective agreements which are binding on its members and directly applicable in enterprises (unless they have rejected the agreement beforehand).

Its representativeness is unchallenged. France has no separate organization for public sector enterprises.

209. **CONSEIL SUPÉRIEUR DE LA PRUD'HOMIE — HIGHER INDUSTRIAL TRIBUNALS COUNCIL**: Tripartite consultative body (comprising representatives of the Ministries of Justice and Labour, representatives of the most representative trade union organizations and representatives of the employers' organizations) responsible for undertaking studies, issuing opinions and making proposals on the organization and functioning of the **Industrial Tribunals**.

210. **CONSEILLER PRUD'HOMME — INDUSTRIAL TRIBUNAL MEMBER**: Old term (still in use) synonymous with **prud'homme**.

211. **CONSTAT DE FIN DE CONFLIT — RECORD OF DISPUTE SETTLEMENT**: Name also given to a **minute of dispute settlement**.

212. **CONSTITUTION — CONSTITUTION**: In terms of form, a body of legal rules accorded special priority and special protection by virtue of the method by which they are drawn up and the position they occupy in the legal system.

In terms of substance, a body of essential rules determining the organization and functioning of the State and establishing the rights and freedoms possessed by those governed by it, as citizens and individuals.

Not all constitutional rules are written down as such. The **Constitutional Court** has recognized as unwritten constitutional rules some of the fundamental principles laid down by the laws of the Republic or principles of constitutional significance which are either mentioned in the preamble to the 1946 Constitution, on which the current 1958 Constitution is based, or expressed in ordinary laws promulgated since the end of the nineteenth century.

213. **CONSULTATION — CONSULTATION**: Act of seeking an opinion. For instance, cases where a Minister is obliged to consult joint or tripartite bodies when their opinion is a necessary

69

preliminary to his or her decision, or an employer is obliged to consult the **works council** before taking any decision concerning the general operation, management or organization of the enterprise.

In the latter case, the law stipulates a procedure which involves the provision of information in advance, a period of time for deliberation, and then an obligation on the employer to respond to the council's comments, giving reasons. The purpose of this consultation is to obtain the works council's opinion, not necessarily its agreement. In this sense, consultation is distinguished from negotiation. However, although enshrined in the law the distinction is to a large extent artificial.

214. **CONTRACTUEL — CONTRACT PUBLIC EMPLOYEE**: One of the three categories of **public employee** who do not possess **established civil servant** status. They work under a contract of employment parallel, as it were, to a private contract but subject to special rules. A typical example is a traffic warden.

215. **CONTRAT À DURÉE DÉTERMINÉE — FIXED-TERM CONTRACT**: Contract of employment incorporating a term, *i.e.* a future event which marks the end of the contract and whose occurrence is beyond the control of the parties. For a long time this definition, arrived at through court decisions, was all that determined the legal regulation of such a contract and distinguished it from a contract of indeterminate duration (which is the only type covered by the law on **dismissal**).

Since the late 1970s, a succession of formal regulations on fixed-term contracts have been introduced under the influence of employment policies. Although of varying rigour depending on the circumstances prevailing at the time, these regulations have been uniform in restricting fixed-term contracts to short-term contracts, limiting the allowable grounds for their use and establishing a degree of equality of treatment between employees hired under such contracts and other employees. As a result, the fixed-term contract has been turned into a written contract, enabling checks and controls on its use, and, above all, into a contractual formula which is the exception, as opposed to the contract of indeterminate duration which is presented as the basic form of employment contract, or typical contract.

The successive introduction of formal regulations has been matched by increased use of fixed-term contracts.

216. **CONTRAT À DURÉE INDÉTERMINÉE — CONTRACT OF INDETERMINATE DURATION**: See **contract of employment, fixed-term contract**.

217. **CONTRAT À TEMPS PARTIEL — PART-TIME CONTRACT**: Type of contract that has been regulated since 1981 to serve as a framework for **part-time work**.

218. **CONTRAT COLLECTIF — COLLECTIVE AGREEMENT**: Term used in the early 1900s, when the contractual nature (hence "contrat") of collective agreements was being emphasized.

It is acquiring renewed popularity in connection with moves in certain quarters among modern-day employers to develop company-level bargaining, notably because it allows extensive divergence from the law. They use the term "contrat collectif d'entreprise" to describe the type of company-level agreement they are promoting.

219. **CONTRAT D'ADAPTATION — EMPLOYMENT AND TRAINING CONTRACT**: Special type of contract of employment provided for by French law which serves as a framework for **combined training and work**. The purpose is to prepare a young person for a job or type of job. Since it must include a training schedule and the cost of the training can be deducted from the employer's compulsory contributions to the funding of combined training and work, such a contract may be concluded only if the employer has official approval from the authorities.

The formula is somewhat on the decline.

220. **CONTRAT D'ENGAGEMENT — SIGNING-ON CONTRACT**: See **seafarer**.

221. **CONTRAT DE QUALIFICATION — EMPLOYMENT AND TRAINING CONTRACT**: Special type of contract of employment provided for by French law which serves as a framework for **combined training and work**. The contrast with the "**contrat d'adaptation**" formula lies in providing an individual with the opportunity to acquire specific occupational skills. Since some general rules are waived (no social security contributions are payable in respect of the remuneration paid) and the employer must undertake certain commitments as regards the provision of training, such contracts may be used only if the employer has official approval from the authorities.

The formula has met with only limited success, although its use is growing considerably.

222. **CONTRAT DE SOLIDARITÉ — JOB CREATION AGREEMENT**: Name given during a certain period (1981-1984) to agreements concluded between the Government and enterprises

which undertook to co-operate with the objectives of policy on work sharing. In fostering work sharing, and hence a form of "solidarité", *i.e.* the philosophy of shared sacrifices, the Government's intention was to create employment for young people, who would be hired either to replace employees who took **early retirement** or chose to reduce their working time (gradual retirement), or as a result of a general reduction in working hours. Under job creation agreements, state funding was provided for the costs incurred by such measures.

The scale of these objectives remained fairly modest. Nowadays they are mainly pursued through forms of funding from the **National Employment Fund**.

223. **CONTRAT DE TRAVAIL — CONTRACT OF EMPLOYMENT**: The necessary source of any employment relationship in France, since the law does not recognize the concept of a *de facto* relationship as an alternative source of this legal relationship. In the absence of a statutory definition, the generally accepted definition of the contract of employment is an agreement whereby an individual, the employee, puts his or her services at the disposal of another, the employer, subjecting themselves to the latter's authority, in exchange for the payment of remuneration.

For a contract of employment to be deemed to exist, three combined elements must be present: personal performance of work (manual or intellectual, but also artistic or sporting), remuneration or pay (in money or in kind) and a relationship of "subordination", *i.e.* subjection to another's authority. (Hence the use of the term "travailleur subordonné" to refer to a person working under a contract of employment.) It is most often this last element of "subordination" that is contested when the existence of a contract of employment comes into dispute. The predominance of disputes on this point has resulted in the accumulation of a body of case law that adopts a very comprehensive definition of "subordination", which is recognized as being present whenever the work performance is supplied as part of a service organized by another party. This means that the category encompassed by the contract of employment is very broad. Teachers, professional sportsmen and sportswomen, doctors (in clinics or in health centres), lawyers, etc., may all practise their occupation under a contract of employment. The courts even accept that a company director may simultaneously be bound to the company by such a contract by reason of performing an activity (technical, commercial, etc.) separate from overall management. In particular, the senior executives of an enterprise (finance manager, sales manager, personnel manager, etc.) are always classed as employees (see **professional and managerial staff**). Furthermore, provisions of the Labour Code expressly define as a contract of employment any agreement under which a journalist, **performing artiste**, fashion model or **sales representative** supplies their services.

In the functioning of legal relationships, the contract of employment plays a twofold role. Firstly, it creates a contractual relationship between the employer and the employee. Secondly, it serves to formalize the employee's position, fitting him or her into the institutional relationships within the enterprise (subjection to the authority of the head of the enterprise and integration into the enterprise's workforce) which give rise to various rights concerning representation or participation in trade union activity. Thus, it has a contractual dimension and an institutional dimension. It is of great practical importance that those elements of the employee's position which are connected with the former (which belong to the contractual sphere) should be clearly established, particularly from the point of view of making any subsequent changes to them, since under the general rules of contract law such changes must be agreed between the parties. These elements are: the nature of the work performance promised (and, correlatively, the occupational skills of the individual concerned), the intensity of this performance (defined, where appropriate, by the identification of specific targets), working time (full-time or part-time), the place where work is to be performed, pay, and the duration of the contract itself (of indeterminate duration or fixed-term), which dictates the continuity or precariousness of employment. These elements constitute the subject of the reciprocal obligations which are entered into when the employee is hired, or the formalities stipulated in order to define their nature or the manner in which they are to be fulfilled.

In terms of its legal status, the contract of employment is governed by ordinary law, *i.e.* the Civil Code. It is, therefore, a consensual contract, which may be confirmed in any form chosen by the parties (*e.g.* signature of a letter of appointment). However, special contracts of employment of a particular type (*e.g.* fixed-term contract, part-time contract) must be in the form of a written document that includes a number of statements enumerated by law. Except in cases where the regulations on the minimum age for entry into employment or on the employment of aliens are applicable, the conditions of validity for the basis of the contract are governed by ordinary law, particularly as regards free and full consent and the lawfulness and compatibility with public morals of the purpose and the consideration. It is, however, extremely rare for the nullity of a contract of employment to be invoked with respect to these requirements. Cases of nullity recorded in court reports essentially concern apprenticeship contracts (with respect to their special rules). These led the courts to pronounce that nullity of the contract of employment, as a contract under which performance by one party is consecutive to performance by the other, did not operate retrospectively, and that remuneration was therefore due for work already done, except in the case of lack of **good faith** on the part of the employee (this is now set out in the Civil Code in relation to foreign workers).

The contract of employment creates reciprocal obligations. On the employer's part, these include the obligations to procure work for the employee (can its fulfilment be enforced via a court order directing the employer to reinstate the employee? See **reinstatement**) and to pay remuneration. On the employee's part, they include the obligation to work. The courts have consistently made any liability on the part of the employee (see **employee liability**) subject to proof of gross misconduct. But the "penalty" for contractual infringements of which the employee is accused by the employer usually takes the form of dismissal or disciplinary sanctions. It is when legal disputes relating to such measures arise that the courts specify the diligence that is required of the employee. In this connection, it seems that Article 1134 of the Civil Code (agreements "shall be performed in good faith") provides a basis for the progressive affirmation of a duty of loyalty (see **trust, loyalty**) from which, for example, the legitimacy of **dismissal** on the grounds of "loss of trust" can be deduced. That being so, as far as the effects of the contract of employment are concerned legal theory focuses less on the obligations created than on the scope of the contract's binding effect, which also influences them: for instance, the question of the intrinsic legal force of this effect, which, according to the Civil Code, excludes unilateral **variation**, and problems of interpretation posed by the legal exception to the principle that this binding effect is limited to the parties (see **transfer of undertaking**).

Nowadays the contract of employment is receiving renewed attention from legal experts. Whereas until quite recently the tendency among legal scholars was to regard the "decline of the contract of employment" (in the sense of voluntarily incurred obligations) as an established fact, current practice in enterprises is demonstrating the vigorous use of this instrument in "human resource management". It represents the preferred vehicle for the **individualization** or "flexibilization" of terms and conditions of employment and for fostering loyalty on the part of employees. All kinds of different contractual clauses are coming into use (performance-related clauses, geographical mobility clauses,

clauses mapping out the employee's career path, commitment by the employee not to leave the enterprise in exchange for training provided by the employer, etc.). As an enduring element in the legal ordering of employment relationships, the contract of employment is flourishing.

224. **CONTRAT DE TRAVAIL INTERMITTENT — INTERMITTENT EMPLOYMENT CONTRACT**: Type of contract of employment that has been regulated since 1986 to serve as a framework for **intermittent work**.

225. **CONTRAT EMPLOI-FORMATION — EMPLOYMENT AND TRAINING CONTRACT**: Name given to a special type of contract of employment which served as a framework for **combined training and work**. The name is no longer used, and other formulas exist (see **"contrat d'adaptation"** and **"contrat de qualification"**).

226. **CONTRAT EMPLOI-SOLIDARITÉ — JOB CREATION CONTRACT**: Special type of contract of employment recently introduced to replace the **youth employment scheme** formula.
      The intention is to provide government aid to encourage the hiring of unemployed young people (aged 16-25), the long-term unemployed or unemployed people aged over 50 in order to develop "activities which fulfil community needs not otherwise met".

227. **CONTRAT PRÉCAIRE — CONTRACT FOR PRECARIOUS EMPLOYMENT**: See **precariousness**.

228. **CONTRAT SAISONNIER — SEASONAL EMPLOYMENT CONTRACT**: See **seasonal work**.

229. **CONTRIBUTION PATRONALE — EMPLOYER'S WORKS COUNCIL CONTRIBUTION**: French law stipulates that the employer must contribute to the financing of the works council's activities (see **works council**). There are two separate contributions nowadays, one towards the **company welfare and cultural facilities** managed by the council and the other towards its day-to-day functioning. This latter contribution is equal to at least 0.2 per cent. of the total wage bill and may be used for the council's administrative expenses and to pay for the services of advisers and experts whom the council may choose to call in.

230. **CONTRÔLE À DISTANCE — REMOTE SURVEILLANCE**: See **electronic identity card**.

231. **CONTRÔLE DES INVESTISSEMENTS — WORKERS' CONTROL OVER INVESTMENT**: Trade union watchword which enjoyed a degree of popularity in the 1970s, denoting the ambition of an enterprise's employees, or their representatives, to have a say in investment decisions. It has disappeared as such, but has left behind as its legacy the demand to be provided with comprehensive economic information.

232. **CONTRÔLE OUVRIER — WORKERS' CONTROL**: See **workforce delegate**.

233. **CONTRÔLEUR DU TRAVAIL — EMPLOYMENT INSPECTOR**: See **labour inspector**.

234. **CONVENTION COLLECTIVE — COLLECTIVE AGREEMENT**: Within the meaning of French law, an agreement between one or more representative trade union organizations on the one hand and a grouping of employers or an employer acting individually on the other, whereby they lay down the regulatory system governing work applicable in the relationships created by the contracts of employment concluded by the signatory employers or members of the signatory grouping of employers.

Three elements in this definition should be emphasized. Firstly, the law spells out, on the employees' side, which agents possess the capacity to conclude a collective agreement: representative unions (see **representativeness**). It is, however, essential to note that, for a collective agreement to be validly concluded and to take full effect, it is enough for it to have been signed by only one such union. Secondly, the legal conception of the collective agreement derives from the historical importance accorded to the industry-wide agreement (see **branch of economic activity**). This is seen as a kind of internal law covering a given area of activity; what counts, therefore, is that it lays down a regulatory system governing work. It is thus a source of law. Although not negligible, the obligations that it places on the signatory parties are nevertheless secondary. Since it regulates work, its purpose is to cover the entire range of terms and conditions of employment, working conditions and social guarantees. If a collective agreement covers only one or more particular topics it is called, instead, an "**accord collectif**", although this name does not alter its status.

Thirdly, its applicability is solely dependent on the employer being bound by the agreement. It governs the contracts of employment concluded by any employer thus bound, irrespective of whether the employees concerned are union members or not, or members of a non-signatory union (see **erga omnes**).

This definition is the outcome of a lengthy evolvement, established by two Laws of 1971 and 1982.

235. **CONVENTION DE CONVERSION — RE-TRAINING AGREEMENT**: Measure introduced by a general multi-industry agreement of 1986 and by law, intended to enable employees faced with the prospect of **redundancy** to prepare themselves for employment in another enterprise.

236. **CONVENTION INTERNATIONALE — INTER-NATIONAL AGREEMENT**: The French Constitution makes a distinction between treaties ("traités") and international agreements not subject to ratification ("accords"). This distinction concerns not their subject-matter, but the negotiation procedure: the President of the Republic holds exclusive authority to negotiate a treaty, whereas he need merely be informed of the negotiation of an agreement not subject to ratification. On the other hand, certain treaties and international agreements, because of their subject-matter, may be ratified or approved by the President only after they have been authorized by a Law (peace treaties, trade agreements, treaties committing the finances of the State, treaties modifying a legislative provision, etc.).

A treaty or an international agreement comes into effect within France only after it has been published in the *Journal officiel* in accordance with a Presidential decree.

Interpretation of a treaty or international agreement may be carried out by the Government, in which case this interpretation is binding on the courts. But it is now a generally accepted principle that, in the absence of a government interpretation, judges hearing a dispute at law have the power to interpret the treaty or international agreement on which settlement of the case depends, unless they consider that "a point of public international law is at issue".

In the event of conflict between a treaty or international agreement and a French Law, the former takes precedence thenceforth; this precedence is readily accepted in cases where the treaty post-dates the national Law, but has taken much longer to become established in cases where the national Law post-dates the treaty, despite a provision to this effect in the Constitution. The superior authority of treaties is recognized both by the civil and criminal courts and by the administrative courts (see **Supreme Administrative Court**).

237. **CONVERSION — RESTRUCTURING/RE-TRAINING**:
The French term is used in reference both to an enterprise or
sector (industrial restructuring) and to employees (re-training).
In both cases, it constitutes a process intended to allow adaptation
to fundamental changes: the adaptation of work units whose
production must be discontinued or altered, and the adaptation
of employees faced with the fact or prospect of their jobs
disappearing and their skills becoming obsolete. Re-training is
at the heart of so-called modernization policies directed at
facilitating industrial change and enabling employees to acquire
new skills. It may be either internal (organized within the
enterprise) or external.

238. **COOPÉRATIVE — CO-OPERATIVE**: Co-operative societies
comply with the following principles laid down by law: their
capital is variable, they work only with their members, they are
non-profit-making, and each member has just one internal vote.
There are three main types: agricultural co-operatives, which are
formed to allow shared use of the means of production; consumer
co-operatives, which may sell their goods to non-members; and
workers' and producers' co-operatives (referred to as SCOP). The
latter have been formed only in certain sectors (building, fishing,
lighterage, printing, taxis). Every member is an employee.
Despite regular attempts to make them viable, they have never
become widely established in France.

239. **COORDINATIONS — OCCUPATIONAL UNITY
ORGANIZATIONS**: In the French context, name given to a
form of organization of workers in an **industrial dispute** which
gives, or seeks to give, prominence to the unity and sovereignty
of the occupational group being mobilized, and to its identity
independent of official union structures. In the light of recent
experience (particularly action taken by nurses), some observers
see these "coordinations" as a characteristic manifestation of a
growing **level of industrial conflict** within individual occupations.

240. **CORPORATISME — CORPORATISM**: Principle of
organization of the labour market based on the central role
accorded to the groupings formed by those who are active in it.
These groupings each delineate an occupation or profession.
   In a broader sense, corporatism is the tendency to protect or
promote the interests of a particular occupational group,
particularly by establishing or developing rules governing access
to or practice of the occupation in question.

241. **COTISATIONS SOCIALES — SOCIAL SECURITY CONTRIBUTIONS**: Traditional method of financing social security schemes. Such contributions consist of a levy on earnings which is allocated directly according to the needs of the various institutions. This dual feature distinguishes them from taxes, whose amount is not based on earnings alone and for which direct allocation according to needs is not possible. The authorities responsible are also different: the legislature votes the level of taxation, whereas the regulatory authorities set the rate of contributions.

For employees, contributions to the general social security scheme represent a certain percentage of their pay. They are either deducted from it ("cotisations salariales", *i.e.* employee's contributions) or they are added to it and chargeable to the employer ("cotisations patronales", *i.e.* employer's contributions); or, for the financing of certain risks, both types of contribution are paid together.

This method of financing comes under constant criticism. It penalizes those enterprises which employ a large workforce and, in particular, the basis of financing no longer matches the philosophy underlying social security, whose benefits are not confined to employees.

242. **COTISATIONS SYNDICALES — TRADE UNION DUES**: Sum that every member of a union is required, in that capacity, to pay to the union in accordance with its rules.

In France the most common practice is still for union members to hand over their own dues or contributions. Only in rare cases is the system used whereby, by arrangement with the unions, the employer deducts these contributions from pay and then pays the money direct to the unions ("check-off").

The unions are entitled to organize the collection of contributions during working hours and on the enterprise's premises. This task is traditionally assigned to "collectors".

The regularity and amount of contributions constitute one of the factors used to assess the representative status of a union (see **representativeness**).

243. **COUR D'APPEL — COURT OF APPEAL**: Courts of second instance (as opposed to the **Supreme Court**) which hear appeals against the decisions of the lower courts.

Appeal, the means by which application is made to these courts, allows a full re-examination of the case. Such right of appeal is open only if the claims brought before the lower courts exhibited certain characteristics (size of the sum that was the subject of the claim, indeterminate nature of the claim). A Court of Appeal is composed of career judges and includes a Division specializing in social matters.

244. **COUR DE CASSATION — SUPREME COURT**: Highest court in the system of civil and criminal courts. France has two separate systems of jurisdiction: the system of administrative courts (see **Supreme Administrative Court**) and the system of civil and criminal courts.

The Supreme Court is divided into five civil divisions, one of which specializes in labour law and social security law (the Social Division), and one criminal division.

Its primary duty is to promote consistent interpretation of the rules of law. Application is made to the Court by way of a form of reference called "pourvoi en cassation", *i.e.* request to have a decision quashed. In accordance with a traditional principle, it may examine only points of law.

245. **COUR SUPÉRIEURE D'ARBITRAGE — HIGHER COURT OF ARBITRATION**: Institution which, having existed briefly in 1936-37, was subsequently revived in 1950. It possesses authority to hear appeals against **arbitration** awards. Since the arbitration procedure, which is always voluntary in France, is very seldom used as the means of settling industrial disputes, applications are made to the Court only very occasionally.

246. **COÛT DE LA VIE — COST OF LIVING**: See **cost-of-living index**.

247. **COÛT DU TRAVAIL — LABOUR COST**: Total financial costs incurred by the use of a labour force. The concept is no longer used to refer simply to pay and **employment-related costs** and has taken on a broader meaning. What has now developed is an economic analysis of rules or normal employment practices, to which a cost is assigned. This analysis is frequently the prelude to criticism of the excessive cost of the rights granted to unions and employees for the expression of their interests, of the rules governing use of the various forms of employment, of pay trend mechanisms, and of the legal provisions on working hours and dismissal.

If it is to go beyond mere generalities or polemic, this economic analysis of rules and normal employment practices requires methods of measurement which at present are still largely lacking.

248. **CRÉATION D'EMPLOI — JOB CREATION**: Increase in the size of the workforce, as assessed either within an enterprise or

in a broader context such as a sector, employment catchment area or entire country.

A first point to note is that it is difficult to measure, since not every person hired represents the creation of a job: there must be a net increase in the number of people employed. Also, a purely quantitative approach is misleading, since jobs created in one place may not compensate for jobs lost in another.

Secondly, active employment policies derive from analysis of those factors which stimulate or discourage job creation. Even though there is relatively broad agreement in France that the level of employment is dependent on general macroeconomic mechanisms, successive Governments have never given up the use of measures to encourage job creation. Rather, the debate begins at the stage of choosing which levels of intervention and instruments are to be used.

Although there have been various forms, particularly from one period to another, aid for job creation (see **employment support**) has generally taken the form of grants, tax exemptions or preferential loan arrangements for enterprises which start up or expand units in regions or areas particularly badly affected by unemployment. These measures are designed to influence the calculation of the viability of enterprises or to modify the financial constraints upon them.

249. **CRÉATION D'ENTREPRISE — ENTERPRISE CREATION**: The starting-up of enterprises is viewed favourably by public policies at both national and local level, since it is simultaneously a form of economic development, an indication of the creation of employment (see **job creation**) and, when done by job-seekers, a way of reducing unemployment.

Simplification of the formalities for setting up a business, preferential taxation arrangements during the early stages and direct aid, particularly in the case of unemployed persons: these are the principal measures which for more than a decade have been directed at encouraging enterprise creation in France.

250. **CRÉDIT D'HEURES — TIME-OFF RIGHTS**: Amount of time granted to every **trade union delegate**, every **workforce delegate**, every elected member of the **works council** and every elected member of the **workplace health and safety committee**, to perform their functions as employee representatives. In practice, especially in large enterprises, these individual entitlements are sometimes cumulated in such a way as to allow particular representatives to take significant amounts of time off. The law sets a minimum number of hours to be granted per month for such time off, which may be exceeded in exceptional

circumstances. These hours are credited as working time and therefore attract pay, to be paid on the normal due date.

There is a legal presumption that such time off is used for its proper purpose. The burden is therefore on the employer to present proof of improper use.

More recently, time-off rights have been introduced for employees who assist or represent other employees before an Industrial Tribunal, and granted to union workplace branches for the purpose of making preparations for company-level bargaining.

251. **CUMUL D'EMPLOIS — MULTIPLE JOBHOLDING**: Term used to refer to the situation where an individual simultaneously carries on several economic activities, at least one of which takes the form of work under a contract of employment. (The term "moonlighting" is also used in English.) It is, therefore, to be distinguished from the situation where an employee has more than one employer for one and the same job.

French law does not discourage multiple jobholding. Rather, it makes provision for the rationalization of **social security contributions** in such a hypothetical case. The only legal restriction is that, with certain exceptions, maximum working hours must not be exceeded overall (although the individual contract of employment may prohibit multiple jobholding by including a sole-employment clause). However, the law does lay down regulations governing the simultaneous occupation of a job as an employee and appointment as an officer of the company within the same company.

252. **CYCLE ÉCONOMIQUE — BUSINESS CYCLE**: Period of a certain duration over which the same phenomena (growth, crisis, depression, recovery) recur in the same order. The theory has been, for instance, that it is possible to identify an intra-annual cycle for what are termed seasonal price rises, a short cycle for crises, a long cycle reflecting the fundamental evolvement of the economy, and minor cycles within these periods.

The theory of cycles has lost some of its explanatory force. Some commentators believe that this decline is due to the vigorous development of public policies.

D

253. DANGER IMMINENT — IMMINENT DANGER: Circumstance which justifies exercise of the **right to notify** and the **right to withhold labour**.

254. DÉBRAYAGE — STOPPAGE: Term popularly used to denote a brief cessation of work, usually intended as a warning or token strike (''grève d'avertissement''). Because of the brief duration of the stoppage, in most cases employees remain on the enterprise's premises. (See **strike**.)

255. DÉCENTRALISATION (DE LA NÉGOCIATION) — DECENTRALIZATION (OF BARGAINING): Movement away from a centralized model of organization and decision-taking towards one at a lower level. In France such a trend has been discernible over the past decade, and has taken the form in particular of a move towards bargaining at company level and away from the generalized and impersonal rules laid down by law and multi-industry bargaining.

As a feature of this trend, the development of company-level bargaining (see **company-level agreement**) has been encouraged by French law; in particular, following a Law of 1982, an obligation to bargain annually within the enterprise was introduced (see **duty to bargain**) and the possibility of concluding **derogation agreements** was recognized in relation to specified matters. Such company-level bargaining is increasingly acquiring a momentum of its own. Initially envisaged as a means of adapting general rules to diverse situations, it has become a management tool, an instrument for combining the interests of the workforce with those of the enterprise itself.

The trend towards decentralization is still a limited one. The traditional role of the industry level (see **industry-wide agreement, branch of economic activity**) has not been abandoned, and both the law and national multi-industry bargaining attempt to promote compromises between a centralized bargaining system and the growth of company-level bargaining.

256. DÉCRET — DECREE: Legal act emanating from the Prime Minister or the President of the Republic. In France, Ministers do not possess any regulatory powers. A decree, an act carrying executive force, may concern an individual (*e.g.* a letter of appointment) or be regulatory (enactment of general provisions). An ordinary decree bears the signature of the Prime Minister or, in exceptional cases, that of the President of the Republic, and is countersigned by a Minister or Ministers; a decree of the Council of Ministers is signed by the President of the Republic.

257. **DÉLAI DE PRÉAVIS — PERIOD OF NOTICE**: See **notice**.

258. **DÉLÉGATION (DE POUVOIR) — DELEGATION OF AUTHORITY**: The existence of a decentralization of authority within an enterprise has two effects that can be clearly pinpointed in terms of labour law. Firstly, the powers which are delegated to the head of an individual establishment within the enterprise determine the extent of the consultative functions of the **establishment-level works council**: it must be consulted at least whenever a decision likely to have an impact on the position of employees emanates from the head of that particular establishment. Secondly, the heads of enterprises (see **head of an enterprise**), who are held responsible for the proper observance of labour laws and regulations, may exonerate themselves from criminal liability by establishing that they have properly delegated their authority to an appropriate subordinate. For such to be deemed to include the avoidance of criminal liability, however, the courts require that authority be delegated to a person ("cadre", *i.e.* professional or managerial staff member) who is competent and invested with the requisite means and powers to ensure effectively that the provisions in force are observed.

Outside these two hypotheses, the delegation of authority provokes debate, particularly in **groups of companies**. Senior management is anxious to prevent interference with the decision-making machinery, while the unions often complain that the managers with whom they have dealings as their opposite numbers do not possess adequate powers of initiative or authority to act on behalf of the group.

259. **DÉLÉGATION À L'EMPLOI — EMPLOYMENT DIVISION**: Central division forming part of the Ministry with overall responsibility for Labour and Employment. In particular, it undertakes the allocation of **employment support** and, for this purpose, administration of the **National Employment Fund**, and supervision of the **National Employment Agency**.

260. **DÉLÉGUÉ D'ATELIER — WORKPLACE DELEGATE**: As the ancestor of the **workforce delegate**, the workshop delegate appeared in a number of large enterprises prior to 1914, before being made a compulsory institution in munitions factories in 1917 by government order. Since the introduction of workforce delegates by law in 1946 the term has largely fallen into disuse, other than in connection with organizational experiments relating, in particular, to the right of expression of employees in public

sector enterprises (see **shop-floor and departmental committee, right of expression**). It is widely, but misleadingly, translated as "shop steward" (*cf.* **trade union delegate**).

261. **DÉLÉGUÉ DE SITE — SITE DELEGATE**: Category of **workforce delegate** whose election may, since a Law of 1982, be imposed by the Labour Inspectorate in cases where a total of at least 50 employees belonging to a number of different small units (establishments each employing no more than 10 employees) but encountering shared problems (transportation, working conditions, etc.) work on a long-term basis at a particular "site" (*e.g.* shopping centre or industrial plant). The site delegate is a multi-enterprise delegate. There are still relatively few of them in France.

262. **DÉLÉGUÉ DU PERSONNEL — WORKFORCE DELEGATE**: Person elected by all of the employees of an establishment (whether union members or not, and therefore not to be translated as "shop steward") to a recognized office which consists in presenting individual and collective **grievances** to management and bringing to the attention of the **Labour Inspectorate** any complaints or comments in connection with the regulations for whose enforcement the Inspectorate is responsible. A very recent Law invests the workforce delegate with the authority, in cases of infringement of the rights and freedoms of individuals, to request the employer to take corrective action and, should it then become necessary, to bring the matter before an **Industrial Tribunal**. Nowadays, this form of workforce representation is required by law in all enterprises or establishments with 10 or more employees. Its origins are complex, since it is simultaneously an extension of the historical practice of delegates chosen by and from among the employees of an enterprise to speak on their behalf in dealings with management, the historical institution of **miners' delegates** (who were originally responsible for health and safety), the institution of **workplace delegates** ("délégués d'atelier") first created in the public sector during the First World War, and the demand for workers' control which, in some of its aspects, the Popular Front Government of 1936 sought to satisfy. The regulations currently governing the election, functions, means of action and protection of these delegates date from 1946 and 1982.

This is the most widespread form of employee representation in France; its legitimacy is very firmly founded, even though the powers and responsibilities of workforce delegates are limited in comparison with those of the **works councils** and **trade union delegates**.

263. DÉLÉGUÉ MINEUR — MINERS' DELEGATE: As the earliest form of employee representation in France and instituted by a Law of 1890, miners' delegates, elected by and from among the (underground) miners in a given district (which consists of a group of pits, galleries and workings), essentially have the task of monitoring the health aspects of physical working conditions and the safety of miners. In law, their title is ''délégués à la sécurité des ouvriers mineurs'' (miners' health and safety delegates).

264. DÉLÉGUÉ SYNDICAL — TRADE UNION DELEGATE/''SHOP STEWARD'': Every representative union (see **representativeness**) which has members in an enterprise employing more than 50 employees is entitled, under a Law of 1968, to appoint a trade union delegate within the enterprise, chosen from among the unionized employees. (The term therefore bears some similarity to the English ''shop steward''.) Since 1982, and only in enterprises with fewer than 50 employees, a **workforce delegate** may be appointed to act simultaneously as a trade union delegate.

The position of these delegates is a complicated one: they represent their trade union in dealings with the head of the enterprise, but have the task of protecting the interests both of the union members and of the enterprise's workforce as a whole. In laying down the manner in which they are appointed (a union designates one of the enterprise's employees) and defining their functions, the law seeks to entrust to trade union delegates the role of reconciling different groups of interests. They necessarily stand at the interface between the rank and file and the union, which generally forms part of a confederal structure (see **trade union confederation**). The idea is that in negotiating company-level agreements, which is one of their functions as members of the trade union delegation, they will not give preference to interests that are either too narrow or too broad.

French law takes account of the size and structure of enterprises, making provision for establishment delegates when the enterprise includes separate establishments, for a central enterprise delegate when such an enterprise has more than 2,000 employees in all (and at least two establishments with more than 50 employees), and for additional delegates to represent ''cadres'' (see **professional and managerial staff**) and certain categories of employee. Provision is also made for a special trade union delegate who sits on the works council in a consultative capacity: the ''représentant syndical'' (union representative on the works council). As a general principle, in enterprises with fewer than 300 employees the trade union delegate also acts as this representative; where the workforce exceeds this number, a different employee may be appointed as such.

Trade union delegates are entitled to move freely about the enterprise and to have paid time off to perform their functions (see **time-off rights**). As employee representatives, they are protected by law against actions on the part of the employer likely to hinder the performance of these functions.

265. **DEMANDE DE TRAVAIL — LABOUR DEMAND**: For any analysis in labour market terms, it is necessary to define the object of exchange and the behaviour of the agents making the exchange. It is impossible to speak of a labour demand in its literal sense from anything but a neoclassical perspective. What is being supplied or demanded is, in fact, a certain working time. The labour demand emanates from enterprises and is determined from the marginal product in labour value, and hence actually fixed by the operating conditions of enterprises. Marxian analyses hold that the object of exchange is not labour but labour power; what is exchanged is, therefore, a potential which is not precisely defined.

Other analyses, based on Keynesian ideas, maintain that labour power is not purchased in its own right. Account must be taken of the constraints on exchange, which, of course, we call employment. This turns the worker, who from the perspective of neoclassical economics is a supplier of labour, into a demander of employment, that is, a demander of a job or post as a means of utilizing his or her labour power.

266. **DEMANDEUR D'EMPLOI — JOB-SEEKER**: See **job**.

267. **DÉMISSION — RESIGNATION**: Termination of a contract of employment of indeterminate duration, by the employee's unilateral act. It must be preceded by a period of notice whose duration is not stipulated by statute law but by collective agreement, custom or the individual contract of employment. It does not give rise to any monetary entitlements for the employee. Also, in the event of a dispute at law its voluntary nature is subject to verification: there is no legal presumption of resignation, and it must result from an unquestionable and unequivocal intention on the part of the employee.

268. **DÉMOCRATIE ÉCONOMIQUE — ECONOMIC DEMOCRACY**: In the French context, term designating a system or form of organization of society based not only on the essential requirements traditionally linked to the democratic ideal, such as individual liberty, universal suffrage and political

pluralism, but also on intervention by the State for the purposes of correcting inequalities between groups. Labour law, as it exists in France today after emerging at the end of the nineteenth century, is the central element of an economic democracy.

269. **DÉMOCRATIE INDUSTRIELLE — INDUSTRIAL DEMOCRACY**: Term used to encompass ideas and reforms whose purpose is to reduce or limit the absolute power of employers and providers of capital and to grant employees or their representatives a place in the decision-making process. The nodal point of industrial democracy is the exercise of authority within the enterprise.

270. **DÉMOCRATIE OUVRIÈRE — WORKERS' DEMOCRACY**: Movement seeking to place power in the hands of the workers themselves, which was widespread mainly at the turn of the nineteenth and twentieth centuries. It was fuelled by the distrust felt by certain groups of workers for the trade union apparatus. The movement in no way repudiated the institution of representatives or, as they are termed, delegates, but demanded that they should be empowered and controlled by the rank and file.

271. **DÉMOCRATIE SYNDICALE — UNION DEMOCRACY**: In a narrow sense, union democracy is to the individual trade union what political democracy is to the political system. The term is used in study and analysis of the internal functioning of the organization and relations between the group and its members, for the purpose of ascertaining whether members participate in the appointment of its governing bodies and have any control over their activities.

In France, the question of whether there is a need to impose democracy within the organization through legislation has received little attention. This caution reflects a real reluctance regarding intervention by the law in this sphere; it is also explained by the fact that the unions have little hold over recalcitrant members, who can always leave the organization, and by the existence of **trade union pluralism**.

Beyond this original sense, the concept has broadened in two directions. Firstly, people have become aware that the issue of democracy concerns not only the internal organization of an individual trade union but also the union movement as a whole, particularly in view of the regulatory powers now held by the **trade union confederations**.

Secondly, the democratic ideal or goal itself has taken on further aspects. It is not merely a matter of promoting majority rule and election mechanisms; it is also a matter of establishing checks and controls on the activities and decisions of governing bodies, and of reconciling the rights of the majority with the rights of the minority.

272. **DÉMOCRATISATION — DEMOCRATIZATION**: Process directed at furthering equality by allowing everybody real access to certain values (education, culture, training), responsibilities and the means of expressing their opinions (see **industrial democracy, union democracy**).

273. **DÉNONCIATION (ACCORD COLLECTIF) — NOTICE OF TERMINATION OF A COLLECTIVE AGREEMENT**: Unilateral legal act whereby one or other of the parties to a collective agreement of indeterminate duration evidences an intention to bring it to an end.

Such termination is regulated by law, as regards both the form it must take and its consequences. Essentially, when notice of termination emanates from only one or some of the signatory unions, it takes effect only with respect to that union or those unions; the agreement remains in force for the remaining parties. When notice of termination emanates from the employers' side (where there is usually only one signatory), the agreement concerned remains in force until it is replaced by a new one or, failing such replacement, for a period of one year.

274. **DÉNONCIATION (USAGE) — NOTICE OF DISCONTINUANCE OF A CUSTOM**: Unilateral legal act whereby an employer evidences the intention to put an end to a **custom** which is established practice within the enterprise. The rules governing such discontinuance are defined by case law: requirement of an adequate period of notice, and obligation to inform the **employee representatives** and every employee who is personally affected. Employees possess no entitlement to the maintenance of terms and conditions but, according to prevailing legal opinion, may invoke substantive **variation of the contract of employment** as grounds for claiming the compensation that is payable in cases of dismissal.

275. **DÉPENDANCE — ECONOMIC DEPENDENCE**: A distinction has been made in some instances between purely economic dependence and **"subordination"** (*i.e.* the employee's subjection to another's authority), for the purpose of extending the scope of application of labour law to cover any worker who is in a position of economic inferiority with respect to another person without their work necessarily being controlled by that

person. Such instances of the extension of labour law have been made possible through formal recognition of certain workers as persons similar to an employee and enactment of the legal presumption of a **contract of employment** in certain circumstances.

276. **DÉQUALIFICATION — DOWNGRADING/DE-SKILLING**: In contexts where the term "qualification" (see **skill**) is used in the sense of the acquired expertise and, more generally, personal competence of an employee or employees, "déqualification" or de-skilling consists in a loss of competence. To employees, this has two related meanings:
1. It is referred to as absolute if competence has declined, for instance as the result of a lengthy absence from work or the effect of working conditions of a damaging nature.
2. It is referred to as relative if personal competence remains unchanged but is no longer used or recognized.

The latter moves close to the meaning which de-skilling carries in legal language. In this context, it denotes downgrading to a skill level ("qualification") lower than the level which was contractually agreed or than the one which corresponds to the post occupied.

277. **DÉRÉGULATION — DEREGULATION**: Movement away from state intervention, perceived in France first as a trend unique to the USA and later as a general trend in all industrialized countries. In French labour law it has mainly taken the form of a shift in the source of the creation of regulations away from the State towards collective bargaining and towards the employer's **managerial prerogative**: possibility of concluding **derogation agreements** (introduced in 1982 and expanded in 1986), abolition of the requirement for prior official authorization of redundancies (1986), widening of the range of different types of employment contract which employers may opt to use, etc. The trend has, in fact, been relatively limited and constrained because the shift towards collective bargaining and managerial prerogative has required detailed and complicated statutory regulation.

278. **DÉSACCORD — DISAGREEMENT/FAILURE TO AGREE**: See **minute of failure to agree**.

279. **DÉTACHEMENT — DETACHMENT/POSTED WORK**: Placing an employee temporarily (*cf.* **job move, change of employer through legal transfer**) at the disposal of an enterprise other than the one in which he or she is usually employed,

irrespective of whether the enterprises concerned belong to the same group.

The original contract of employment is not broken off in such a situation, which constitutes a manner of performing that contract or involves the conclusion of a second contract, sometimes with suspension of the first.

280. **DÉTENUS — PRISONERS**: There are at least two points of contact between labour law and prison. Firstly, the effect of the imprisonment of an employee on the contract of employment must be specified. The French courts tend, with shades of interpretation, to deem it a justifiable ground for **dismissal**. Secondly, it is important to determine the rules applicable to work performed in prison. Detailed regulations exist which prohibit, in principle, work by detainees remanded in custody while awaiting trial, and prohibit all forms of forced labour. Prisoners who work are still far from being treated in law as employees.

281. **DEVOIR DE PAIX — PEACE OBLIGATION**: In France, no peace obligation exists between the signatories to a collective agreement. This means that strikes are lawful during the lifetime of such an agreement, even if the claims in question relate to the matters regulated in it. French law establishes only a duty of loyal performance, which is interpreted as a requirement to perform the agreement in **good faith**.

According to case law collective agreements may, however, stipulate adjustments to exercise of the **right to strike**, provided this does not effectively amount to its denial.

282. **DIALOGUE SOCIAL — SOCIAL DIALOGUE**: See **concerted consultation**.

283. **DIFFÉRENTIEL — DIFFERENCE OF LEVEL**: Modern expression referring to the margins between two levels, *e.g.* rates of inflation.

284. **DIPLÔME — DIPLOMA**: Document which confers and certifies a formal qualification or degree and, by the same token, attests to a certain level of knowledge or aptitude.

The French tradition of national diplomas and a system of official accreditation (and hence harmonization) of diplomas have made the diploma an important factor in the use of grading systems (see **skill**) and the construction of **job classifications**.

In fact, the development of **further vocational training** is making it necessary to accredit new forms of training and to devise new diplomas or amend the conditions governing the acquisition of formal qualifications.

285. **DIRECTION DU PERSONNEL — PERSONNEL MANAGEMENT**: In a substantive sense, activity which consists in giving practical effect to the employer's prerogative rights relating to the hiring, management, supervision and dismissal of employees, and also in determining policy and practice regarding consultation and negotiation with employees and the relevant institutions.

In an organizational sense, personnel management is the department within an enterprise or group of companies which is responsible for this activity. It is one of the functions grouped under the heading of "direction fonctionnelle" (functional management), which share the characteristic of being primarily responsible for the smooth running of the enterprise and participating only indirectly in the achievement of its objective.

A recent development emerging is that some enterprises, instead of a department called "personnel management", have one called "direction des ressources humaines" (human resource management, or HRM) or "direction des relations sociales" (employee relations management). These new titles reflect a desire (if not always a concrete plan) to make more efficient use of employees' abilities and to promote dialogue and discussion rather than impose authority.

286. **DIRECTIVE — DIRECTIVE**: Term with two different meanings:
   1. As a concept deriving from French administrative practice, a directive is a document, usually issued by a Minister, which codifies to a varying extent the freedom of action of his or her administration or of a body subject to its supervision. Such a directive is not of a generally regulatory nature, since Ministers do not possess regulatory powers (see **decree**). It is, however, similar to a general regulation in that its provisions are generalized and impersonal. The persons to whom it is addressed retain the right of derogation imposed by the principle of individual examination inherent in discretionary authority.
   2. At EC level, a Directive is one of the types of instrument which the Community authorities are entitled to adopt in connection with the performance of their functions. It is binding upon the Member States as regards the result to be achieved but, as a general principle, leaves them free to choose the manner in which it is to be brought about.

287. **DIRECTOIRE — MANAGEMENT BOARD**: See **supervisory board**.

288. **DIRIGEANT D'ENTREPRISE — EXECUTIVE MANAGER**: The French system of law does not offer a uniform treatment of the manager as such. It distinguishes between:
1. the manager of a company or officer of a company, which are concepts of company law, and
2. the **head of an enterprise** or his or her representative, by definition a "cadre" (see **professional and managerial employee**), which are concepts of labour law.

In company law, the company manager or company officer is a person who is, in principle, invested with full powers to act on behalf of the company in dealings with third parties. In public limited companies with the traditional structure of a single board of directors, this refers to the chief executive ("directeur général"); this chief executive may be the chairperson of the board, and may also be chosen by it. In public limited companies with the new two-tier structure (a supervisory board and a management board), it refers to the members of the management board. In other commercial companies it refers to a manager who is specifically given the name "gérant".

The head of an enterprise is, in principle, the company manager. Some of this person's powers may, however, have been delegated to a "cadre" (see **delegation of authority**), as is frequently the case in enterprises with a number of **establishments**. In this situation, the managerial prerogative is exercised by an employee.

But the point to be noted is the advantage of being covered by labour law, as perceived by managers: many combine the capacity of company officer with a contract of employment, for the manifest purpose of benefiting from the protection provided by such a contract. This combination is to some extent regulated by company law. But the restrictions imposed by law relate only to the situation where the two capacities of company officer and employee are combined within one and the same company. Hence, in **groups of companies** it is common practice for an officer of one company to be an employee of another.

289. **DIRIGEANT SYNDICAL — SENIOR FULL-TIME OFFICIAL**: When analysing trade unionism it is useful to distinguish, according to their level of participation, between members ("adhérents"), activists ("militants"), **full-time officials** and senior full-time officials. This latter term is usually reserved for the higher-ranking officials of the **trade union confederations**, whose task is to guide the movement as a whole and to implement the policy guidelines adopted at congresses. The confederations have been identified with the public profile of some of their highest-ranking officials (called, depending on

93

the particular confederation and the convention at the time, either union president or general secretary). The actual composition of a confederation's executive appears to follow complex rules dictated partly by ability and experience but also by the need for balance (between different industries, between the sexes, etc.) and by a historical tendency towards continuity of the leadership structure. This continuity is encouraged by the rules on the incompatibility of trade union office with political office and by the difficulties in re-entering employment faced by a departing full-time official.

290. **DISCIPLINE — DISCIPLINE**: Term with two distinct meanings:
1. Branch or field of learning. Since they constitute a specialized area of knowledge, labour law and industrial relations are disciplines in this sense.
2. Rules and decisions applied in a group with the purpose of maintaining order within it. By extension, discipline covers actual compliance with these rules and decisions. In this sense, an enterprise is a site of discipline (and, to all intents and purpose, a trade union likewise).

Discipline within the enterprise is the subject of rules of legal origin, in some instances supplemented by collective agreements. Under French law disciplinary rules, collected together in a compulsory written document called the "règlement intérieur", *i.e.* works rules, are drawn up by the employer (who must consult the works council) and subjected to detailed scrutiny by the Labour Inspectorate, which has powers to modify or reject.

Disciplinary decisions are also subject to legal regulation. A particular procedure must be followed, and certain sanctions (such as the imposition of **fines** by employers) are expressly prohibited while the others are subject to a form of examination by the courts which was made more rigorous by a Law of 1982.

291. **DISCRIMINATION — DISCRIMINATION**: Unlawful distinction. Not every difference in treatment, therefore, constitutes discrimination. An anti-discrimination rule prohibits the assignment of the persons it concerns to a separate category for the purpose of making them subject to a special form of regulation.

French labour law contains numerous anti-discrimination rules. Some guarantee the free exercise of a legal prerogative which is otherwise recognized (trade union freedom, right to strike, freedom of opinion, etc.), while others are rules giving specific protection to groups or categories who are in a vulnerable position or in some way excluded (prohibition of differential treatment based on race, sex (see **equality between men and women**), state of health, etc.).

292. DISCRIMINATION POSITIVE — POSITIVE DISCRIMINATION: Compensatory measure introduced to promote effective equality in contexts where purely legal equality actually masks or justifies existing inequalities of treatment. The concept arose from deliberations on equal treatment for men and women at work. In France today, in this area the State confines itself to encouraging positive discrimination.

293. DISTRIBUTION D'ACTIONS — PROFIT-SHARING (DISTRIBUTION OF SHARES): Over the past 20 years or more in France a number of legislative measures have been aimed at encouraging the distribution of shares to employees or the acquisition of shares by employees on preferential terms. For instance, during the wave of privatizations which took place in 1986 and 1987, 10 per cent. of the shares released for issue by the Government were allocated to a priority right of acquisition reserved for employees. In the private sector, a favourable financial and fiscal regime was established to stimulate the purchase or free distribution of shares.

At present, two formulas are used with a measure of success. First, the system of **company savings schemes** has been renewed by the law to favour the investment of employees' savings in shares in the company. The sums deriving from employees' **pay related to company performance** and **profit-sharing** may be paid into these schemes, which thus constitute forms of their implementation.

Secondly, the law encourages the grant of share purchase options to employees and company officers (see **executive manager**), since the price fixed for the shares may be substantially reduced and the capital gains achieved are, subject to certain conditions, eligible for tax relief. In practice, this formula tends to be offered to specific categories such as **professional and managerial staff**.

294. DIVERSIFICATION DES CONTRATS — DIVERSIFICATION OF EMPLOYMENT CONTRACTS: Although the existence of a range of different types of contract of employment is not a new phenomenon, recent years have seen a sudden increase in the types of contract as regulated or organized by law: fixed-term contract (Law of 1979), part-time contract (Law of 1981), intermittent employment contract (Law of 1986), etc.

This legislative intervention embodies a dual purpose: to allow and facilitate diversity, but also to provide the employees

95

concerned with guarantees. (See **fixed-term contract, intermittent employment contract, precariousness, restructuring.**)

295. **DIVERSIFICATION PRODUCTIVE — DIVERSIFICATION OF PRODUCTION**: In contrast to the standardization of goods and services, the diversification of production consists in differentiating between them. Diversification processes can take numerous different forms (in terms of their specification, their appearance, their price, etc.). The present-day process, according to some analysts, is one of growing diversification in terms of the quality of products and services. Product diversification has led in the 1980s to pressure for greater flexibility, including new forms of work organization and employment contract (see **diversification of employment contracts**).

296. **DIVISION DU TRAVAIL — DIVISION OF LABOUR**: Term designating a system in which individuals specialize, to a greater or lesser degree, in one particular phase of the production process (see **Taylorism**).

In France, analysis of the division of labour lies at the heart of the work of Durkheim (1893), who saw the division of labour as a means of reducing social imbalances when a society becomes more complex and its population more numerous. The division of labour not only engenders specialization; it co-ordinates functions, creates links between individuals and so gives rise to a sense of solidarity between them.

Durkheim noted, however, that it could have invidious effects: inequality, bureaucracy, etc. These criticisms of the division of labour have, subsequently, been considerably expanded by other commentators. Denouncement of its major disadvantages, and the search to correct them, underlie the debate on the organization of work.

Following on from Durkheim, the division of labour has been studied not only in the sphere of industrial production but also in political, cultural and other spheres.

297. **DOCKER — DOCK WORKER**: Manual worker employed in the loading and unloading of ships. Dock workers are characterized by two unusual features. Firstly, their work is covered by a special set of regulations incorporated in the Maritime Ports Code. Secondly, in connection with the organization of work dock workers' trade unionism is still a form of occupation-based trade unionism, seeking to control the labour market on a unified basis. A Law passed in 1992 has sought to weaken the union monopoly over the labour market.

298. **DOMESTIQUE — DOMESTIC WORKER**: Domestic workers are employees who are employed by private individuals to perform work relating to the housekeeping needs of the employer and the employer's family. Nowadays, they are referred to in law as "employés de maison". They are excluded from the scope of many legal provisions whose application presumes the existence of an enterprise (the law on redundancy, supervision by the Labour Inspectorate, etc.). They do have an employer, but they do not work in an enterprise.

299. **DONNÉES NOMINATIVES — PERSONAL DATA**: Synonym of **information nominative**.

300. **DROIT À L'EMPLOI — RIGHT TO EMPLOYMENT**: See **right to work**.

301. **DROIT ADMINISTRATIF — ADMINISTRATIVE LAW**: In France, the separate body of legal rules which regulate the activity of the **public administration**.

302. **DROIT D'ALERTE — RIGHT TO NOTIFY**: See **notification**.

303. **DROIT AU TRAVAIL — RIGHT TO WORK**: Constitutionally protected principle which forms the foundation for active intervention in the labour market by the State, in particular the enactment of measures designed to give preference to the employment of workers who are disadvantaged in comparison with others, *i.e.* positive discrimination. It has to be reconciled with the principle of **freedom of labour**, which, in its turn, entitles everyone to apply for a given job.

304. **DROIT D'EXPRESSION — RIGHT OF EXPRESSION**: The right of all employees to voice their opinion and comments on employment and working conditions, the organization of work and the quality of production within their work unit (see **shop-floor and departmental committee**) and in the enterprise. This right, which was established by a Law of 1982, is of complex origin: it is part of the movement to improve terms and conditions of employment and working conditions but at the same time, because of its links with experiments using such techniques as **quality circles** and quality control, it is implicated in the evolvement of company management methods.

Although the right established by the Law is an individual right, and although its exercise as such is protected, such expression must be collective. It takes place at work unit level, through the formation of groups called "groupes d'expression", in accordance with arrangements defined by collective agreement. This guarantees a role for the unions, even though some of them were or remain distrustful of direct expression by employees (*i.e.* outside the institutionalized channels of employee representation).

305. DROIT DE GRÈVE — RIGHT TO STRIKE: Right recognized in the Preamble to the Constitution of October 27, 1946, to which the present Constitution expressly proclaims its attachment. Such recognition, which makes the right to strike a constitutionally protected principle, limits the restrictions that could be placed by the law on the exercise of this right. But there has been no real legislative regulation: the scope of the right to strike and the conditions governing its exercise have been defined principally by case law.

The holder of the right to strike is the individual employee. It is not a union prerogative. This means that strikes by a minority of employees, strikes confined to a single workshop and lightning strikes without advance notice (except in the case of the **public service** sector) are all lawful forms of its exercise.

Since strike action is a right, it merely implies a suspension of performance of the contract of employment. Dismissal of an employee who takes part in a lawful strike is automatically null and void and gives rise to entitlement to reinstatement.

306. DROIT D'INFORMATION — DISCLOSURE OF INFORMATION/RIGHT TO INFORMATION: The upsurge of a right to know the reasons for, content of and foreseeable consequences of any decisions proposed within the enterprise is one of the major trends of contemporary labour law.

This approach is exemplified in the organization of a procedure which must be followed prior to the imposition of any disciplinary sanction (see **disciplinary power**) or to any **dismissal**, and in particular **redundancy**. The same is true of the obligations imposed on heads of enterprises with respect to the works council and, likewise, their obligations to provide the unions with relevant information at the outset of compulsory annual bargaining (see **duty to bargain**).

307. DROIT DE RETRAIT — RIGHT TO WITHHOLD LABOUR: Since 1982, statutorily recognized right of employees, when they have good reason to believe that some condition at work poses a serious and imminent danger to their life or health, to stop work without incurring any penalty or deduction from pay. It complements the right to notify (see **notification**).

308. DROIT DU TRAVAIL — LABOUR LAW: Term which may be interpreted in three senses:
1. Branch or subset of statute law encompassing all the rules relating to employment relationships and industrial relations. This subset has only gradually, over the past century, acquired sufficient volume and coherence to be referred to specifically as labour law.
2. Since the regulation of employment relationships and industrial relations does not have the provisions which are grouped together in a separate branch as its sole source, but also rules deriving from constitutional law, public law, private law, etc., international regulations and, in particular, rules generated by the actors of industrial relations (by collective agreement, for instance), labour law also refers to this entire system of legal organization.
3. In a third sense, labour law comprises the knowledge or expertise of those who, by profession, study and deal with labour law in either or both of the above two senses.

309. DROIT SYNDICAL — TRADE UNION LAW/RIGHT TO ORGANIZE: Term with two distinct meanings:
1. In the sense of trade union law, the legal system covering unions. It thus denotes all the legal rules governing the formation, organization, functioning and activities of trade unions.
2. In the sense of the right to organize, a fundamental right of citizens to organize themselves and act collectively. In this sense, much used in the language of politics, the concept is not recognized as such by statute law. This is doubtless because the law has given separate, successive recognition to the **freedom of collective industrial organization**, which in France refers only to employee or employer groups possessing the legal form of a **"syndicat"** and in the case of employees is often termed "trade union freedom", and to the **right to strike**.

310. DROITS ACQUIS — ACQUIRED RIGHTS: Synonym of **avantages acquis**.

311. DUALISME — DUALISM: See **segmentation**.

312. DURÉE DU TRAVAIL — WORKING HOURS: Amount of time for which employees perform their work activity on behalf of the employer.

French law lays down statutory workings hours; since 1982 the length of the working week has been specified as 39 hours. This is not a maximum, since it may be exceeded if employees work **overtime**, nor is it a minimum, since **part-time work** is lawful and widespread. Nevertheless, the statutory working hours serve as a central point of reference for the application of the rules governing overtime and part-time work. They therefore represent "normal" working hours.

In calculating working hours, only actual hours of work are counted, *i.e.* the periods during which employees are subject to the employer's authority. Travel-to-work times ("temps de trajet"), preparation times, mealtimes and breaks are not included. Some of the latter may, however, attract pay in accordance with custom or under a collective agreement.

The law does set some maximum limits: directly, by restricting the length of the working day to 10 hours (with exceptions), and indirectly, by specifying the length of **annual holidays**.

Since 1982 actual working hours have been one of the matters subject to compulsory annual bargaining at enterprise level, in conjunction with the organization of working time. The required procedure for fixing them still includes consultation of the works council, the display of schedules, and notification to the Labour Inspectorate.

In essence, the underlying trends are, firstly, a gradual reduction of actual working hours as calculated on a weekly basis; secondly, the option of ceasing to take weekly hours as the reference point for calculating overtime (see **annualization of working hours**); and lastly, greater importance attached to diversification of patterns of working time.

E

313. **ÉCHELLE MOBILE — SLIDING PAY SCALE**: Arrangement whereby pay follows changes in the cost of living. In France, the national **minimum wage** (now referred to as the SMIC, *i.e.* "salaire minimum interprofessionel de croissance") is index-linked to the cost of living. On the other hand, the introduction of a sliding pay scale arrangement under a collective agreement or individual contract of employment is in principle prohibited (see **index-linking**).

314. **ÉCONOMIE DU TRAVAIL — LABOUR ECONOMICS**: Branch of the discipline of economics which is concerned with labour. In France it has traditionally stressed the view that the phenomena of heterogeneity and discontinuity in the activity rate, employment, unemployment, pay and terms and conditions are the result of fluctuations in external factors that lie outside the scope of the discipline. More recent institutional approaches which attempt to explain and analyse the variables that produce difference and change of direction have emerged to challenge this dominant view.

315. **ÉCONOMIE SOUTERRAINE — HIDDEN ECONOMY**: Term used to refer to concealed economic activity, that is, activities which are not openly declared in accordance with the regulations on taxation, labour law, social security law, etc. This hidden (or "black") economy is also known as the "économie informelle" (informal economy).

316. **ÉDUCATION OUVRIÈRE — WORKERS' EDUCATION**: Training provided by the trade unions. French law has made it possible for the unions to organize such training for workers who are in active employment by allowing provision for workers' educational leave, replaced since 1985 by **leave for education in economic, social and union affairs**.

317. **ÉDUCATION PERMANENTE — LIFELONG EDUCATION**: Conception of education as a process that continues throughout one's life. Such a view entails introducing changes in institutions, procedures and practices in order that every individual's needs may be met, whatever their age, abilities, standard of education or occupational level.
    Further vocational training falls within the notion, but does not convey it fully.

318. **EFFECTIF — WORKFORCE**: Term used in two senses:
    1. The actual number of employees of an enterprise or

101

establishment; calculation of the size of the workforce is an essential element of the **threshold** technique.

2. The employees of an enterprise or establishment as a collective body; hence, an employee may be referred to as being (or not being) a member of the workforce.

319. **EFFICACITÉ JURIDIQUE — LEGAL FORCE**: In general, a rule is regarded as having legal force when it carries a penalty that is applied either directly by the public authorities or under their supervision. A more exact definition of what characterizes a rule possessing legal force (*i.e.* a legal rule) is the fact that it has the capacity to serve as an instrument of assessment for the courts in the settlement of legal disputes.

320. **ÉGALITARISME — EGALITARIANISM** Belief that all workers should be treated in the same way. It is central to the trade union movement. Such a belief has never been made an absolute watchword, but rather used as a battle-cry against excessive inequalities (particularly in terms of pay) and against the arbitrary authority of employers.

321. **ÉGALITÉ ENTRE LES FEMMES ET LES HOMMES — EQUALITY BETWEEN MEN AND WOMEN**: French law contains numerous provisions whose purpose is to guarantee the absence of discrimination and to promote equal treatment for men and women. Equality before the law is a constitutional principle; and the law specifies and extends this principle, in terms not only of pay but also of all working conditions and terms and conditions of employment. There are still three major weaknesses in the implementation of the provisions on equality. Firstly, court cases are rare, and when disputes are actually brought before the court judges hesitate to impose penalties for forms of indirect discrimination, *i.e.* where the undifferentiated application of a rule has the effect, in fact, of penalizing women. In particular, numerous terms in collective agreements relating to **job classification**, promotion, career paths and bonuses appear to harbour forms of indirect discrimination. Secondly, the standard of proof is still rudimentary and it is only with regard to pay that employers are obliged to furnish evidence capable of justifying the difference in question. Lastly, although since 1983 certain measures have been in existence which attempt to promote equality, in particular by offering incentives for enterprises to draw up plans on equality (containing action on **positive discrimination**), they are rarely used.

322. ÉLECTION — ELECTION: The preferred method whereby employees select representatives from among their number to conduct their affairs, following the principles forged in the name of the democratic ideal (equal and universal suffrage, secret vote, etc.). In France it has wide application: members of **Industrial Tribunals**, members of the management committees of **social security offices**, workforce delegates and works council members are all elected in this manner. These elections make it possible, in particular, to gauge the strength of influence of the unions. The individuals instituted by election are representatives of interests rather than delegates in the literal sense.

Within the enterprise, the law gives the right to vote to all employees in the case of workforce delegates (election annually) and works council members (election every two years). The responsibility for organizing elections lies with the head of the enterprise; those representative unions (see **representativeness**) which have members in the enterprise play an important role, since they negotiate an electoral protocol which is a virtual charter for the conduct of the elections and are alone in possessing the right to nominate a list of candidates for the first ballot. The voters are divided into electoral bodies. Voting, which is for several candidates on a list, takes place in two successive ballots, following the principle of proportional representation.

323. ÉLECTIONS PROFESSIONNELLES — WORKPLACE-LEVEL ELECTIONS: Term designating the elections which are organized within the enterprise or establishment in order that employees may choose their representatives (see **workforce delegate, workplace health and safety committee, works council**).

324. EMBAUCHE — HIRING: As a synonym of **recrutement,** this popularly used French term emphasizes the freedom which the employer had (and still has to a large extent) in choosing employees and specifying their pay and employment conditions. The term "embauchage" is similarly used.

325. EMPLOI — EMPLOYMENT/JOB: Term used in two senses:
1. Access to the labour market, including its forms, procedures and results. Hence the expressions "plein emploi" (full employment), "politique de l'emploi" (employment policy) and "l'emploi des statistiques" (employment statistics).
2. Activity involving labour (*i.e.* work), viewed as a job in terms of status and role. Hence the description of workers who are offering their labour as "demandeurs d'emploi" (job-seekers), and the phrase "l'emploi des petites annonces" (classified job advertisements in the press).

326. **EMPLOYÉ — WHITE-COLLAR WORKER**: Historically defined as category of employee whose work is connected with the administration of the enterprise or who deals with its customers. The distinction between white-collar workers and "ouvriers", *i.e.* **manual workers**, no longer carries the significance it once did when their mode of payment and the level of their pay and benefits differed. Nowadays, neither the law nor collective agreements establish any substantial differences. The distinction remains in **job classifications**, with manual worker grades still usually shown separately from the others.

327. **EMPLOYÉ DE MAISON — DOMESTIC WORKER**: Synonym of **domestique**.

328. **EMPLOYEUR — EMPLOYER**: The employee's contracting partner in the contract of employment. The term belongs to contract terminology and designates a natural person (individual entrepreneur) or legal person (company or other grouping) who is both under an obligation ("débiteur") and owed an obligation ("créancier"). In France, the courts reserve the power to attribute the capacity of employer to a person other than the one named in the contract, since under French law the employer is the person to whose authority the employee is subject. It may therefore happen that there are two or more employers in cases where, as in some **groups of companies**, the employer's prerogative rights are divided between several companies.

329. **ENCADREMENT — PROFESSIONAL AND MANAGERIAL STAFF**: The collective body of **professional or managerial employees**.

330. **ENFANTS (TRAVAIL DES) — CHILD EMPLOYMENT**: France's first social Law (1841) regulated child labour in manufacturing industry. Nowadays, except for certain exemptions (theatrical performances, light work during school holidays, periods of practical work experience) the law prohibits the hiring of children who have not yet completed their compulsory schooling, *i.e.* under the age of 16. Children may, however, "help out" informally in a family business (referred to as "entraide"), within bounds where there can be no question of a contract of employment.

331. **ENRICHISSEMENT DES TÂCHES — JOB ENRICHMENT**: See **work organization**.

332. ENTRAVE — INTERFERENCE: General term alluding to a series of criminal offences which have all been created by the law for the purpose of preventing and punishing any action that impedes the exercise of a fundamental freedom or right.

Protection under criminal law against interference with trade union activities and representatives is a fundamental aspect of French labour law. The rules governing the establishment and functioning of the institutions of employee representation within the enterprise all carry penal sanctions. Interference with the creation of representative bodies, interference with the free selection of their members, interference with their functioning or with exercise of the right to organize collectively: these offences, covering what is termed elsewhere anti-union behaviour, have been the subject of a considerable body of case law specifying the extent of the rights of employee representatives.

333. ENTREPRISE — ENTERPRISE: As a term in general usage, basically deriving from economic theories, the enterprise is a grouping of factors of production, combined and utilized with a view to producing goods and services for exchange on a market, or a decision-making centre possessing the capacity to pursue an autonomous strategy.

In labour law, the enterprise does not constitute a legal concept. Rather, it serves as a reference point, a category which orders thinking. It therefore defies definition. In some instances, the enterprise is one and the same thing as the employer (that is, as a general rule, the company which has concluded the contracts of employment): this is the sense in which the word should be interpreted in the expression "négociation d'entreprise" (see **company-level bargaining**). However, in instances where the enterprise is taken as the unit of employee representation, *i.e.* the context for the formation of a **works council**, the installation of **workforce delegates** or the appointment of **trade union delegates**, it is not always identified by the employer: the courts may recognize a single enterprise behind several separate companies. For this purpose, they make use of the concept of the **unit of economic and employee interest**. And in still other instances, the enterprise is interpreted as meaning an organized activity, "an economic entity endowed with an identity": this is so where the word "entreprise" is used in French in defining those cases of the transfer of ownership of a business undertaking (see **transfer of undertaking**) in which the law provides for contracts of employment to be maintained.

334. ENTREPRISE ARTISANALE — CRAFT TRADES ENTERPRISE: Enterprise in the **self-employed craft sector**.

105

335. **ENTREPRISE DE TENDANCE — IDEOLOGICALLY ORIENTED ENTERPRISE**: Enterprise established not so much for the production of goods and services as to defend and promote an ideology. The concept has little recognition in French law, but it does allow labour law to be applied only partially, in various attenuated forms, within political parties, trade unions or religious educational establishments. The point is sometimes stressed that it must be possible for the exercise of employees' individual freedoms to be restricted in order that the special objective and nature of such bodies may be observed. The matters on which such debate has bearing are disciplinary procedures and dismissal.

336. **ENTREPRISE FAMILIALE — FAMILY ENTERPRISE**: Private business held in joint possession by, or company whose entire capital is held by, members of a single family. Family enterprises used to play an important role in France's economy, but their relative importance is now declining.

337. **ENTREPRISE INTERMÉDIAIRE — INTERMEDIARY ENTERPRISE**: Association, with official authorization from the State and in receipt of government aid, which hires workers who are having difficulty in gaining access to active employment (see **absorption into employment**) in order to arrange forms of work for them in enterprises or public authorities and establishments which under market conditions would not otherwise be available.

This type of structure, which has been encouraged over the past few years and for which French law now makes provision, is characteristic of a policy to create socially useful jobs. Intermediary associations have in fact been set up on only a limited basis.

338. **ENTREPRISE MULTINATIONALE — MULTI-NATIONAL CORPORATION**: A **group of companies** or enterprise made up of separate establishments located on the territory of different countries. These multinationals are also referred to as "transnationals".

339. **ENTREPRISE PUBLIQUE — PUBLIC ENTERPRISE**: Commercial or industrial enterprise which is separate from the State but under its control (or under the control of other public authorities). Such enterprises do not necessarily provide public services. In France, banks and insurance companies which have been nationalized are typical examples.

340. **ÉQUIPE AUTONOME — AUTONOMOUS WORK TEAM**:
See **autonomous work group**.

341. **ÉQUIPE DE SUPPLÉANCE — RELIEF (WEEKEND) SHIFT**: Group of employees whose function is to continue the work of others during the rest period which the latter are granted at the weekend. The use of a relief shift presumes exemption from the rule stipulating that Sunday should be a rest day (see **Sunday rest**). Since 1982, "derogation" to this effect (*i.e.* contracting out of the legal provision) has been possible under a collective agreement that has been decreed generally applicable (see **extension of collective agreements**).

342. **ÉQUIPES SUCCESSIVES — SHIFTS**: Different groups of employees who successively occupy the same jobs, thereby enabling the enterprise to operate on a prolonged basis, or even uninterruptedly. When the shifts succeed each other without interruption, round the clock and including Sundays and public holidays, the system is called continuous working (*e.g.* electricity and gas). When there is an interruption at weekends (and on public holidays) it is called semi-continuous, and when work halts every night it is called discontinuous.

After having declined, the use of shiftwork has recently shown renewed growth in France, particularly in semi-continuous and continuous forms.

There are some legal provisions regulating this system of work organization: an employee may not work two consecutive shifts, and in the case of shiftworkers the statutory weekly **working hours** are reduced to 35 hours as averaged over the year.

343. **ÉQUIVALENCE — EQUIVALENCE**: Term applicable in two contexts:
1. In some occupations, for the purposes of calculating **working hours** levels of equivalence have been established by decree between hours of attendance, *i.e.* hours during which an employee is present at work, and actual hours of work. The reason for this is the existence of "heures creuses", *i.e.* slack or intervening periods when no actual work is performed. The modern tendency is to abolish this practice.
2. Equivalence denotes a trend in legal and trade union policy towards replacing the quest for uniformity of rights and guarantees with room for a degree of diversity, provided that the outcome is the same.

344. ***ERGA OMNES***: Latin expression meaning "in relation to all", used to describe the general force of a collective agreement. Its

clauses automatically apply to all contracts of employment concluded by an employer who is bound by the agreement. The reference in the word *"omnes"* (all) is therefore to employees, and not to employers, who, except in the case of **extension of collective agreements**, are bound by an agreement only if they have signed it, are members of a signatory organization or are applying it voluntarily.

The principle of the *erga omnes* force of collective agreements has been enshrined in French law since 1950. It thus reduces the advantage of union membership, a consequence which for a long time, because of the system of distributive or zero-sum bargaining, was accepted without provoking much debate, but which the upsurge in concession bargaining (see **concession bargaining, derogation agreement**) is now making more problematical.

345. **ERGONOMIE — ERGONOMICS**: Discipline created with a practical objective: the search to adapt human beings to their work and to adapt work to human beings. It is a discipline that brings together diverse areas of expertise such as physiology, anatomy, psychology, etc. Initially focused on working hours, the pace of work, the organization of work and physical movements, modern-day ergonomics is now attempting to make use of the cognitive sciences in order to analyse the transmission of information, the meaning of messages, etc.

346. **ESSAI — TEST/PROBATION**: Term with two distinct meanings:
    1. A selection test: in certain sectors and for certain skill levels, it is common practice during the recruitment procedure to require applicants to undertake a brief test, that is, a test piece of work or task. This test does not form part of a contract of employment, even though the applicant frequently receives payment for the time spent on it.
    2. Probation, in the sense of a probationary period ("période d'essai"), which, by contrast, is part of a contract of employment (which is thus concluded on a trial basis). Its existence and duration must be laid down by the contract, custom or collective agreement. It is subject to certain legal limits set out in the regulations governing fixed-term contracts.

    During the probationary period, the contract of employment may in principle be terminated at any time by either party without needing to comply with the rules on dismissal. However, since the sole purpose of this probationary period is to assess the employee's suitability for the job, the courts do penalize termination for unlawful reason (*i.e.* infringement of a right).

347. **ÉTABLISSEMENT — ESTABLISHMENT**: Subdivision of an enterprise which, in cases where it exists, constitutes the context for exercise of the employer's prerogative rights (formulation of works rules) and in particular for employee representation, and, optionally, for collective bargaining. The establishment also serves as the basis for determining the geographical jurisdiction of the **Industrial Tribunals**.

Where the establishment consists of a production unit without legal personality, its legal definition, as developed by case law, differs according to which particular, compulsory institution of employee representation is being considered. Its definition is described as relative and functional.

348. **ÉTAT MINIMUM — MINIMALIST STATE**: By contrast with the welfare state, the minimalist state is the ideal of those commentators who criticize social legislation (labour law and social security law) as a source of rigidity which damages competitiveness at international level. This philosophy has inspired various economic analyses of the law which have never really struck a chord in France. The term "nighwatchman state" is also used in English.

349. **ÉTRANGER — ALIEN**: See **immigration**.

350. **ÉVALUATION (DU PERSONNEL) — STAFF APPRAISAL**: Assessment of employees' characteristics, abilities and performance. Appraisal has come into widespread use under the influence of two factors: the practice of setting objectives for employees (on an individual or group basis) in the quest for higher productivity, and the wish on the part of some employers to involve individual employees in the definition of their own career path and future prospects.

Appraisal is a necessary prelude to the individualization of both pay and career paths. It entails regular interviewing and the development of criteria or rating scales to ensure that judgments are objective.

351. **EXPERT — EXPERT**: French labour law and social security law have been widely affected by the spreading impact of scientific expertise and accepted norms. Thus, it frequently happens that the tasks of resolving a crisis situation or drawing up a reform are entrusted to experts who possess specialized scientific knowledge and, as such, are regarded as being distinct from the social protagonists.

Within the enterprise, increased numbers of experts are now

stipulated by law, either on a permanent basis (see **company medical service**) or called in as occasion requires. The latter are selected by the institutions of employee representation, *i.e.* the workplace health and safety committee and, in particular, the works council, but it is often the enterprise that is responsible for paying them. This applies to the "expert-comptable" (chartered accountant) whose services every works council is entitled to enlist for its annual analysis of the enterprise's financial position, and to the experts who may be consulted in the event of an emergency relating to safety at work (serious danger), a financial crisis (disquieting situation justifying the **notification** procedure), an employment crisis (where redundancies are proposed) or an organizational crisis (major technological change).

352. **EXPRESSION — EXPRESSION**:
   1. All employees in principle possess the right, in their capacity as employees, to voice their opinion on their employment and working conditions (see **right of expression**).
   2. As citizens, they in principle possess, even within the enterprise, freedom of expression. Its boundaries are, nevertheless, uncertain, since French law tolerates, subject to certain conditions, restrictions on fundamental freedoms within the enterprise. It has been more strongly protected since the courts ruled that acts constituting infringements of fundamental freedoms had no legal effect and imposed an obligation on the employer to restore the *status quo ante*.

353. **EXPULSION — DEPORTATION/EVICTION**: Term used in two distinct senses:
   1. Deportation is an order to leave the country, addressed to an alien whose presence constitutes a serious threat to public law and order.
   2. Eviction is an order issued by the ordinary courts to striking employees who are occupying the enterprise's premises (*i.e.* a "sit-in" or "work-in"), directing them to leave the premises.

354. **EXTENSION — EXTENSION OF COLLECTIVE AGREEMENTS**: Technique whereby a collective agreement is rendered compulsorily applicable in all enterprises falling within its occupational and territorial scope. Failing such extension, an agreement is binding only on those enterprises where the employer is a member of the signatory employers' association.
   First introduced in 1936, when it could be used only for **industry-wide agreements**, the technique may now also be used for **general multi-industry agreements**. It is effected by an act of public administration, *i.e.* a directive from the Minister for

Labour; the conditions to which it is subject and the procedure which must be followed are specified by law in considerable detail. In particular, the **National Collective Bargaining Commission** must be consulted. The ministerial directive preserves the private nature of the collective agreement, and may not affect its substance in any way.

The effect of extension is to make a collective agreement a kind of internal law for the industry or industries concerned.

355. **EXTÉRIORISATION (DE L'EMPLOI) — EXTERNALIZATION OF EMPLOYMENT**: Term which features in analyses of the segmentation of the labour market (see **segmentation**) and the diversification of forms of employment (see **diversification of employment contracts**), used to emphasize the distance which may exist between certain workers and the enterprise that gainfully utilizes their work.

The distance may be spatial, in which case externalization is geographical. Examples of this are **homeworking** and, more generally, **telework** (which is made increasingly possible by information technology). Alternatively, the distance and externalization may be purely legal when between the enterprise and the employees there is a second enterprise, either acting as a subcontractor of the first enterprise or commissioned to hire employees and place them at the disposal of the first enterprise. This latter hypothesis (for which the English term "distancing" is also used) encompasses the legal model of **temporary-employment agency work**, but also forms of supplying labour which may or may not be lawful (see **hiring-out of labour**).

F

356. FAILLITE — BANKRUPTCY: Name traditionally given to the procedure set in motion to ensure settlement of the claims of creditors of an enterprise which is unable to pay its debts (and is thus said to be "en faillite", *i.e.* bankrupt). The term disappeared from legislative terminology at the same time as the aims of the legal system applicable to an enterprise which is "en état de cessation de paiement", *i.e.* insolvent, were altered. Since 1985, the aim of the **compulsory administration** procedure has been to save the enterprise, where it is viable, to maintain the employment it provides and to discharge its debts. Only when it is impossible to arrange (by the continuation or the total or partial change of ownership or control of the enterprise) for its activity to be carried on, is compulsory liquidation declared.

This change of approach has led to closer involvement of the employees and their representatives in the court procedure and better control over the accompanying dismissals.

357. FAUTE — MISCONDUCT/FAULT: Failure to meet an obligation. In this connection, the first special feature of French labour law is the existence of a "scale" of possible forms of misconduct committed by an employee. Misconduct without any further qualification incurs a **disciplinary sanction**. To justify dismissal which is accompanied by entitlements to **compensation in lieu of notice** and **compensation for dismissal**, the misconduct must constitute **genuine and serious cause** for termination of the contract of employment. Serious misconduct ("faute grave") not only justifies dismissal but absolves the employer from payment of compensation in lieu of notice and compensation for dismissal. Lastly, gross misconduct ("faute lourde"), which is necessarily deliberate, deprives a dismissed employee of entitlements to the above payments and, in addition, of entitlement to compensation in lieu of paid **annual holiday**. Only gross misconduct entitles the employer to institute civil liability proceedings against the employee (see **employee liability**) and justifies dismissal of an employee who is on strike.

The second special feature of French labour law with respect to misconduct or fault concerns the employer's civil liability in the event of an accident at work or occupational illness. Employers are liable only in the event of deliberate or inexcusable fault on their part; in all other cases, the employee is protected solely by the social security system.

358. FAVEUR POUR LE SALARIÉ — FAVOURABILITY TO THE EMPLOYEE: Principle applied in settling disputes arising from conflict between the law and a collective agreement, between two collective agreements, or between the law or a collective agreement and the individual contract of employment. It is, however, a purely legal principle. It can therefore be set aside by the law, as is evidently the case with **derogation agreements**.

Application of the principle involves making comparisons. Comparison between a clause in the individual contract and a provision laid down by law or collective agreement is straightforward, since only the employee's individual interests need be considered. Comparison between the law and a collective agreement or between two collective agreements entails isolating a coherent group of rules and identifying the interests of all the employees governed by them.

359. FÉDÉRATION DE L'ÉDUCATION NATIONALE — FEDERATED EDUCATION UNION: Federation (referred to as FEN) which serves as an umbrella organization for unions of established civil servants, and more particularly unions of personnel employed in the education sector. It occupies a special position in French trade unionism, firstly because it has more members than any other federation, and secondly because in 1947 it refused to accept the split between the **CGT** and the **CGT-FO** (see **trade union confederation**) and opted for autonomy. Consequently, it is not affiliated to any confederation.

360. FÉDÉRATION PATRONALE — EMPLOYERS' FEDERATION: See **employers' organization**.

361. FÉDÉRATION SYNDICALE — TRADE UNION FEDERATION: Grouping at national level of trade unions according to a "vertical" logic, *i.e.* by industry or sector. It has been the typical form of grouping in French trade unionism since the choice was made to foster solidarity within given industries or sectors. There are, nevertheless, still some "fédérations de métiers", *i.e.* occupation-based federations.

362. FEMMES — WOMEN: French law contains a set of rules whose purpose is to ensure equal treatment for men and women at work (see **equality between men and women**), as well as special provisions on what is referred to as protection for women at work, such as those relating to **maternity**. But how far can special measures go? This is the question running through the debate provoked by the traditional rules governing night work for women (see **night work, female employment**). Rules on equality still, in fact, meet with considerable resistance.

363. FEN: Abbreviation of Fédération de l'éducation nationale (**Federated Education Union**).

364. FERMETURE D'ÉTABLISSEMENT — CLOSURE OF ESTABLISHMENTS: Term used in two contexts:
1. Sanction that may be applied in the event of infringements of certain regulations (particularly those on the sanitary conditions of premises).
2. Measure that may be taken by a Prefect to preserve competition between sole traders who work alone and are therefore able to open their shops on Sundays, and commercial enterprises which have employees. An order allowing establishments to open on Sundays ("Sunday trading") presupposes that an agreement to this effect has been reached and that the majority of the enterprises concerned are in favour.

365. FÊTE — OFFICIAL HOLIDAY: See **public holidays**.

366. FIDÉLITÉ — LOYALTY: Synonym of **loyauté**.

367. FILIALE — SUBSIDIARY: In commercial law, a company in which another company holds more than 50 per cent. of the share capital. French law has moved away from this purely structural image of the **group of companies**: a company may be deemed a subsidiary without there being any such linking arrangement of capital. Instead, some provisions focus on the exercise by one company of effective and permanent control over another, which is then called a subsidiary.

368. FISCALISATION — TAX FUNDING OF SOCIAL BENEFITS: Recourse, for the financing of social protection, to public revenues other than those directly levied on earnings alone. It is thus contrasted to financing on the basis of **social security contributions**. This latter model was adopted when the present-day social security system was set up in France in 1945. The criticisms levelled against it have so far failed to persuade the authorities to transfer financing to general public revenue, although a proposal for partial "fiscalization" of this kind is being examined.

369. FLEXIBILITÉ — FLEXIBILITY: The concept of flexibility first assumed prominence in the late 1970s in analyses of the economic crisis, in the form of strong criticisms of the organization of work, the hierarchy of skill levels and guarantees relating to employment, methods of calculating pay and the system of social protection.

Setting aside these criticisms, which were often too sweeping, it becomes evident that flexibility can take several forms. It may concern the organization of production, the mobility of employees, hiring and dismissal, or methods of pay determination.

From a more legal perspective, it would appear that flexibility may be measured by the degree of importance accorded to autonomy, both collective and individual. It is a matter of sources and mechanisms. Here, unquestionably, the part played by the employer's managerial prerogative and the contract of employment is very important in the French system, in practice at least. On the other hand, the favourability principle (see **favourability to the employee**), which requires a detailed examination of the sources of rules, and applies the most favourable, may limit moves towards decentralization.

370. **FLEXIBILITÉ DU TEMPS DE TRAVAIL — FLEXIBILITY OF WORKING TIME**: Since the expression originated from a wish to criticize, its opposites are what give it meaning. Where the aim is to break away from the uniformity of time patterns, flexibility is a call for diversity. Where the aim is to have the possibility of deviating from constant rhythms, flexibility is a call for variability.

Since 1973, and particularly since 1981, a number of legislative measures have made more diversity possible in patterns of working hours. For instance, the rule on identical scheduling of working hours may be disregarded under certain conditions, in the shape of **shiftwork, individualized working hours, part-time work** and **intermittent work**.

Varying the actual number of hours worked is subject to more control. Although mechanisms exist which allow temporary variations (upwards with overtime, downwards with compensation for **partial unemployment**), they do not leave the employer total discretion. Variability has been sought by other means: via the recognized option of adjusting working time over the year by collective agreement (see **annualization of working hours**), with no financial consequences.

371. **FLEXIBILITÉ DU TRAVAIL — LABOUR FLEXIBILITY**: In a general sense, term referring to the scope for action available to the management in order to adjust the organization and deployment of the workforce to any changes which appear to be made necessary by the enterprise's circumstances. Such action may affect many different areas: policy on hiring (use of temporary workers, etc.), working time (see **flexibility of working time**), pay, dismissals, etc. In France, a distinction is usually made

between the terms "internal flexibility" (which does not affect the volume of employment, but rather its conditions) and "external flexibility".

In a narrower sense, labour flexibility denotes the adaptability of the organization of work, *i.e.* both variation of the utilization of plant and equipment and the mobility of employees.

372. **FO**: Abbreviation of "**Force ouvrière**" as in **CGT-FO**. See **trade union confederation**.

373. **FONCTION — FUNCTION**: Often synonymous with "**emploi**" (in the sense of job or work). An attempt is sometimes made to distinguish between them, to the effect that a function is a role in a concrete system of work, as an element of its organization, whereas a job consists of the collection and share of functions entrusted to a given employee. The distinction, where it is made, is based on the rules of **job classification**.

374. **FONCTION PUBLIQUE — CIVIL SERVICE**: Term used to designate either the activity performed by civil servants, in a broad sense or in a more technical sense (see **established civil servant**), or the collective body of these civil servants. As most widely understood, the term refers to the central administration ("fonction publique de l'Etat"), which at the present time represents approximately 2.6 million budgetary jobs. But it also covers local administration ("fonction publique territoriale"), as referring to the activities or civil servants of the local public authorities (at regional or département level).

375. **FONCTIONNAIRE — ESTABLISHED CIVIL SERVANT**: In popular usage, the term "fonction publique" (**civil service**) covers all employees of the administrative apparatus of the State and of other public authorities.

But it has a more technical meaning: only those employees of the (central or local) administration who have been appointed in accordance with special regulations and thereby attain special status are "fonctionnaires" in the strict sense, *i.e.* established civil servants. This means that there are public employees who are not established civil servants; referred to as "non-titulaires", they fall into one of three categories: "auxiliaires" (**auxiliary public employees**), "temporaires" or "vacataires" (occasional or **temporary public employees**) and "contractuels" (**contract public employees**).

Established civil servants, in the strict or technical sense, are not deemed to be bound to the administration by a contract: they are described as being in a statutory position, and are subject to rules deriving from **administrative law**. Consequently, the general rules applicable to contracts of employment are in principle not applicable to them. Disputes arising from their relationships with the administration do not come under the jurisdiction of the usual labour courts, *i.e.* the **Industrial Tribunals**, but that of the administrative courts.

376. **FONDS D'ACTION SOCIALE — SOCIAL ACTION FUND**: Public service body responsible for aiding the social and occupational integration of foreign workers, but also for helping to organize their return to their country of origin.

377. **FONDS D'ASSURANCE FORMATION — TRAINING INSURANCE FUND**: Joint body set up by collective agreement to cover the cost of training arrangements and trainees' pay. Membership may be made compulsory for enterprises under an agreement.

These funds are financed by contributions which may, subject to certain conditions, be deducted from the compulsory payments which enterprises are required to make towards the general funding of **further vocational training**.

Nowadays, they mainly finance initiatives which form part of an enterprise's **training plan**.

378. **FONDS NATIONAL DE L'EMPLOI — NATIONAL EMPLOYMENT FUND**: Not a body, but a set of budgetary credits grouped under this heading and made available to the Minister responsible for employment policy. The measures which may be financed from this source are defined by law and include, for example, such important matters as early retirement, re-training and assisting geographical mobility.

379. **FONDS SALARIAUX — EMPLOYEE INVESTMENT FUNDS**: Term referring to a form of fund established in an enterprise from employees' contributions and used for financing investments in production or arrangements to reduce working hours, and for job creation. Funds of this kind may be set up only under a collective agreement approved by the Government. Their creation was encouraged by tax advantages until these were discontinued in 1986.

380. **FORCE DU TRAVAIL — LABOUR POWER**: According to some analyses, labour power is the object of the exchanges that take place on the labour market. See **labour demand**.

117

381. *FORCE MAJEURE*: Event which releases obligors from their obligation or exonerates parties causing damage from their liability. In order to have such effect, the event must in principle be unforeseeable, irresistible and outside the control of the person who invokes it (*cf.* frustration of contract in general law).

This concept plays little part in the employment relationships of employees, because the employer is held liable for a certain degree of foresight and must bear the risks of carrying on a business. Nevertheless, a natural disaster may constitute an instance of *force majeure* (in which specific case it is referred to in English as an "act of God").

It finds more singular expression in the procedure relating to industrial disputes. Here, the courts accept that where there are "compelling circumstances", as a kind of attenuated form of *force majeure* (see **lock-out**), employers are released from their obligation to provide work for employees and, by the same token, from their obligation to pay them. (See also **compensation for dismissal**.)

382. "FORCE OUVRIÈRE": Popular term for **CGT-FO** (abbreviation of **General Confederation of Labour-"Force ouvrière"**). See **trade union confederation**.

383. FORDISME — FORDISM: Term designating the form of integration of wage-earners into a capitalist economy which is characterized by the spread of Tayloristic methods (see **work organization**) in conjunction with access for employees to mass consumption. In the specific context of France, Fordism is represented by the phase of growth of the French economy during the 1960s. And the recession that began in the early 1970s illustrates the disruption of Fordism.

384. FORMALISME (CONTRACTUEL) — FORMALIZATION OF EMPLOYMENT CONTRACTS: The law has imposed additional requirements relating to the issue of written particulars of employment as the diversity of employment contracts has increased (see **diversification of employment contracts**): all contracts, unless they correspond to the basic type (full-time contract of indeterminate duration), must be in written form. The purpose is to enable employees to be properly informed of their terms and conditions of employment, and to make it easier to keep a check on the observance of legal requirements. If a contract is not in written form, there is a general legal presumption that it corresponds to the basic type of employment contract.

385. **FORMATION PROFESSIONNELLE CONTINUE —
FURTHER VOCATIONAL TRAINING**: Training defined by
its scope, substance, target audience and method of organization.
In scope, it differs from initial training, which is organized by
the school and university system for those who have not yet
entered working life. Its substance is very broad, ranging from
preparation for entry into employment to adjustment to change,
and taking in occupational, social and cultural advancement. It
is targeted at adults and young people who are already in active
employment or about to enter it. Lastly, since by law it constitutes
a national obligation, its organization involves the participation
of the State, enterprises, trade unions and employers' associations.
It is not subject to centralization, uniformity or a given statutory
model, but is organized on a decentralized basis via collective
bargaining and joint or tripartite administration, the role of the
State being essentially to provide impetus, co-ordination and
financial incentives.

   Such, at any rate, are the features which further vocational
training has acquired with the upsurge, since 1970, of a collection
of rules and institutions, established by law and collective
agreement, sufficiently detailed and coherent to warrant being
referred to as the law on vocational training (see **educational
leave, training insurance fund, training plan**).

386. **FORMATION SYNDICALE — TRAINING IN UNION
AFFAIRS**: The training of union activists and full-time officials
is encouraged by the State, in the form of **leave for education
in economic, social and union affairs** and the regular allocation
of aid to training centres run by the representative trade union
organizations. In addition, specialized institutes exist within the
university system.

387. **FORMES D'ACTION — FORMS OF INDUSTRIAL
ACTION**: Numerous typologies have been devised to describe
and analyse the methods used by employees in their efforts to
ensure that an industrial dispute ends in their favour. The
definition of the **strike** as given by case law provides an initial
guide on lawful forms of industrial action. Within this framework,
however, the status of certain forms of action, such as **false
imprisonment**, picketing (see **picket**) and **occupation of the
workplace**, is controversial.

388. **FORME D'EMPLOI — FORM OF EMPLOYMENT**: In the
study of the changes overtaking the labour market and
employment, the concept of form of employment continues to

play an important role. It serves as the logic for analysis in terms of a standard model: significant deviations from this model are grouped into large categories each constituting diverse or particular forms of employment.

The substance of the standard model features a strong link between employer and employee (with its continuity providing the basis for a career path), full-time work, a single employer, a specific place where work is performed, and the employee's dependence on the financial resources gained from it. The status of this standard model is more difficult to define, since it has never, with all its elements combined, been established as a positive legal type; rather, it is a social representation, a paradigm. The growing diversity of forms of employment therefore signals the disappearance of a paradigm.

389. **FRACTION (SYNDICALE) — UNION FACTION**: A faction, like a "minorité" (minority group) or "courant" (current of opinion), is an organized tendency within a trade union. Under this name, however, it is a tendency which is denounced, opposed or even disallowed, whereas under the other names it is tolerated and sometimes acknowledged.

390. **FRAGMENTATION — FRAGMENTATION (OF THE LABOUR MARKET)**: See **segmentation**.

391. **FRAIS PROFESSIONNELS — EXPENSES**: Expenses incurred by employees in and for the purpose of performing their work. Since in many instances they are then reimbursed and this may give rise to arguments about the rules governing the sums allowed for this purpose by an enterprise, it has become customary to use the word "expenses" in the sense of the actual sums judged to correspond to expenditure arising from work.

392. **FRANCHISAGE — FRANCHISING**: Neologism coined to avoid the use in French of "franchising" as a loan word. It relates to a contract ("contrat de franchise", *i.e.* franchise contract) whereby one party, the franchiser, undertakes to make available to another, the franchisee, a particular expertise, the right (as a general rule) to use a particular trademark, and (more often than not) the supply of certain goods; the franchisee, in return, undertakes to make use of the expertise and the trademark and to procure supplies from the franchiser.

In French law, franchisees are treated as self-employed traders: their situation is not one of **"subordination"** even though they are in a position of relative **economic dependence**. (See also **concessionnaire**.)

393. **FUSION DE SOCIÉTÉS — COMPANY MERGER**:
Operation whereby two or more separate companies are combined
to form a single company. French law recognizes two forms of
merger: merger by absorption, which is the more usual, and
merger by the creation of a new company. It is above all a means
of industrial or financial concentration; the transfer of assets and
partial contribution of assets may serve the same purpose, but
it is only when there is a change of legal identity that such
operations are properly called mergers.

394. **FUSION DE SYNDICATS — UNION MERGER/
AMALGAMATION**: Not envisaged, as such, by French law.
The combination of two or more unions into a single one
presupposes that some or all of the unions involved are disbanded
and that their members join the surviving grouping or a new
grouping.

G

395. GARANTIE D'EMPLOI — GUARANTEE OF EMPLOYMENT: In the strict sense, an undertaking by the employer to maintain the size of the workforce at a certain level or to continue to employ a particular employee. In the former case, there is no identified beneficiary and the question of penalization is uncertain. In the second case, the undertaking is valid in law provided that it is for a specified period: the contract of employment becomes a contract with a stipulated minimum duration.

The expression is also sometimes used to describe the substance of certain company policies which give priority to stability of employment.

396. GARANTIE DES SALAIRES — GUARANTEE OF PAY: See **wage guarantee insurance**.

397. GÉRANT — MANAGER (OF A PRIVATE COMPANY)/ AGENT: In French company law, a "gérant" is a person entrusted with the management of, specifically, certain private companies.

In a strictly legal sense, a "gerant" is a person (agent) responsible for administering the assets or affairs of another person. Depending on the circumstances, they may be employees (which, under French law, does not exclude them from also being an officer of the company), or self-employed. Certain categories of agent who are not employees are deemed, through the operation of the law, to fall within the scope of the rules of labour law.

398. GESTION DU PERSONNEL — MANAGEMENT OF PERSONNEL: As an activity, there is little real difference between this term and "direction du personnel" (**personnel management**). In French, the latter suggests the use of rules, instructions and decisions, while "gestion du personnel" is associated with needs and resources, targets, means and results.

399. GESTION PRÉVISIONNELLE (DES EMPLOIS ET DES COMPÉTENCES) — HUMAN RESOURCE PLANNING: The purpose of human resource planning is to devise (on the basis of medium-term objectives), implement and evaluate plans of action whose aim is to reduce, by anticipating them, discrepancies between the enterprise's needs and available human resources. It implies, in principle, the involvement of all employees in the definition of their own career development.

This ambition places change at the heart of the enterprise's mode of functioning. It calls for the establishment of new dynamic links between skill levels, training and the organization of work, and sets updating training and mobility as priorities. It has developed in France over the past 15 years, as the conviction spread that demographic trends would make it essential to achieve better utilization of existing staff.

It has given rise to a number of company-level agreements which state the ambitions and methods, the procedures that may be used and the resultant rights and obligations for enterprises and employees.

400. **GESTION DES RESSOURCES HUMAINES — HUMAN RESOURCE MANAGEMENT**: See **contract of employment, personnel management**.

401. **GRATIFICATION — DISCRETIONARY BONUS**: Element of remuneration whose payment is at the employer's own discretion. It changes its nature and becomes part of pay when it exhibits the three qualities of being general (paid to all employees or a given category of employee), permanent (paid regularly) and fixed (a set amount or percentage).

402. **GRÈVE — STRIKE**: In France, the scope of the right to strike is determined by the courts. According to the existing formula, the only defined characteristic of what constitutes a lawful strike is as a concerted stoppage of work for the purpose of backing employment-related demands. Hence, legal protection does not depend on who initiates the strike, the timing of its initiation, its duration or the number of employees involved.

There is some debate in part of the trade union movement as to whether the strike is any longer relevant as the preferred form of industrial action. Certainly, since the mid-1970s the changes which are affecting the world of work, the context of unemployment and the weakening of the unions have led to a decrease in the number of strikes. They are mostly concentrated in the public services and those industrial sectors which are undergoing decline or restructuring.

403. **GRÈVE BOUCHON — SELECTIVE STRIKE**: Synonym of **grève thrombose**.

404. **GRÈVE D'AVERTISSEMENT — TOKEN STRIKE**: See **stoppage**.

405. **GRÈVE DU ZÈLE — WORK-TO-RULE**: Scrupulously detailed observance of all working rules, with the aim of delaying or disrupting production. The French courts hold that this form

of action is not covered by the protection of the right to strike, because it does not involve a stoppage of work. It does not, however, constitute defective performance of work provided that minimum production is maintained.

406. **GRÈVE GÉNÉRALE — GENERAL STRIKE**: Strategy proposed by the French trade union movement at the beginning of the century, founded on the belief that a concerted and generalized work stoppage on the part of the workers would be the surest way of forcing the employers to give in (or, for some, of changing the entire social order), or of preventing the slide into war. The frustration of this proposed strategy by the events of 1914 put an end to the doctrine.

Nowadays, the term designates any nationwide strike action whose purpose is essentially, in practice, to protect jobs or protest against government measures. Participation by an employee within an enterprise, even in the absence of a claim directed against the particular employer, is deemed to be legitimate exercise of the right to strike.

407. **GRÈVE PERLÉE — GO-SLOW**: A slowing-down of the pace of work which does not involve a total cessation of activity and which is, therefore, held by the courts to constitute defective performance of obligations under the contract of employment, and not a form of exercising the right to strike. It renders employees liable to a cut in pay and a disciplinary sanction.

408. **GRÈVE POLITIQUE — POLITICAL STRIKE**: Strike which is not directed at employment-related ("industrial") objectives, and which for that reason is excluded from legal protection. The complex nature of the organization of society means that the distinction between a strike relating to industrial objectives and a political strike is not altogether clear. Indeed, whenever the government measures being denounced by strikers have an impact on the position of employees (nationalization or privatization, social protection, etc.), the courts tend to recognize such action as lawful.

409. **GRÈVE SAUVAGE — UNOFFICIAL STRIKE**: Term used to emphasize in French the spontaneity of a stoppage of work and/or the absence of any trade union backing. (The American term "wildcat strike" is also used in Britain.) As a corollary of the French conception of the right to strike of which every employee is an individual holder, in the private sector an unofficial strike constitutes legitimate exercise of the right to strike. The courts do, however, impose one restraint: the employees'

demands must be known to the employer when the strike commences.

In the public services, on the other hand, the initiative must come only from a representative trade union, which is required to observe a period of advance notice (see **public service**).

410. GRÈVE THROMBOSE — SELECTIVE STRIKE: Stoppage of work affecting just one workshop, department or occupational category, but one without whose activities the enterprise is brought to a halt (*e.g.* the computer department in a bank). This form of strike (also called "grève bouchon") is in principle lawful, provided it does not involve any abuse of the law.

411. GRÈVE TOURNANTE — ROTATING STRIKE: Form of action involving stoppages of work successively affecting either different occupational categories (horizontal rotating strike) or different areas of activity (vertical rotating strike). Its effectiveness derives from the interdependence which exists between the various departments of an enterprise: the enterprise may suffer substantial losses, whereas the loss of pay for particular employees is only small. Consequently the courts, applying a principle of "proportionate damage", have sometimes interpreted it as an abuse of the right to strike.

Rotating strikes are prohibited by law in the public services.

412. GROSSESSE — PREGNANCY: A range of provisions ensure the protection of female employees who become pregnant. The key institution is an exemption from performance of the contract of employment (see **maternity leave**) accompanied by protection against dismissal which is absolute during maternity leave and relative during the period of pregnancy and during the four weeks following the end of statutory maternity leave. Other measures complement this system of protection: an employee "in a condition of evident pregnancy" is entitled to terminate her contract of employment without notice while still retaining a preferential right to be re-hired; arrangements are provided for making adjustments to an employee's job at the start of pregnancy and again when she returns to work at the end of maternity leave; and when maternity leave expires, the employee may opt instead for a further suspension of the contract of employment by taking up an entitlement to **parental childcare leave**.

413. GROUPE AUTONOME — AUTONOMOUS WORK GROUP: Name given to experiments conducted by enterprises in which the planning of work and rest periods is left, within certain limits, to the employees concerned, in some cases along with quantity and quality control, with a concomitant relaxation of supervision and discipline. Such experiments, which have been in decline over the past 15 years, are experiencing renewed interest in some industrial and commercial enterprises.

414. **GROUPE DE SOCIÉTÉS — GROUP OF COMPANIES**: Various legal consequences have progressively become attached to the existence of a group of separate companies joined under uniform control. For instance, the courts accept that:
1. in the event of successive job moves within such a group the same contract of employment remains in force, and
2. in some cases the employee may make application to different companies within the group for the purpose of securing payment of wages or of entitlements due on termination of the contract of employment.

Statute law itself, since 1982, has stipulated the formation of a **group-level works council**, a body federating the works councils established in the individual companies of a group. Although for the purposes of instituting this latter body the law gives a suggested definition for a group of companies (combining criteria on financial structure with criteria on interrelations or modes of action), the courts adopt a more empirical approach.

415. **GROUPE SEMI-AUTONOME — SEMI-AUTONOMOUS WORK GROUP**: See **work organization**.

416. **GROUPEMENT D'EMPLOYEURS — EMPLOYERS' POOL**: Association set up by enterprises which must each have no more than 100 employees and, in principle, be bound by the same industry-wide agreement, the purpose being to hire personnel who will then be placed at the disposal of its members (see **provision of labour**). This "collective employer" formula has been encouraged by French law since 1985, in the hope that it would meet the needs of small and medium-sized enterprises and allow the creation of secure jobs. In practice, it has been little used.

417. **GROUPEMENT SYNDICAL — TRADE UNION GROUP(ING)**: See **trade union organization**.

H

418. **HANDICAPÉ — DISABLED PERSON**: Access to paid employment is the pivot of policies concerning disabled adults. Thus, French law establishes employment priorities in favour of the disabled, making it compulsory for enterprises with 20 or more employees to reserve a quota (6 per cent.) of jobs for disabled persons. This obligation is, however, moderated by alternatives to actual hiring: conclusion of a subcontract with specialist establishments that employ disabled workers, application of a state-approved collective agreement stipulating an action programme in favour of disabled persons, or payment of a contribution to a development fund for their absorption into active employment.

The law does not define disability and merely refers to a registration procedure conducted by a technical commission (COTOREP). It is this Commission that is responsible for defining and assessing disability.

419. **HARCÈLEMENT (SEXUEL) — SEXUAL HARASSMENT**: A recent French statute, adopted in a climate of vigorous debate, seeks to protect individuals against sexual harassment at work. Within the meaning of this Law, sexual harassment presupposes a relationship of authority in the work hierarchy; it emanates from a person who is invested with an authority conferred by their function and consists in issuing orders, proffering threats, imposing constraints or exerting pressure of any kind on a lower-ranking employee with the aim of obtaining sexual favours for themselves or for a third party.

The new Law protects victims and witnesses of sexual harassment and places the head of an enterprise under an obligation to take the measures necessary to prevent the acts it so defines.

420. **HEURES DE DÉLÉGATION — TIME-OFF RIGHTS**: Synonym of **crédit d'heures**.

421. **HEURES SUPPLÉMENTAIRES — OVERTIME**: Hours worked at the employer's request in excess of statutory working hours, which in France have been set since 1982 at 39 hours, in principle calculated over a weekly period.

Also since 1982, employers have had the option of freely arranging a certain quota of overtime, fixed by regulation or collective agreement, provided that they inform the works council and the Labour Inspector and pay the employees concerned an enhanced rate of pay (whose minimum rate is set by law) and, in addition, grant them time off in lieu. Authorization from the Labour Inspector is not required unless this quota is exceeded.

422. **HIÉRARCHIE — HIERARCHY**: Term borrowed from religious language and applied to organizations in which power relationships, *i.e.* asymmetrical relationships, exist. Thus, the hierarchy of an enterprise indicates the distribution of power within it.

To hierarchize is to arrange in classes ranked one above the other. Hence the expressions "pay hierarchy" or "social hierarchy" (the latter often being equivalent to "social stratification").

423. **HORAIRE DU TRAVAIL — SCHEDULING OF WORKING HOURS**: The pattern of working time in an enterprise. Under French law, two principles regulate this pattern. First, hours of work are collective, *i.e.* the same for the entire workforce; various exceptions to this first principle are possible (see **individualized working hours, relief (weekend) shift, shifts**). Secondly, the pattern is a weekly one: working time is distributed within the framework of the week, in accordance with certain models laid down by decree; this second principle is also being eroded (see **annualization of working hours, flexibility of working time**).

424. **HORAIRE FLEXIBLE — FLEXIBLE WORKING HOURS**: (See **flexibility of working time**.) Patterns of working time are subject to detailed regulations (see **scheduling of working hours**). They may be described as flexible where there is a permitted deviation from any element of the regulatory models.

425. **HORAIRE INDIVIDUALISÉ — INDIVIDUALIZED WORKING HOURS**: System of scheduling working hours under which employees are free to arrange their own pattern of working time provided they are present at work during a specified "core time" ("période fixe"). The system is also referred to as "horaire variable" (flexitime). It constitutes a departure from the rule that the timing of working hours should be collective, *i.e.* identical for the entire workforce. This is not left to the employer's discretion; the introduction of individualized working hours presupposes that the works council does not object or, where no works council exists, that the Labour Inspector, having ascertained that the workforce is in agreement, has authorized it.

426. **HYGIÈNE DU TRAVAIL — OCCUPATIONAL HEALTH**: A range of rules and institutions are directed at safeguarding

employees' health. The rules are essentially based on a philosophy of prevention: they make the employer responsible for meeting certain obligations whose purpose is to reduce the risks of harmful effects on health. The institutions are partly internal to the enterprise (see **company medical service, workplace health and safety committee**) and partly external.

The conception of risks to health has widened to include aspects other than actual cleanliness and healthy conditions in workplaces: the work environment, workload and pace of work are all factors which receive attention in thinking on employees' health. (Nowadays, the word "santé" tends to be used in French in this connection rather than "hygiène".)

129

I

427. **IMMIGRATION — IMMIGRATION**: Term which first came into general use in France in the early years of the twentieth century, when it became tempting for some to see the size of the foreign population in the country (around 2.5 million in 1926) as one of the factors explaining its economic weakness and difficulties. This led to the call for an immigration policy, that is, measures to control the entry of aliens into France, their length of stay and their access to employment.

Today, with the exception of EC nationals, aliens may be hired only if they hold an official work permit (very few of which are issued). If this condition is not met, any such contract of employment is null and void and the employer is rendered liable to penal, administrative and civil sanctions.

A second consideration has now taken over from the first. Since French enterprises by now employ very large numbers of foreign workers who have been legitimately settled in France over the past 30 years, it is important to decide on a policy concerning them.

428. **IMPLANTATION SYNDICALE — UNION PRESENCE IN THE ENTERPRISE**: See **representativeness**.

429. **INAPTITUDE PHYSIQUE — PHYSICAL UNFITNESS**: An employee's incapability, for reasons of health, of performing the job for which they were hired. When this incapability is the result of an **accident at work** or **occupational illness**, French law makes it compulsory for the employer to offer the employee an alternative job; if this is not practicable or if the employee refuses the alternative post offered, a special form of compensation for dismissal is stipulated.

Where there is no work-related cause, the employer is not under an obligation to offer the employee an alternative job, but is merely required to take account of any suggestions made by the company doctor (see **company medical service**). The legal treatment of termination of the contract of employment on the grounds of physical unfitness includes a number of distinctions which have been developed by the courts. Temporary incapacity for work does not, in principle, justify dismissal; permanent but partial incapacity obliges the employer to take account of the company doctor's suggestions but, if it is not practicable to follow these suggestions, termination is lawful without incurring the payment of any form of compensation; the same applies in the case of permanent total incapacity.

430. **INAPTITUDE PROFESSIONNELLE — INCOMPET-ENCE**: An employee's inability to perform his or her job. The terms "insuffisance professionnelle" (occupational inadequacy) and "inadaptation à l'emploi" (unsuitability for the job) are frequently used in the same sense, as a means of designating reasons for dismissal without making specific reference to any shortcoming on the part of the employee. Their relatively widespread use is due to the reluctance of some judges to pronounce on an employee's professional competence.

431. **INCITATION — INCENTIVE**: Encouragement or invitation to act in a particular manner. A number of measures introduced under employment policies (see **employment support**) constitute incentives, in reserving a particular advantage for those enterprises which adjust their actions to fit the government's objectives.

432. **INDEMNITÉ — COMPENSATION**: Sum of money intended to make amends for loss or harm suffered. Two very different categories exist. In the conventionally accepted sense of the term, compensation makes amends for loss or harm suffered as the result of a wrongful act or irregularity; in this case the term more often used is "dommages-intérêts" (damages). Examples include the compensation payable by the employer for failure to observe the correct dismissal procedure (see **dismissal**) and the compensation due for dismissal without **genuine and serious cause**.

Secondly, some forms of compensation are also due to the employee to make amends for loss or harm suffered without the employer having committed any wrongful act. For instance, employers are obliged to pay **compensation in lieu of notice** when they exempt an employee who has resigned or been dismissed from continuing to perform their work during the period of notice, and to pay an "indemnité de congés payés" (compensation in lieu of paid **annual holiday**) to make good the loss of pay resulting from an employee's absence from work during the period of annual holiday. Such forms of compensation represent the price, as it were, of rights which are claimable without any wrongful act on the part of the employer. In general, therefore, they fall under the legal and tax regulations applicable to pay.

433. **INDEMNITÉ DE CHÔMAGE — UNEMPLOYMENT BENEFIT**: Synonym of **allocation de chômage**.

434. **INDEMNITÉ DE CLIENTÈLE — GOODWILL INDEMNITY**: See **sales representative**.

131

435. INDEMNITÉ DE LICENCIEMENT — COMPENSATION FOR DISMISSAL/SEVERANCE PAY: Sum of money, determined on a lump sum basis, which is intended to compensate the loss or harm suffered by the employee as a result of employer decision to end a contract of employment of indeterminate duration. It is not payable in cases of resignation by the employee, *force majeure* or **dismissal** on the grounds of serious misconduct (see **misconduct**). Both the basic entitlement to and the amount of such severance pay are strictly dependent on length of continuous service, which therefore serves as its justifying ground for claims. It is regulated by law and collective agreement and, sometimes, the individual contract of employment. Statutory severance pay, which is a minimum, does not become payable until after two years of continuous service; it is not payable cumulatively, *i.e.* in addition to any more favourable compensation provided for under a collective agreement or individual contract of employment.

Severance pay is not, in principle, treated as pay. It does not attract social security contributions, nor is it taxable.

436. INDEMNITÉ DE MALADIE — SICK PAY: Under French law, illness leads to suspension of the contract of employment. In principle, therefore, employers are thereby exonerated from their obligation to pay wages. Employees, in their turn, are entitled to claim the benefits paid via the social security system known as "indemnités journalières" (daily allowances), but these are far smaller than the lost earnings. For this reason, collective agreements often stipulate that the employer is liable to continue paying all or part of an employee's pay for the duration of a certain period of absence; this "sick pay" is also called "indemnité compensatrice de perte de salaire pour cause de maladie" (compensation for loss of earnings caused by illness). As a substitute for pay, it is treated in law as such.

All employees who are paid under a **monthly pay system** are entitled to this financial protection.

437. INDEMNITÉ DE PRÉAVIS — COMPENSATION IN LIEU OF NOTICE: Compensation for the loss of earnings suffered when, following the termination of a contract of indeterminate duration, the employer has exempted an employee from continuing to perform their work during the **period of notice**. It falls under the legal, social and tax regulations applicable to pay.

438. INDEMNITÉS DE RUPTURE — ENTITLEMENTS PAYABLE ON TERMINATION OF THE EMPLOYMENT CONTRACT: Also referred to as "end-of-contract payments". See, for example, **wage guarantee insurance, dismissal**.

439. **INDÉPENDANT — SELF-EMPLOYED PERSON**: See **self-employment**.

440. **INDÉROGABILITÉ — "INDEROGABILITY"**: Term little used in France, designating the nature of a rule of statute law which parties may not agree between themselves, by exercising discretion under a collective agreement or individual contract of employment, to amend or set aside (*i.e. jus cogens*). Such rules are more usually described as being "d'ordre public" (a matter of public policy).

   In labour law, however, a distinction must be made between relative "inderogability" (an alternative regulation may be applied, but only if it improves the position of employees) and absolute "inderogability" (no alternative regulation may be applied under any circumstances). Examples of the latter include the rules which define the jurisdiction of the labour courts and the Labour Inspectorate, and those which restrict the **index-linking** of pay.

441. **INDEXATION — INDEX-LINKING/INDEXATION**: A system whereby levels of pay are linked automatically to changes in the cost of living. Such a link, although only partial, is operated in the calculation of the SMIC (national guaranteed **minimum wage**). It is, however, prohibited by law to index-link the pay scales contained in collective agreements to the general cost of living and the SMIC; these scales may use only indices relating directly to the form of activity of the parties. Numerous automatic index-linking practices have nevertheless existed, but are now much less common, having been replaced by procedures for reviewing pay at regular intervals or as dictated by circumstances.

442. **INDICE DU COÛT DE LA VIE — COST-OF-LIVING INDEX**: Index which serves as a measure of employees' purchasing power. To fix the SMIC, *i.e.* the national guaranteed **minimum wage**, use is made of one of the general consumer price indices calculated and published by a public body, the Institut national de la statistique et des études économiques (National Statistical and Economic Research Institute), known as INSEE.

443. **INDIVIDUALISATION — INDIVIDUALIZATION**:
   1. In a general sense, a tendency which consists, within the enterprise, in calling rules (and particularly customs) into question in order to establish differences in treatment between employees. Reference is made, for instance, to the individualization of employment relationships. However, it appears to exist on only a limited scale.

2. In the specific context of pay, individualization consists in reserving a growing proportion of the employee's total remuneration, or any increase, for the "récompense des performances individuelles" (reward of individual performance).

444. **INDUSTRIE — INDUSTRY**: Term used in two senses:
1. In the traditional tertiary division of economic activities, industry is the subdivision which groups together all those activities concerned with the exploitation of mineral resources and energy resources and the transformation of raw materials. In this generic sense, it is the industrial sector as opposed to the commercial sector and the agricultural sector.
2. In the specific sense, "an industry" is a particular branch (see **branch of economic activity**) of industry in the generic sense. By extension, any branch of economic activity of whatever kind may in fact be referred to as an industry; it is within this context that French trade unionism developed from industry-based groupings.

445. **INFORMATION — INFORMATION**: It is as the subject of an obligation on employers that information has become a central element of employment relationships and labour relations.

Within the employment relationship, French law obliges the employer, prior to any **disciplinary sanction** (other than a trivial one) or any form of **dismissal**, to provide the employee concerned with information on the reasons for and nature of the action envisaged.

In labour relations, the law obliges the head of an enterprise to supply the works council with regular data and prior information on management decisions that are likely to have an impact on the position of employees. Collective bargaining, where compulsory (see **duty to bargain**), must also begin with the provision of certain items of information by the enterprise.

There are basically two aims behind the evolving requirement to supply compulsory information: firstly, to provide employees with some degree of protection against arbitrary treatment, and secondly, to establish a better balance in relations between the enterprise and the unions or other institutions of employee representation.

446. **INFORMATION NOMINATIVE — PERSONAL DATA**: A key concept of the French procedure, established by a Law of January 4, 1978, for controlling the creation and use of computerized data processing systems. Personal data is defined as any data which allows "the identification, in any form

134

whatever, directly or otherwise, of the natural persons to whom" it relates (see **National Commission for Information Technology and Civil Liberties**).

447. **INFORMATION SYNDICALE — UNION INFORMATION**: See **union communications**.

448. **INFORMATIQUE — INFORMATION TECHNOLOGY**: Information technology has aroused deliberations and reactions in essentially three directions. The first is its impact on employment. Nowadays, the utmost caution is observed in studies which attempt to analyse the changes that information technology has caused or is likely to cause. Before new technologies are introduced into an enterprise the works council must, by law, be informed and consulted, and the council is entitled to request the appointment of an expert to provide assistance. Various collective agreements arrange for employee representatives to be allowed closer involvement in studying and designing the computerization of production. The second direction is the impact of information technology on working conditions. Analyses have concentrated in particular on work at VDU screens. Some collective agreements stipulate procedures for monitoring its use and its effects on employees' health. The third direction concerns the threats which computerization may pose to employees' individual liberties. A Law of January 4, 1978 granted new rights to the individual and regulated the computerized processing of personal data (see **National Commission for Information Technology and Civil Liberties**).

449. **INFORMEL — INFORMAL**: Adjective designating something which is not governed by any rule, or something which is not governed by any positive rule but may be governed by rules deduced from an analysis of conduct (**custom**, for example), or something which represents an evasion of certain rules (in which last sense the **hidden economy** is also referred to as the "informal" economy).

450. **INFRACTION — OFFENCE/INFRINGEMENT**: Conduct which is prohibited by the law and, as such, punishable by the criminal courts.

451. **INGÉNIEUR — ENGINEER**: Individual who has received a course of training evidenced by a formal qualification (usually a degree in engineering, although enterprises sometimes recognize equivalent qualifications) which makes them fitted for functions entailing, because of their technical nature, initiative and

responsibility. A prototype of the "cadre" (**professional or managerial employee**).

452. **INSAISISSABILITÉ — IMMUNITY FROM SEIZURE/ IMMUNITY FROM ATTACHMENT**: Special protection of certain of a person's assets, making them unavailable to creditors (*i.e.* not subject to "execution"). Their seizure is thus prohibited. Such immunity may be only partial. This is so in the case of pay (where seizure is referred to specifically in English as "attachment of earnings"); hence, an employee's pay is attachable by a creditor only to an extent permitted by law. The assets necessary to the functioning of a trade union are immune from seizure (also referred to in this context as "sequestration").

453. **INSERTION PROFESSIONNELLE — ABSORPTION INTO EMPLOYMENT**: Term designating the goal and certain features of procedures which have now been instituted in France for more than 10 years in order to reduce unemployment among young people or disadvantaged social categories. The purpose is to place them in active employment. But since enterprises do not hire them and they need to acquire training necessitating close supervision, their employment takes place within the framework of "stages" (special training schemes) or employment contracts of a special type whose cost is partly or wholly financed by the State.

454. **INSPECTEUR DU TRAVAIL — LABOUR INSPECTOR**: Name given to the established civil servants belonging to the **Labour Inspectorate**. At enterprise and establishment level, the labour inspector is the official who has direct dealings with enterprise managers, unions and workforce representatives and employees. Although the title "labour inspector" has been retained since the creation of the Labour Inspectorate in 1892, the administrative division to which these inspectors belong is called the "Administration du travail, de l'emploi et de la formation professionnelle" (Labour, Employment and Vocational Training Division), organized on a département basis (each headed by a Département Director of Labour, Employment and Vocational Training) and a regional basis (each headed by a Regional Director of Labour, Employment and Vocational Training). Alongside the labour inspectors, there are employment inspectors who are empowered to perform the same functions; in practice, responsibilities are allocated between the two on the basis of the size of enterprises.

455. INSPECTION DU TRAVAIL — LABOUR INSPECTOR-ATE: Specialist administrative division whose name evokes its original function of monitoring and enforcing the application of social legislation. Its monitoring function has been extended to include compliance with provisions deriving from collective agreements. In addition to this, it also performs advisory and information functions, has responsibilities in the settlement of disputes and possesses certain decision-making powers, particularly in matters where the law stipulates prior administrative authorization for a private initiative (*e.g.* dismissal of an **employee representative** and, between 1975 and 1986, redundancies).

This administrative division comes under the Minister for Labour, but there are special inspectors for transport and agriculture. Outside the central office, there are external offices grouped into Directorates of Labour and Employment at both regional and département levels.

456. INTEMPÉRIES — BAD WEATHER: In the building and public works sector, there is a compulsory insurance scheme in operation which guarantees employees compensatory payment for hours lost when weather conditions bring work to a halt. It is known as "chômage intempéries" (bad-weather unemployment insurance scheme).

457. INTÉRESSEMENT — PAY RELATED TO COMPANY PERFORMANCE: Range of methods introduced by French law since 1967 which link the allocation of benefits to employees to improvement in the enterprise's results.

The law encourages the introduction of cash-based profit-sharing schemes, both by exempting the sums allocated to employees from social security contributions and taxes levied on pay and by permitting their deduction from the company's taxable profits. The introduction of such schemes is, however, subject to control. The concessionary legal arrangements are available only if certain conditions are fulfilled; in particular, schemes must be established by collective agreement. The law also stipulates that the sums in question may not take the place of existing components of pay.

458. INTÉRÊT COLLECTIF (DE LA PROFESSION) — COLLECTIVE INTEREST (OF AN OCCUPATIONAL GROUP): Consideration in the name of which a trade union is entitled to institute legal proceedings without needing to establish that its members are affected. Under French law, a union's legal capacity is not confined to defending the interests of its actual members. It is also authorized to defend the interests of all those who, under its rules, are eligible to become members. Together, they constitute an occupational group (see **occupation**).

459. **INTÉRIM — TEMPORARY-EMPLOYMENT AGENCY WORK**: Synonym of **travail temporaire**.

460. **INTERMÉDIAIRE — INTERMEDIARY**: Person who establishes relations between two other persons with a view to the conclusion of a contract. On the labour market, private enterprises are prohibited from performing this function if it constitutes **job placement**.

461. **INVALIDITÉ — DISABILITY**: Long-term reduction (at least two thirds) of the capacity for work or earning capacity which, if the employee concerned is aged under 60, entitles them to special benefits called "prestations de l'assurance invalidité" (disability benefits).

462. **INVENTION (DE SALARIÉ) — INVENTIONS BY EMPLOYEES**: Term referring to the discovery of a scientific innovation which, if it is patentable, is subject to rules on attribution laid down by a special Law. An invention produced as part of the employee's job ("invention de service", *i.e.* job-related invention) is the property of the employer; an invention which is totally unrelated to the employee's job ("invention hors service", *i.e.* independent invention) is the property of the employee; and an invention produced outside the context of the employee's actual job but falling within the enterprise's field of activity ("invention à l'option", *i.e.* invention subject to option) entitles the employer to at least a right of use.

J

463. JEUNE TRAVAILLEUR — YOUNG WORKER: As distinct from the child (see **child employment**) and the **minor**, the young worker is one of the central figures of policies on **employment support** and **absorption into employment**. The concept is defined by the scope of application pronounced for these measures; at present, it refers to a job-seeker aged, in general, from 16 to 25.

464. JOURNÉE — WORKING DAY: The number of hours that an employee may be required to work in a day (*i.e.* during the 24-hour period calculated from midnight to midnight) was first regulated in 1919. Nowadays, daily working time, or the working day, may not exceed (except in cases of exemption) 10 hours, or 8 hours for apprentices (see **apprenticeship**) and young people under the age of 18.

465. JOURS FÉRIÉS — PUBLIC HOLIDAYS: The law lists the 11 "fêtes légales" (official holidays) which are public holidays in France, only one of which, May 1, must compulsorily be "chômé", *i.e.* a day off work, with pay. The listing of the other 10 holidays would be of little relevance were it not for the fact that collective agreements and custom have in many cases ensured that such public holidays entitle employees to dispensation from work at the normal rate of pay.

466. JURIDIFICATION — JURIDIFICATION: Process whereby industrial relations become increasingly subject to legal rules. The term "juridicisation" is also used in French. The process may be interpreted in at least two different ways: either as the increased production of rules, or as more frequent recourse by those concerned to existing rules, which need not necessarily increase in number.

If the concept is to be usable, it is necessary to make clear which rules are being considered. Is reference being made only to rules of statutory origin, in which case juridification is taken as synonymous with legislation? Or are rules deriving from diverse sources being included, which presupposes that the State is not seen as the sole source of law? A distinction may be made between juridification and the French term "judiciarisation" (*i.e.* judicialization); the latter concept indicates increased recourse to the courts.

467. JURISPRUDENCE — CASE LAW: In popular usage, the body of court decisions delivered in a particular area of law (commercial case law, social case law, etc.).

139

As a practice, case law is a system of law, or customary manner of ruling on cases. Consequently, it originates both from judges, who repeat decisions delivered in previous cases, and from the authors of collected law reports, who select those to be published, and lawyers who comment on court decisions and pinpoint the continuities and divergences between them. Together, they forge a tendency, demonstrate that a case law has been established and reveal developments and reversals.

Case law carries the authority attached to repeated judgments. It is powerful, since lawyers and judges place reliance upon precedents. In France, however, although judges are inclined to follow precedents they are not (as in the common law) bound by them.

L

468. **LABEL SYNDICAL — TRADE UNION LABEL**: See **trade union mark**.

469. **LÉGISLATION INDUSTRIELLE — INDUSTRIAL LEGISLATION**: Scholarly term used at the turn of the century to describe, analyse and systematize the body of regulations, of statutory origin, relating to economic activity. Because no clear distinctions had yet been made, rules concerning work under a contract of employment and rules concerning the entrepreneur and the enterprise were studied together.

470. **LÉGISLATION PROMOTIONNELLE — LEGISLATIVE PROMOTION OF COLLECTIVE BARGAINING**: See **promotion**.

471. **LÉGISLATION SOCIALE — SOCIAL LEGISLATION**: Body of statutory rules dealing with employment relationships and the social protection of employees. The term has become obsolete as labour law and social security law have ceased to be presented as forming a whole and as rules of non-statutory origin have come to be taken into consideration.

472. **LÉGITIMITÉ — LEGITIMACY**: In one sense, conformity with the law or lawfulness. In a broader sense, justification, *i.e.* conformity not so much with legality or legal rules as with a principle or principles of justice.

473. **LIBERTÉ DES SALAIRES — FREEDOM TO NEGOTIATE PAY**: The right of individual parties (employer and employee) or collective parties (trade unions and employers' organizations) to fix rates of pay. Although a major issue in social and political debate, particularly criticism levelled against government intervention, this freedom is not constitutionally guaranteed in France. The principle of the introduction by law of a national guaranteed **minimum wage** is not disputed as such, and this has also been the case with various statutory measures on pay controls or temporary pay freezes.

474. **LIBERTÉ DU TRAVAIL — FREEDOM OF LABOUR**: Recognized right of every individual to practise the occupation of his or her choice. It is central to the French conception of the right to organize collectively and the right to strike. It constitutes the legal basis which prevents the unions from either controlling hiring or imposing an *a priori* monopoly on hiring. In addition, it represents the origin of and explanation for the general

applicability of **collective agreements**. It constitutes the legal basis of the restrictions placed on the activities of strikers, who are not permitted to prevent others from working. However, there is a legal presumption that the offence of prejudice to freedom of labour exists only if forms of violence have been employed against non-strikers.

It has been criticized as an abstract freedom, and has been supplemented by a **right to work** or right to employment.

475. **LIBERTÉ INDIVIDUELLE — FREEDOM OF THE INDIVIDUAL**: Sphere of autonomy which is deemed essential, is recognized as the right of every individual and, as such, enjoys powerful statutory protection. The term is virtually synonymous with ''liberté civile'' (civil liberty). In principle, this freedom may not be prejudiced either by the State or by any person such as an employer. In practice, infringements or restrictions are permitted, on the grounds of the need to reconcile one freedom with another or with certain legal prerogatives.

476. **LIBERTÉ SYNDICALE — FREEDOM OF COLLECTIVE INDUSTRIAL ORGANIZATION**: Constitutional principle proclaimed for the first time by a Law of March 21, 1884. (Strictly, since it specifically covers organizations possessing the legal form of a **''syndicat''**, this freedom relates to employers' organizations as well as to trade unions, and the term must be translated with care. In practice, it tends to be used in the sense of what is often termed ''trade union freedom'', notably as regards its exercise by employees within the enterprise.)

It has two dimensions, one individual and the other collective. For the individual, it represents both the ''positive'' right of all employees to join the union of their choice and their ''negative'' right to abstain from union membership or withdraw from membership at any time.

Collectively, it has reference to relations between employee organizations, the State and employers. It denotes the freedom to form and operate trade unions without any interference by the State or restriction by employers.

As an individual freedom, it is strongly protected: any action by an employer on grounds relating to trade union membership is unlawful and constitutes a criminal offence. Its absolute nature is, however, lessened by the fact that the unions have been granted special rights, including a monopoly of collective bargaining.

477. **LICENCIEMENT — DISMISSAL**: Termination of a contract of employment of indefinite duration which originates from the employer. This may be as a result either of a decision by the

employer to end it, or of a ruling by the courts, on application from the employee, that the employer is responsible for the termination (*e.g.* through failure to meet contractual obligations), which is therefore classed as dismissal.

Except in cases of serious **misconduct** on the part of the employee, dismissal is subject to a period of notice and entitles the employee to severance pay or compensation for dismissal whose amount and conditions of eligibility are specified by collective agreement, custom or the individual contract of employment, above and beyond the minimum rules established by law.

French law has gradually established a special regulatory system governing dismissal which distinguishes it from unilateral termination in the purely general terms of contract law (see **dismissal for reasons relating to the individual**) and lays down specific rules on **redundancy**.

478. **LICENCIEMENT POUR MOTIF ÉCONOMIQUE — REDUNDANCY**: Whether it is individual or collective, redundancy (*i.e.* dismissal for economic reasons) is governed, at least in part, by specific rules. This special feature of French legislation dates back to a Law of 1975 which made all redundancies subject to prior official authorization. The requirement for prior authorization was abolished in 1986 but the special treatment of redundancy remains in force.

The regulatory system as currently laid down by law has three main components whose extent differs according to the number of employees to be dismissed: consultation of the works council or, where no works council exists, of the workforce delegates; an invitation to rationalize the selection of the particular employee(s) to be dismissed; and a requirement to provide for accompanying measures including at least a **re-training agreement**. As with any dismissal the courts, if application is made to them, verify the existence of genuine and serious cause.

The existence of a special regulatory system for redundancy means that the term must be clearly defined. French law lays down two essential criteria: the reason for dismissal must not relate to the person of an individual employee, and termination of the contract must derive from the abolition or alteration of a post or from refusal to accept a substantive change to the contract of employment.

479. **LICENCIEMENT POUR MOTIF INDIVIDUEL — DIS-MISSAL FOR REASONS RELATING TO THE INDIVIDUAL**: It is only recently that rules have been laid down by law in France formally governing under what conditions and

in what forms the employer may unilaterally terminate a contract of employment of indefinite duration. The principal innovations stem from a Law of 1973, specifying a particular procedure and defining the supervision by the courts of the juristic act of dismissal.

Nowadays, the employer's decision to dismiss an employee must be preceded by a preliminary interview, and the act must be a formal one and duly justified. The courts, for their part, are responsible for verifying that there is genuine and serious cause for dismissal. If any doubt remains after a period of one month, the employee is given the benefit of the doubt.

Under French law, the obligation to reinstate the employee (see **reinstatement**) is not a universal sanction for cases of unjustified dismissal. The scope of this sanction, which is sometimes expressly provided for, remains unclear. Where it is not applicable, the sole sanction imposable is the payment of compensation.

480. **LIMITE D'ÂGE — AGE LIMIT**: Age above which a person may no longer take part in a competitive examination organized for access to a post or continue to be employed in a certain capacity. In France, a statutory age limit exists only for **established civil servants**. In other cases, an age limit may be stipulated, under certain conditions, by collective agreement or under the individual contract of employment (see **retirement**).

481. **LIQUIDATION — SETTLEMENT/LIQUIDATION**: Term used in both a general and a specific sense:
1. In a general sense, operation whereby accounts are paid and balanced following the definitive establishment of their elements.
2. Compulsory liquidation ("liquidation judiciaire") is the outcome of a compulsory administration procedure (see **bankruptcy**) when there is no longer any real possibility that the enterprise concerned can survive. Also called "winding-up" in English.

482. **LITIGE DU TRAVAIL — LABOUR DISPUTE AT LAW**: As opposed to a "conflit" (**industrial conflict** or dispute), which is a social issue, a "litige" is a matter of legal proceedings in which opposing claims are brought before a court (see **Industrial Tribunal**).

483. **LIVRE DE PAIE — PAYBOOK**: Document in which the information contained in **itemized pay statements** must be recorded in order to allow verification of compliance with the rules governing pay.

484. **LOCAL SYNDICAL — UNION ROOM**: Room placed at the disposal of union **workplace branches** within an enterprise. Employers are obliged by law to provide this facility when the enterprise is of a certain size (200 employees). And in enterprises with 1,000 or more employees, a separate room must be provided for each trade union branch.

485. **LOCK-OUT**: Decision whereby the employer, in the event of an **industrial dispute**, denies all or some employees access to the enterprise or establishment and refuses to pay them their wages.

   As a general principle, under French law the lock-out is deemed to be unlawful. It is not covered by any specific legal provision, but analysed in the light of the obligations deriving from the individual contract of employment: a lock-out constitutes a breach of the contract by the employer, who cannot evade the obligation to pay wages. However, the courts allow that the employer is in some instances released from the obligation to supply employees with work and, consequently, from the obligation to pay them. This is so in the case of "compelling circumstances", a concept representing an attenuated form of *force majeure*, or in the event of a strike which is itself unlawful or an improper use of the right to strike.

486. **LOGEMENT (DU SALARIÉ) — HOUSING FOR EMPLOYEES**: Except in the case of caretakers in residential buildings (concierges) and of foreign workers who are admitted into France at the enterprise's request, there is no legal obligation on the employer to provide employees with housing accommodation. Such provision constitutes a form of **payment in kind**. As the subject of an agreement accompanying the contract of employment, it must be continued for as long as the contract remains in force but may be withdrawn when the contract ends.

487. **LOGICIEL — SOFTWARE**: Since 1985, software has been classed in French law as an intellectual "work" in the copyright sense and is governed by the relevant rules (see **author**).

488. **LOI — LAW/STATUTE**: Term embodying several distinctions:
   1. In the sense of a statute, a text enacted by vote of Parliament or by referendum.
   2. This first meaning is linked with another, *i.e.* a rule of law which occupies the pre-eminent position. The Constitution is a law in this sense, whereas it does not fall within the definition of a statute.
   3. Sometimes designates the law in the sense of the entire body of rules issued by the State, encompassing not only statute law but also **regulations**.

4. As contrasted with custom, in another sense it is also any written rule of law.

In labour law, it is the third meaning which applies when an attempt is made to define the importance of the various sources. In France, the law is a predominant factor because, whilst accommodating the principle of diverse sources, it seeks to rank them (see **multiplicity of sources of law**).

489. **LOYAUTÉ — LOYALTY**: Although every contract must be performed in good faith, the meaning of this requirement in the context of employment relationships is controversial, given the complexity of reconciling the duty of loyalty on the one hand with, on the other, the responsibility for taking the initiative incumbent on certain employees such as **professional and managerial staff** and the freedom of expression. Professional and managerial staff who make their disagreement with the enterprise's top management publicly known are sometimes subjected to sanctions. Yet it could not be claimed that they are under any obligation to evince constant agreement with its policies. Also known as "fidélité".

M

490. MALADIE — ILLNESS: The effect of illness on the contract of employment is defined by the courts and by collective agreement. It is only when illness is of occupational origin (see **accident at work, occupational illness, physical unfitness**) that French law provides special protection for the employee. As a general principle, illness merely entails suspension of the contract of employment (see **sick leave**). This suspension, and the continued payment of all or part of the employee's pay, are regulated by collective agreement. **Dismissal** is, however, possible when repeated or prolonged absence from work on grounds of ill health seriously disrupts the functioning of the enterprise.

A very recent Law, whose scope is still difficult to determine, prohibits any discrimination on the grounds of an employee's state of health.

491. MALADIE PROFESSIONNELLE — OCCUPATIONAL ILLNESS: Illness resulting from the performance of certain activities by the employee in the context of employment. For the purposes of compensation, it is treated as similar in law to an **accident at work**.

In France, as in many other countries, the principle of a selective list of recognized occupational illnesses has been established. This principle is not without its critics.

492. MANIFESTATION — DEMONSTRATION: Mass meeting or procession whose purpose is, according to circumstance, to show the strength of support for a demand, express a protest or celebrate the memory of a past event. As a traditional form of industrial action by the labour movement, demonstrations are covered by police regulations which are considered liberal.

493. MARCHANDAGE — LABOUR-ONLY SUBCONTRACTING: Old form of the subcontracting of labour at reduced rates of pay which French law has sought to restrict since 1948. Nowadays, the law prohibits the supplying of labour on a profit-making basis when it has the effect of causing loss or harm to the employee or evading legal rules and collectively agreed provisions. See **hiring-out of labour, provision of labour**.

The term may also be used in the sense of "haggling", *i.e.* discussion or negotiation aimed at lowering another party's financial demands.

494. MARCHÉ DU TRAVAIL — LABOUR MARKET: In its simplest interpretation, the place where labour supply and demand meet. Nowadays, there is virtually unanimous agreement that labour should not be seen as a commodity lending itself to trading exchanges whose trends and equilibrium are governed by a price and its movements. Analyses of dualism or **segmentation** stress the dispersion of labour demand and supply. Studies also highlight a geographical dispersion of the market, and close links between training and the labour market. A wide variety of explanatory models have emerged, some seeking to enrich the classic model of equilibrium and others seeking to break away from it.

495. **MARIAGE — MARRIAGE**: French law prohibits any discrimination on the grounds of an employee's marital status.

It makes provision for a period of marriage leave (see **special family leave**) which permits employees to be absent from work, without loss of pay, for four days for their own marriage and one day for a child's marriage.

496. **MARIN — SEAFARER**: Person who is hired by a shipowner to perform work on board a ship. The relevant contract of employment (called a "contrat d'engagement", *i.e.* ship's articles or signing-on contract), is regulated by a set of special provisions, some of which are grouped together in a Maritime Labour Code.

497. **MARQUE SYNDICALE — TRADE UNION MARK**: Symbol affixed to a product to demonstrate that the employer complies with the stipulations of social legislation and collective agreements. Known as a "trade union label" in the printing industry, it is little used in France. A collective agreement imposing the obligation to affix a trade union mark or label does not, under French law, affect the freedom of every employee to decide whether or not to join a union, and if so which one.

498. **MATERNITÉ — MATERNITY**: See **pregnancy, sick leave**.

499. **MÉDECINE DU TRAVAIL — COMPANY MEDICAL SERVICE**: Service within the enterprise, or catering jointly for several enterprises, whose role as laid down by law is to prevent any impairment of employees' health as a result of their work. It monitors **occupational health** conditions, and issues its formal opinion on employees' fitness: at the recruitment stage (see **hiring**) on the fitness of potential employees to occupy their intended job, and after a cessation of work because of illness or accident (see **accident at work, illness**) on an employee's fitness to resume work. It is responsible for suggesting organizational changes to take account of employees' state of health.

500. MÉDIATION — MEDIATION: Process for settling collective labour disputes whose special feature lies in the appointment of a third party, the mediator, charged with the task of seeking the bases for an agreement and recommending them to the parties.

French law makes provision for a mediation procedure whose implementation is voluntary. It is, in fact, seldom used. However, for the past 20 years or so a number of judges, when dealing with cases arising in the course of **strikes**, have been adopting an approach whereby they appoint an agent of the court for the more or less explicit purpose of achieving a kind of mediation.

501. MENSUALISATION — MONTHLY PAY SYSTEM: System under which wages are paid at monthly intervals. For manual workers, it was introduced in France through collective agreements before being made generally applicable by a national multi-industry agreement of 1977 and a Law of 1978. In particular, this system has brought with it a guarantee of a minimum monthly wage. It has reduced the significance of the distinction between **manual workers** and **white-collar workers**.

502. MÉTIER — OCCUPATION: Synonymous with the term **profession**. But whereas the latter, in one of the senses in which it is used, has come to designate a form of activity in the overall context of the division of labour, the term "métier" has retained a narrow meaning.

One of the special features of French trade unionism is that, with a small number of exceptions, it has not encouraged solidarity within particular occupations nor, therefore, groupings on a "craft" or occupation basis.

503. MICROCONFLICTUALITÉ — "MICROCONFLICT" (LEVEL OF): Neologism coined to draw attention to the number of disputes which occur in labour relations at the most local level.

504. MILITAIRE — MILITARY: Employment relationships within the armed forces are subject to special regulations. As a general principle, trade unionism is not permitted. The effect of compulsory **national service** (formerly called "service militaire", *i.e.* military service) on an existing contract of employment is governed by special rules intended to ensure young men a right to **reinstatement** in their former job or, at least, a preferential right to be re-hired.

505. MINEUR — MINOR: In France, the age of majority (nowadays, 18) is of little significance in the legal regulation of employment relationships, which places more emphasis on youthfulness in general (see **age, child employment, young worker**) and on the categories targeted by employment policies. The latter are based on age groups, such as 16-21 or 18-26 (see **absorption into employment**).

506. **MINES — MINES**: Numerous special provisions regulate work in mines (mineral or fossil deposits), particularly work underground (see **miners' delegate**). This sector, nowadays in decline, has been marked by an unusual pattern of industrial relations as a result, in particular, of the nationalization of some mines, an old-established and strong trade union tradition, the power of the occupational groups concerned and the influence of mining engineers.

507. **MINIMUM GARANTI — GUARANTEED MINIMUM WAGE**: See **minimum wage**.

508. **MINISTÈRE DU TRAVAIL — MINISTRY OF LABOUR**: Group of administrative divisions placed under the authority of the Minister responsible for labour. A Ministry of Labour was first created in France in 1906. Since then, depending on priorities, political bias and circumstances, the divisions responsible for labour, health, social security, employment and vocational training have been either grouped together in a single Ministry or separated into several different ones. At present, labour, employment and vocational training are grouped together.

509. **MISE À DISPOSITION — PROVISION OF LABOUR**: Act whereby one enterprise places an employee's services at the disposal of another enterprise, while itself remaining the employee's employer. The operation is lawful when it complies with the regulations governing **temporary-employment agency work**. Otherwise, it may be counter to the ban on **labour-only subcontracting** or the **hiring-out of labour** on a profit-making basis.

510. **MISE À L'INDEX — BLACKLISTING**: See **boycott**.

511. **MIXITÉ — EQUALITY IN EMPLOYMENT**: Term used in analyses of the status of women to describe a situation attained in which men's and women's roles are identical. It therefore constitutes an objective of policies aimed at establishing equality of men and women at work (see **equality between men and women, positive discrimination**).

512. **MOBILITÉ DU TRAVAIL — LABOUR MOBILITY**: Designates the movement of workers between local job markets (regions, districts, catchment areas or markets) or between the various establishments of an enterprise or group of companies, and also the adjustment of workers to changes in the content of jobs. Each of these forms of mobility, *i.e.* external geographical mobility, internal geographical mobility and occupational mobility, lends itself to different analyses which attempt to take account of the factors determining each of the obstacles it encounters, and of the organizational structure into which it fits.

513. **MODÉRATION SALARIALE — PAY RESTRAINT**: Term used to describe a tendency towards the reduction of rises in pay (see **pay increase**) or, at least, towards the disappearance or restriction of automatic pay increases (see **automatic effect**).

514. **MODERNISATION — MODERNIZATION**:
1. Term used as a watchword by the Government to encourage improved productivity, investment and growth in the number and quality of jobs. At present, the Government is advocating a negotiated form of modernization whereby any sacrifices demanded of employees in terms of pay or the organization of work may be offset by better prospects in terms of employment and skill levels.
2. At enterprise level, term used to refer, rather loosely, to changes in organization, technologies and the skills required of employees.

515. **MODIFICATION — VARIATION OF THE CONTRACT OF EMPLOYMENT**: Partial change made to the conditions of performance of a contract of employment. Amendment affecting its substantive terms ("dispositions substantielles") is referred to as "révision" (revision). The legal presumption, derived from the binding force of the contract, is that when variation is imposed unilaterally it is null and void. If the employee refuses to accept it, the employer is obliged to maintain the pre-existing conditions or to decide, at his or her own risk, to proceed with **dismissal**.

   The term may also signify change in the sense of the emergence of a new situation (see **transfer of undertaking**).

516. **MOUVEMENT OUVRIER — LABOUR MOVEMENT**: Popular expression associated with the idea that the workers, as a body, are pursuing a collective endeavour to change the established order. The expression "mouvement social" (social movement) has sometimes been preferred as a way of emphasizing the advent of new protagonists (women's movement, youth movement, "green" movement).

517. MOUVEMENT SYNDICAL — TRADE UNION MOVEMENT: Collective endeavour of workers organized into groupings or unions. The term is virtually synonymous with "syndicalisme" (trade unionism).

518. MUTATION — JOB MOVE: Term which designates either a change in an employee's geographical assignment within the same enterprise, or the formal transfer of an employee from one enterprise to another (see **change of employer through legal transfer**). The former case entails **variation of the contract of employment**; in the second case, the contract may be either transferred or replaced by a new one.

519. MUTILÉS — DISABLED EX-SERVICEMEN: Recipients of a military disability pension, for whom enterprises in France are obliged by law to reserve a quota of jobs.

520. MUTUALITÉ — MUTUAL INSURANCE:
1. Method of assuring cover against risks by the creation of a mutual benefit fund made up of the premiums paid in by members. The members ("mutualistes") are thus both insurers and insured.
2. Viewed collectively, the societies and groupings established on the basis of this method of insurance. They are grouped into powerful federations, are covered by special regulations and in some cases have been made compulsory (*e.g.* in the agricultural sector).

N

521. **NATIONALISATION — NATIONALIZATION**: Government decision (which must be voted by Parliament) to transfer to the nation (in practice, the State) assets belonging to private individuals. In France's recent history, there have been two major waves of nationalization: in 1945-1946 and in 1982. The latter was followed in 1986-1987 by a privatization programme.

At present, the trading public sector comprises some 2,000 enterprises (if enterprises directly under state control and their subsidiaries or sub-subsidiaries are counted separately), employing close on 1.5 million employees. The main areas of activity are energy, intermediate products and capital goods, transport, banking, insurance and certain commercial services.

522. **NÉGOCIATION ARTICULÉE — ARTICULATED BARGAINING**: Organized system of bargaining levels creating a hierarchy or distribution of the issues covered by collective bargaining.

French law contains no provisions overtly aimed at this: there is overlap between the various bargaining levels. The law does, however, contain a principle which establishes the co-ordination of collective agreements. This principle is based on the concept of favourability: the collectively agreed clause which is applicable is that which is the most advantageous to all the employees concerned (see **favourability to the employee**).

The past few years have seen attempts to hierarchize collective bargaining. In sometimes permitting the parties to contract out of statutory provisions (see **derogation agreement**), the law gives formal priority in certain cases to industry-wide agreements, with bargaining at company level ranked lower. Also, **framework agreements** concluded at national multi-industry level outline, for specific issues, a distribution of bargaining roles between the industry and company levels.

523. **NÉGOCIATION COLLECTIVE — COLLECTIVE BARGAINING**: Process or method of negotiation between employees' representatives and employers (or employers' representatives) for the purpose of establishing rules.

Although the phenomenon is well-known and has been extensively analysed, the concept is an unusually complex one. As the drawing-up of rules by parties other than the public authorities, it is contrasted with legislation; yet the law is in many instances negotiated. It is contrasted with unilateral decision-making by the employer; yet in many cases it merely sets limits to such decision-making. It is contrasted with conflict, in that it is a peaceful form of action; yet some commentators see it as conflict in a different guise. It is a manifestation of **collective autonomy**; yet it is, in France, a right belonging to the employees. In addition, the law has recently given specific reinforcement to the right of employees to bargain collectively by imposing bargaining obligations on employers and employers' organizations at industry level (see **duty to bargain**). In more general terms, the law identifies which agents are empowered to bargain (see **representativeness**) and defines the status of **collective agreements**, although for the most part not stipulating **bargaining levels** or the issues to be covered.

524. **NÉGOCIATION DE CONCESSION — CONCESSION BARGAINING**: A product of the past decade, concession bargaining has (partly) taken over from distributive or zero-sum bargaining ("négociation distributive"), which, historically and in trade unionist thinking, was bound up with the close link between bargaining and straightforward improvements in the workers' position.

Concession bargaining has profoundly affected the geometry of collective agreements, with the appearance of so-called "give-and-take" or "win-win" agreements in which reciprocal exchange is strongly emphasized: in return for an undertaking to limit the number of redundancies or reduce general working hours, for example, the employees' side accepts the reopening of discussions on pay structure or the pace of work. In practice, undertakings on the part of the employer are not always specific; they sometimes constitute general objectives, usually relating to employment. This leads to one of the awkward questions raised by concession agreements: their applicability to employees as individuals. As collective agreements that have been properly negotiated and signed by representative unions (see **representativeness**), they automatically govern all current contracts of employment. They are, after all, assumed to bring reciprocal advantages for employees. But the choices effected with the signatory unions may run counter to aspirations or customary practices. If so, must it be acknowledged that, as individuals, employees may refuse to accept the change to their terms and conditions of employment entailed by a concession agreement? The tendency is to regard resistance on their part as legitimate if the terms and conditions concerned were laid down in their contracts of employment.

525. **NÉGOCIATION DÉCENTRALISÉE—DECENTRALIZED BARGAINING**: See **decentralization (of bargaining)**.

526. **NÉGOCIATION D'ENTREPRISE — COMPANY-LEVEL BARGAINING**: Collective bargaining which takes place at company or enterprise level (see **bargaining level**).

Since its purpose is to conclude **collective agreements**, it is partly regulated by the law. Thus, the bargaining agents are defined by law: only the representative unions in an enterprise possess such capacity (see **representativeness**). Also, it is compulsory for bargaining to take place annually on certain issues (see **duty to bargain**). Outside this legal framework, negotiations are conducted with other parties such as works councils and workforce delegates; these cannot lead to collective agreements within the meaning of the law.

Bargaining at this level is undoubtedly acquiring growing importance, as evidenced by the actual number of company-level agreements. This can be attributed, in particular, to the shift in bargaining towards issues such as work organization and working hours, **pay related to company performance** and profit-sharing, and, more recently, training and company employment policies.

527. **NÉGOCIATION DISTRIBUTIVE — DISTRIBUTIVE BARGAINING/ZERO-SUM BARGAINING**: See **concession bargaining**, *erga omnes*.

528. **NÉGOCIATION INTÉGRATIVE — INTEGRATIVE BARGAINING/POSITIVE-SUM BARGAINING**: See **reduction of working hours**.

529. **NÉGOCIATION INTERPROFESSIONNELLE — NATIONAL MULTI-INDUSTRY BARGAINING**: Bargaining whose purpose is to conclude a **general multi-industry agreement**.

530. **NÉOCORPORATISME — NEO-CORPORATISM**: Theoretical model for analysing relations between the State and society, used sometimes for descriptive and sometimes for prescriptive purposes. In essence, it consists in the participation of intermediate bodies in social regulation. And in the 1970s at least, it was put forward as one of the responses to the crisis of legal intervention in the modern State.

Neo-corporatism constitutes, on the one hand, a system of interest representation which is reduced to a limited number of units or intermediaries to whom the State offers a recognized monopoly, in return for the control which it exercises over their activities. On the other hand, it embodies a form of participation by these recognized groups in the development of public policies:

the formulation and application of policies become the product of social concertation, of a pact based on the exchange of mutual advantages between the State and private groups. This interaction fosters the institutionalization of interest groups and entails the delegation of public authority to private actors, which blurs the dividing line between the private and the public spheres.

It could not be said that France has had any real experience of neo-corporatism, given the absence of any global organization of social interests and of general and permanent processes of bargaining. The State, by way of a technostructure which is strong and equipped with a modernization programme, retains a very real autonomy; furthermore, French society is strongly "sectorized", a situation which engenders, rather, a phenomenon of sectoral (neo-)corporatisms.

531. **NÉOLIBÉRALISME — NEO-LIBERALISM**: Doctrine or, rather, set of proposals which seek to adapt liberalism, in its economic sense, to the demands of modern society. According to one of its proponents in France, modern-day liberalism is a system based on *laissez-passer*, and no longer one based on *laissez-faire*.

This philosophy, which rehabilitates the concept of the market and challenges the effectiveness, and even the legitimacy, of state intervention to regulate the economy, has struck powerful chords in France, although the tradition of the strength of the State and the criticisms aroused by some of the initiatives inspired by the philosophy have tempered its widespread acceptance.

532. **NIVEAU DE NÉGOCIATION — BARGAINING LEVEL**: Territorial and economic context or unit in which collective bargaining takes place. By tradition, and in some respects as laid down by law, three separate levels are distinguished: national level, industry level (see **branch of economic activity, industry-wide agreement**) and company or enterprise level, together with the subdivision represented by establishment level. There are, in fact, other levels; the company group is one such example.

As a general principle, there is still free choice of bargaining level. Since 1982, however, this has been modified by the introduction of legal obligations to bargain on particular issues at particular levels (see **duty to bargain**) and by the assignment of authority to particular levels to contract out of statutory provisions by way of framework agreements (see **articulated bargaining, framework agreement**).

533. **NIVEAU DES SALAIRES — WAGE LEVEL**: Indicates a gradation in a scale of amounts of pay. Since a scale may cover

various contexts (enterprise, industry or sector, all sectors combined, European Community), the pertinence of a given level depends on what it is measured against.

534. **NOMENCLATURE — NOMENCLATURE**: Systematic list of titles for classifying the elements of a whole (see **job classification, occupational category**).

535. **NON-CONCURRENCE — RESTRAINT ON COMPETITION**: Obligation, which exists only if expressly stipulated (*e.g.* by a covenant), requiring an employee to refrain from practising a particular activity until a certain period of time has elapsed after the contract of employment ends. It is not regulated by French law; the courts accept its validity with liberal interpretation, insisting only that it should be subject to a time limit and restricted to a specified geographical locality and a specified form of activity.

536. **NON-TITULAIRE — NON-ESTABLISHED PUBLIC EMPLOYEE**: See **established civil servant**.

537. **NOTE DE SERVICE — SERVICE MEMORANDUM**: Explanatory document drawn up by an enterprise's management. It often contains rules which either specify the way in which management intends to act (*e.g.* in fixing rates of pay) or impose obligations on employees (rules on discipline or on health and safety). In this latter case, the procedure laid down for the formulation of **work rules** must be followed and the same checks and controls are applicable.

538. **NULLITÉ — NULLITY**: Penalty consisting in the pronouncement of a juristic act to be null and void, incurred when it is irregular. For a long time the French courts resisted the application of this penalty to unilateral juristic acts by the employer, *i.e.* an act imposing a **disciplinary sanction**, and **dismissal**. The law has broken down this resistance in some instances; for example, it provides for irregular disciplinary sanctions or discriminatory acts to be pronounced null and void. However, dismissal without **genuine and serious cause** is not voidable: the penalty here is financial compensation. The same is no longer automatically true of unlawful dismissal, which is sometimes pronounced null and void.

O

539. OBLIGATION DE NÉGOCIER — DUTY TO BARGAIN: Following a Law of November 13, 1982, collective bargaining is not merely a recognized freedom held by the social partners. Legal obligations relating to bargaining have been introduced. These obligations bear on specified issues; other issues therefore remain within the sphere of the freedom to bargain.

Some of the obligations relate to the industry-wide context (see **branch of economic activity**). Employers' organizations and trade union organizations which have already concluded a collective agreement at this level must reopen pay negotiations every year and examine the need to revise **job classifications** every five years.

In particular, however, these obligations relate to the context of the individual enterprise (see **company-level bargaining**). In all enterprises where union **workplace branches** have been formed, the employer must enter into negotiations every year on actual pay, working hours and patterns of working time. Since recent Laws of 1989 and 1990, this compulsory annual bargaining has covered, in addition, the examination of forecast levels of employment and trends in the use of **contracts for precarious employment**. Training is also the subject of compulsory bargaining, both at industry level and at enterprise level. Other obligations relating to bargaining have been imposed by law with the aim of preventing industrial disputes; examples include the obligation to give **notice of termination of a collective agreement** and **notice of strike** in the **public sector**. The duty to bargain does not amount to an obligation to conclude a collective agreement. It merely signifies that employers or employers' organizations may not refuse to take part in discussions, that they are required to examine the proposals put forward by the unions and that the negotiations must be conducted in good faith, even though the implications of this duty to abide by the principle of good faith remain uncertain.

The law outlines a system governing the duty to bargain at enterprise level: it places the onus on employers to initiate bargaining, propose a timetable and provide the information required, and prohibits them from taking any unilateral action on the issues under discussion while bargaining is in process. If negotiations break down, a **minute of failure to agree** must be drawn up which must state the unilateral measures that the employer intends to take.

540. OBSTRUCTION — OBSTRUCTION: Obstacle wilfully created to impede the proper course of a process (*e.g.* bargaining) or procedure (*e.g.* inspection by a Labour Inspector) or the exercise of a right or freedom (freedom of movement about the workplace for employee representatives, or employees' access to their workplace). It is not a legal concept, but is sometimes deemed to constitute an element of a criminal offence (see **interference**).

541. **OCCUPATION DES LIEUX DE TRAVAIL — SIT-IN/OCCUPATION OF THE WORKPLACE**: Form of industrial action, relatively common in France, which is taken during a strike to increase its effectiveness and, in many cases, to demonstrate employees' commitment to their work. Its legal status is uncertain; the tendency is for a sit-in to be deemed unlawful only if it is accompanied by palpable interference with the freedom to work of other employees who are not on strike. In such cases, the employer may seek an eviction order under an emergency procedure.

Over the past 20 years, occupation of the workplace has also become a form of protest by employees in reaction to an announcement that the enterprise is to be closed down or taken out of operation. Here, it may be interpreted as a way of their securing a solution to an employment crisis (and may constitute what is also known in English as a "work-in").

542. **OEUVRES SOCIALES — COMPANY WELFARE FACILITIES**: Name formerly used for **company welfare and cultural facilities**.

543. **OFFICE DES MIGRATIONS INTERNATIONALES — INTERNATIONAL MIGRATION OFFICE**: Public body set up in 1945 under the name of Office national d'immigration, or ONI (National Immigration Office) and then renamed in 1988, which is responsible for implementing immigration policy (see **immigration**) and in particular has monopoly control over the entry into France of foreign workers who are not EC nationals. It is also responsible for assisting workers who settle abroad and enterprises which need to recruit staff to work outside France.

544. **OFFRE D'EMPLOI — JOB VACANCY**: Public offer of employment made by an enterprise. It must be deposited with the **National Employment Agency**, although the enterprise is in no way prevented from making use of other recruitment channels such as employment agencies, newspaper or TV advertising and speculative applications.

A job vacancy advertised in the press may not contain any discriminatory (including sexist) statements.

545. OPPOSITION (DROIT D') — RIGHT OF OBJECTION:

1. Legally recognized prerogative of trade union organizations which are not signatories to a **derogation agreement** (provided they obtained half the votes in the most recent works council elections in an enterprise) to veto the agreement in question. This is a mechanism for *a posteriori* control made necessary by the *erga omnes* force attributed in principle to collective agreements concluded by any representative union. The right of objection, which was introduced in 1982, enshrines the disconcerting notion of negative majority representativeness. Its legitimate exercise deprives the agreement of all legal force.

2. Legally recognized prerogative of two organizations acting on behalf of employees or on behalf of employers to block, temporarily, the extension of a collective agreement by the Minister for Labour, when it is being considered by the National Collective Bargaining Commission. They must invoke failure to satisfy the legal conditions governing extension. The effect of such objection is to oblige the Minister to consult the Commission again; this time the Commission's opinion is not binding.

546. ORDONNANCE — ORDINANCE/ORDER:

1. In the present French Constitution, designates in general a **regulation** enacted by the executive authorities but carrying the force of law.

2. Name given to certain rulings issued by a judge sitting alone (see **procedure in chambers**).

547. ORDRE PUBLIC — PUBLIC POLICY/LAW AND ORDER:

1. Term which emphasizes the special importance of certain mandatory rules, signalling that they cannot be departed from by anyone and that in principle the courts must apply them automatically.

2. In labour law, rules which rank as "d'ordre public", *i.e.* a matter of public policy, may normally be contracted out of (see **"inderogability"**) only if the alternative provision is more advantageous for employees (see **favourability to the employee**).

3. In rules relating to aliens, the meaning approximates more closely to "law and order", designating a reservation of sovereignty in the name of which the executive authorities may take steps obliging an alien to leave French territory.

548. ORGANIGRAMME — ORGANIZATION CHART:
Ordered representation, usually in a graphically depicted form, of the internal structures of an enterprise. It shows the division of tasks and the hierarchy.

549. ORGANISATION D'EMPLOYEURS — EMPLOYERS' ORGANIZATION: To protect their shared interests, employers have formed their own organizations (sometimes also referred to as "organisations professionnelles"). The coverage of these organizations varies, both in terms of geographical territory (town, conurbation, département, region, the country as a whole) and in terms of the activities concerned: a single small-scale activity such as the bakery trade; a group of allied activities which together make up an industry or **branch of economic activity** (often called a "fédération d'industrie" or "fédération de branche", *i.e.* industrial federation); or most or all economic activities (see **General Confederation of Small and Medium-Sized Enterprises, National Council of French Employers**).

Many of these organizations have the status of a formal association, but some take the form of a "syndicat" (see **collective industrial organization**), since in France this form (although generally translated as "union") is not in fact confined to employees but may be used by all groups who have shared occupational interests.

One of the special features of the employers' organizations is that in very many cases they act simultaneously as bodies to protect their members' economic interests, mainly in dealings with the public authorities, and as agents of collective bargaining with the employees' trade union organizations; in France, there is no rigid compartmentalization between organizations with an economic function and organizations with an industrial relations function.

550. ORGANISATION DU TRAVAIL — WORK ORGANIZATION: The purpose of work organization is to replace improvisation, empiricism and disorder in the functioning of enterprises with scientifically based principles.

This approach is still associated today with the name of Taylor and the idea of the "scientific" organization of work. (The French acronym for this "organisation scientifique du travail", OST, formerly tended to be translated as O&M, *i.e.* organization and methods.) The Tayloristic principles that have been retained are, in particular, the separation of design and planning from the actual execution of tasks, the introduction of a specialization system for defining performance times and rates of pay, and the linking of payment systems with rules relating to time.

Widely used in French industry for the past 50 years, the scientific organization of work is nowadays the target of criticism in certain circles who advocate greater emphasis on human relations and have suggested or implemented job enrichment and the creation of semi-autonomous work groups. Such opposition is far from radical, however, since the past decade has seen the emergence of a movement in favour of a form of scientific work organization or Taylorism "with a human face".

551. **ORGANISATION PATRONALE — EMPLOYERS' ORGANIZATION**: Synonym of **organisation d'employeurs**.

552. **ORGANISATION SYNDICALE — TRADE UNION ORGANIZATION**: Term used synonymously with "groupement syndical", *i.e.* in the sense of both a group and a grouping. It therefore designates, according to context, either a primary group (company union or area union at local level) or a combined grouping at secondary level (see **trade union confederation, trade union federation**).

553. **ORIENTATION PROFESSIONNELLE — VOCATIONAL GUIDANCE**: Assistance in choosing a type of training or occupation that suits the abilities of the individual concerned. France has long-established institutions and regulations intended to ensure that young people receive vocational guidance. Some enterprises now make this a central element of their human resource management (see **management of personnel, human resource planning**), with provision for employees of all ages.

554. **OS**: Popular term for **semi-skilled worker (ouvrier spécialisé)**.

555. **OUVRIER — MANUAL WORKER**: Person who physically performs industrial work. Although the distinction between **white-collar workers** and manual workers has lost its former significance, it is still preserved in most **job classifications**.

556. **OUVRIER AGRICOLE — AGRICULTURAL WORKER**: Person who physically performs agricultural work.

557. **OUVRIER PROFESSIONNEL — SKILLED WORKER**: Manual worker who has completed a formal apprenticeship or training in a craft or trade. In the classified lists used as **job classifications**, the skilled worker ranks above the **semi-skilled worker**. Various categories of skilled worker are frequently differentiated.

558. **OUVRIER QUALIFIÉ — SKILLED WORKER**: Synonym of **ouvrier professionnel**.

559. **OUVRIER SPÉCIALISÉ — SEMI-SKILLED WORKER**: Manual worker who, despite the implication of the French term, is not qualified for any particular specialization. A semi-skilled worker (popularly referred to as OS) is a manual worker who has not completed a formal apprenticeship or training in a craft or trade.

P

560. PAIE — PAYMENT: Shortened form of the word "paiement", traditionally used to refer to the paying over of wages or salary (see **itemized pay statement, monthly pay system**).

561. PANIER — MEALS ALLOWANCE: Historically (in reference to employees needing to bring packed meals to eat at work), the "prime de panier" corresponds to the reimbursement of **expenses**.

562. PARITARISME — PARITY PRINCIPLE: Organizational principle implying strictly joint decision-making mechanisms in which the representatives of two groups with differing interests carry equal weight (see, for example, **Industrial Tribunal**). Its development is associated with collective bargaining. Thus, the bodies which administer institutions created by collective agreement are usually joint bodies composed of equal numbers of representatives of the two sides.

563. PARITÉ (DES ARMES) — BALANCE OF BARGAINING POWER: Equivalence of the forms or procedures of collective action lawfully available to employers and trade unions respectively. The concept may influence the legal interpretation of **strikes** and **lock-outs**. In France, it has not really penetrated the sphere of positive law.

564. PARTAGE DU TRAVAIL — WORK SHARING: See **job creation agreement**.

565. PARTENAIRES SOCIAUX — SOCIAL PARTNERS: Popularly used term which designates the employers' organizations on the one hand and the trade unions on the other and indicates that, above and beyond their differing objectives, they also have some shared interests.

566. PARTICIPATION — PARTICIPATION/WORKERS' PARTICIPATION/SHAREHOLDING:
1. In a general sense, the act of taking part in or being associated with an activity.
2. In labour relations, a term vague enough to serve simultaneously as an analytical framework for studying the degree of institutionalization of collective bargaining, a slogan (indicating financial participation by employees) for those who advocate a **philosophy of capital-labour co-operation**, and a means of reference to the Constitution. The Preamble to the 1946 Constitution, which has been expressly preserved in the

present Constitution, establishes the right of all workers to participate, through the intermediary of their representatives, in the collective determination of terms and conditions of employment and in the management of enterprises.

3. In a technical sense, the term refers to the holding by one company of some of the share capital of another. French company law defines it as the situation arising from the holding of shares representing 10-50 per cent. of the capital.

567. **PARTICIPATION AU CAPITAL — SHAREHOLDING (BY EMPLOYEES)**: See **employee share ownership**.

568. **PARTICIPATION AUX ORGANES — PARTICIPATION IN COMPANY ORGANS**: Inclusion of employees of an enterprise in the bodies responsible for its administration and for the supervision of its management (see **worker member of the board, co-determination**).

569. **PARTICIPATION AUX RÉSULTATS — PROFIT-SHARING**: Generic term for receipt of a proportion of the enterprise's profits, established by French law as an entitlement for employees of enterprises normally employing more than 100 employees. It is calculated on the basis of taxable profit (see **profit-sharing agreement**).

570. **PATERNALISME — PATERNALISM**: Doctrine or practice of organizing relations between employers and employees on the model of domestic relationships (within the family). It implies an approach combining employer or managerial authority and spontaneous protectiveness.

571. **"PATRON"**: Traditional name for the employer, as the person who wields authority or hierarchical power. By extension, a hierarchical superior to whom an employee is directly answerable. The most appropriate colloquial translation is "boss".

572. **PATRONAGE — SPONSORSHIP/PATRONAGE**: Financial or symbolic support given by a well-known personage or by an enterprise. (Formerly, a charitable guild concerned with the religious or civic education of young people.)

573. **"PATRONAT"**: Term used in French for "employers" collectively (see **employers' organization**).

164

574. PAUSE — BREAK: Brief interruption of work for rest or a meal. The existence and duration of breaks, but at the same time their effect on pay, are traditional sources of disputes and negotiation.

575. PENSION — PENSION: Regular payment made to a retired worker (**retirement** pension) or disabled worker (**disability** pension).

576. PÉRIODE D'ESSAI — PROBATIONARY PERIOD: See **probation**.

577. PERMANENT SYNDICAL — UNION EMPLOYEE: Member of a trade union invested with a long-term office who has usually, for this reason, become an employee of the union.

578. PERSONNALITÉ JURIDIQUE—LEGAL PERSONALITY: Capacity to enjoy rights and to be subject to obligations. It is also referred to as "personnalité morale" when it is accorded to an artificial person such as a group.

A trade union is recognized as possessing legal personality, provided it has completed the formalities of declaration to the **works council** and, according to case law, to the **group-level works council**.

579. PERSONNEL — PERSONNEL/STAFF: All the employees of an enterprise, as a collective body (see **workforce**).

580. PIQUET DE GRÈVE — PICKET: Gathering of a group of strikers at the entrance to an enterprise's premises for the purpose of dissuading non-strikers from going to work. This practice does not constitute an offence under French law if the presence of the picket is confined to the application of moral pressure; it does constitute an offence if entry to the workplace is physically prevented.

581. PLACEMENT — JOB PLACEMENT: Activity consisting in identifying job vacancies and preparing job-seekers to fill them. In France this activity is, in principle, a public monopoly (see **National Employment Agency**). Recently, however, some adjustments have been made to this monopoly. Also, the distinction is a fine one between job placement, which is unlawful if it is provided by a private fee-charging bureau, and **recruitment**, which is lawful and frequently entrusted to specialist private agencies.

165

582. **PLAFOND — CEILING/LIMIT**: Maximum amount of pay taken into account for calculating social security contributions ("plafond de la sécurité sociale", *i.e.* earnings limit for chargeable social security contributions), or maximum level of income compatible with the granting of certain benefits ("plafond de ressources", *i.e.* means-test limit).

583. **PLAN D'ENTREPRISE — BUSINESS PLAN**:
1. Set of measures concerning the settlement of debts, future activity and employment that the court orders when, at the end of the observation procedure instituted by the Law on the compulsory administration of enterprises (see **bankruptcy**), there is a serious chance of survival for the enterprise in question.
   The Law refers to a "plan de redressement" (rescue plan) and states that it may arrange either for the enterprise to continue in its existing form or for a total or partial **change of ownership or control**.
2. Programme, or document detailing it, drawn up by some enterprise managements to establish targets, the foreseeable stages of their attainment and the measures they necessitate.
   In general, the purpose is to explain a strategy and build a degree of consensus around it.

584. **PLAN D'ÉPARGNE D'ENTREPRISE — COMPANY SAVINGS SCHEME**: Mechanism provided for by law as a possible form of **profit-sharing**, whereby a portfolio of marketable securities is built up for employees' benefit and managed by the enterprise.

585. **PLAN DE FORMATION — TRAINING PLAN**: Formally, a document submitted for consultation with the works council, setting out the aims and measures which the enterprise intends to pursue as regards employee training.
   The measures included in the plan are decided upon by the employer, who meets the cost but may, subject to certain conditions, deduct the expenditure thus incurred from the compulsory payments which employers are required to make towards the general funding of vocational training.

586. **PLAN SOCIAL — REDUNDANCY PROGRAMME**: Organized set of measures offering alternatives to dismissal, assistance in arranging re-employment elsewhere and compensation, whose purpose is to limit the number of dismissals and soften the impact of those which are to take place.

Redundancy programmes, which first featured in a 1974 general multi-industry agreement, are now compulsory by law in cases where an enterprise with 50 or more employees plans to dismiss at least 10 of them for economic reasons (see **redundancy**). Drawn up by the employer, the programme must be submitted, for their opinion, to the works council and the Labour Inspectorate.

587. **PLATE-FORME — "PLATFORM"**: Major elements of the programme of one or more trade unions, when they have arrived at an agreement.

588. **PLURALISME NORMATIF — MULTIPLICITY OF SOURCES OF LAW**: Coexistence, within a given unit of analysis, of a range of different regulatory systems. French labour law meets this definition, since it represents a combination of rules of statutory origin, as applied in particular industries (see **branch of economic activity**), rules of international origin and rules originating from collective bargaining. Statute law tends, however, to establish a hierarchy of these diverse sources.

589. **PLURALISME SYNDICAL — TRADE UNION PLURALISM**: Coexistence of more than one union within the same occupation or for the same category. It is a fundamental feature of French trade unionism. There is, in fact, very strong legal justification for pluralism: it reflects the principle of the French conception of **trade union freedom**. Consequently, no analysis of trade unionism in France can afford to ignore this structural feature, whether directed at studying the movement's strength or weakness, examining the strategies of the **social actors** or interpreting the rules of trade union law.

The expansion of the role of the unions, particularly in the general regulation of society, has led to the establishment of a modified form of pluralism via the concept of **representativeness**. However, this concept still allows for pluralism; the majority principle still does not prevail, since several unions may all be representative.

590. **POLITIQUE DANS L'ENTREPRISE — POLITICS WITHIN THE ENTERPRISE**: No provision is made by French law regarding the formal presence of political parties within the enterprise. The general view is that it is purely a matter of tolerance.

The employer may not infringe an employee's freedom of political opinion. Here again, a distinction is often made between opinion, which is protected, and action, which is not.

Disputes usually concern any restrictions on the activities of trade unions or works councils (see **company welfare and cultural facilities**). In 1982 the law recognized the unions' right to perform a broad range of functions, extending to the protection of employees' moral interests, and the right of works councils to organize cultural activities and information sessions on topical issues. To this extent, at least, politics represent a civil right within the enterprise.

591. **POLITIQUE DE L'EMPLOI — EMPLOYMENT POLICY**: Collective range of measures adopted by the public authorities with a view to intervening in the labour market (see **employment support, National Employment Fund**).

592. **POSTE — POST/JOB**: Popular term used to refer either to an employment position within an organization, or the functions performed by an employee (virtually synonymous in this case with **emploi**), or these functions plus an indication of their location.

593. **POURBOIRE — TIP/GRATUITY**: Sum of money given to employees by one of their employer's clients with whom they have come into contact in performing their work. As part of the legal regulation of the employee's position, tips and gratuities are covered by special rules to prevent their being retained, in part or in full, by the employer.

594. **POUVOIR DE DIRECTION — EMPLOYER'S MANA-GERIAL AUTHORITY**: Expression used by the courts to designate the scope of the discretionary powers held by the heads of enterprises. It includes the right to issue instructions concerning legal and technical structures and operating conditions, the organization of work, trends in the numbers employed and the recruitment and posting of staff, all of them areas in which these powers may sometimes be restricted by the individual contract of employment, rules laid down by collective agreement or legal rules such as the principle of the equality of men and women in employment (see **equality between men and women**).

595. **POUVOIR DISCIPLINAIRE — DISCIPLINARY POWER**: Recognized authority of the head of an enterprise to lay down disciplinary rules for the enterprise (see **works rules**) and to impose sanctions when those rules are contravened (see **disciplinary sanction**). Its exercise is regulated by law.

596. POUVOIR DU CHEF D'ENTREPRISE — MANAGERIAL PREROGATIVE: Recognized prerogative rights of the heads of enterprises which give them fundamental authority to set rules or take decisions which are binding on employees, *de jure* or *de facto*, without their having given their assent.

The exercise of these prerogative rights is regulated by law to a varying extent (see **employer's managerial authority, disciplinary power**). They may also be restricted by collective agreement.

597. POUVOIR SYNDICAL — UNION POWER: The strength of the trade union organizations. The expression, although vague, has fuelled serious debate on the resources, forms of activity and basis of legitimacy of the **trade union confederations**. As management and organizational tasks have been progressively entrusted to them, so the confederations have, according to some commentators, stopped drawing their strength from the vitality of their member groups and now draw it, instead, from the support of the Government and prevailing opinion.

598. PRÉAVIS — NOTICE: Period of time that elapses between the notification of **dismissal** or announcement of **resignation** and the date on which the contract of employment ceases to have effect. The terms "préavis de congédiement" or "préavis de licenciement" (notice of dismissal) and "préavis de démission" (notice of resignation) are used. Only notice of dismissal is subject to a minimum period laid down by law; this need not, however, be observed in cases of serious **misconduct** on the part of the employee.

599. PRÉAVIS (GRÈVE) — NOTICE OF STRIKE: Period of time that elapses between the declaration of a strike and the actual stoppage of work. Such notice is required by law in the **public sector**; the period stipulated is five clear days, which in practice means seven days. During this period, the parties have a duty to bargain.

The term also designates the act of declaration of a strike. Only a representative union (see **representativeness**) may issue such a declaration, which must state the place, date and time and duration (limited or unlimited) of the proposed strike.

Outside the public sector, some collective agreements have introduced periods of notice prior to strike action. These periods must be put to good use in seeking a settlement of the dispute. However, since the right to strike is an individual right in France, collective agreements can never, by stipulating lengthy periods of notice and preliminary procedures, deprive employees of what is one of their constitutional rights (see **right to strike**).

600. PRÉCARITÉ — PRECARIOUSNESS: Characteristic trait of something that is insecure or unstable. Employment is precarious when it is under a short-term contract or when it can be terminated at the will of the employer. (Not to be confused with the English term "casual work".)

According to new legislative terminology in France, the term "contrat précaire" (contract for precarious employment) covers **fixed-term contracts** and the contracts of temporary workers (see **temporary-employment agency work**), which are always for a fixed term.

601. PRÉPOSÉ — AGENT AND SERVANT: Person who performs an act or carries on an activity under the authority of another (the principal). This terminology is still in use in the law on civil liability, which, to the benefit of the injured party, makes principals liable for acts committed by their agents and servants. Every employee is an agent and servant; but the situation of being such may exist without a **contract of employment**.

602. PRÉRETRAITE — EARLY RETIREMENT: Resources guaranteed to employees who leave their employment at a certain age, until the date when they become eligible to draw their retirement pension. These resources may be provided by the enterprise ("préretraite d'entreprise", *i.e.* company early retirement scheme). Alternatively, they may be financed jointly by the enterprise, the employee concerned and the State (or the unemployment insurance scheme). It is this latter formula which, under diverse arrangements, has been widely used since 1972. Nowadays, the State allocates payments out of the **National Employment Fund**, provided that an agreement has been concluded with the enterprise. There is awareness of the limitations of employment policies that overemphasize the use of early retirement as an approach, which is referred to as "ageist" (*i.e.* discriminating against older workers).

603. PRÉROGATIVES PATRONALES — MANAGERIAL PREROGATIVE: Synonymous with **pouvoir du chef d'entreprise**.

604. PRESCRIPTION — LIMITATION OF ACTIONS: Failure to bring a legal action before a certain period of time specified by law has expired means that the right to bring such action lapses. For legal actions concerning the payment of an employee, the limitation period is five years.

605. **PRESTATION DE SERVICES — PROVISION OF SERVICES**: Operation directed at supplying any benefit other than a product, under a contract for services, agency contract, lease, etc. When accompanied by the provision of personnel (see **provision of labour**), it may be counter to the ban on **labour-only subcontracting** or the **hiring-out of labour** on a profit-making basis when this does not comply with the regulations governing **temporary-employment agency work**.

606. **PRESTATION SOCIALE — SOCIAL BENEFIT**: Benefit granted by a **social protection** institution to offset a loss of income, reimburse expenditure or end a condition of need.

607. **PRÊT DE MAIN-D'OEUVRE — HIRING-OUT OF LABOUR**: French law prohibits the hiring-out of labour for profit-making purposes unless it occurs within the framework of the regulations on **temporary-employment agency work**. The criterion for distinguishing between the hiring-out of labour and the provision of services is the existence or absence of a transfer to the recipient enterprise of the employee's relationship of "subordination".

French law has recently regulated, and hence rendered lawful, the hiring-out of labour as undertaken by a group of employers (see **employers' pool**) or by an association set up with government approval to meet needs that the market fails to satisfy, called an **intermediary association**.

608. **PREUVE — PROOF**: Demonstration of the existence of an act (contract of employment, resignation, dismissal) or fact (loss or harm), to a standard required by law.

609. **PRÉVENTION (DES CONFLITS) — DISPUTE PREVENTION**: All measures and institutions whose purpose is to avoid the outbreak of open conflict. French law does not stipulate any particular measures, but organizes voluntary **conciliation**, **mediation** and **arbitration** procedures for the protagonists to use if they so choose. In the **public services**, where notice of the intention to strike is compulsory (see **notice of strike**), a duty to bargain during this period of notice is imposed by law.

There is, however, a widely held belief that effective prevention can be achieved only if potential causes of conflict are identified and eliminated, and this entails making prevention an integral part of management in the form of various processes such as communication, information, consultation, etc.

610. **PRÉVOYANCE SOCIALE — SOCIAL WELFARE**: Term which designates, in French law, any protection scheme established, over and above the coverage provided by social security, to ensure cover against risks other than old age. It is therefore to be distinguished from supplementary pension schemes and individual provident schemes which are not based on the principle of risk-sharing between the members of a group.

A recent Law has attempted to lay down some guidelines that will introduce order into a rapidly growing market.

611. **PRIME — BONUS**: Name given to various components of remuneration paid in addition to basic pay. Since these payments are not linked to working time alone, it is sometimes difficult to determine whether they are due. Everything hinges on the existence and intepretation of the criteria for eligibility. Numerous names are used: "prime de rendement" (output bonus), "prime de bilan" (performance bonus), "prime de productivité" (production bonus), "prime d'assiduité" (attendance bonus), "prime d'incommodité" (inconvenience bonus), "prime d'insalubrité" (bonus for unhealthy working conditions), etc.

612. **PRIME ANTI-GRÈVE — ANTI-STRIKE BONUS**: Name given to attendance bonuses (see **bonus**) which, in order to discourage absenteeism, are reduced or withdrawn in the event of unauthorized absence from work. Since this type of mechanism could penalize striking employees, French law stipulates that they may be deprived of a bonus only if absence for any other reason actually has the same effect on payment of the bonus as being on strike.

613. **PRINCIPE — PRINCIPLE**:
   1. Political proposition of a normative nature which dictates or inspires the content of legal rules.
   2. Legal rule which occupies a position in the hierarchy such that it is a bar to the validity of other rules. Several different categories of principle in this sense can be distinguished: principles carrying constitutional force (see **constitutional principle**), the fundamental principles of labour law, which only statute law may establish, and the general principles of law that must be followed by the regulatory authorities (see **regulations**).
   3. Rule that is held to be absolute (see **public policy**).

614. **PRINCIPE CONSTITUTIONNEL — CONSTITUTIONAL PRINCIPLE**: In a broad sense, any constitutional rule.

In a directly narrower sense, any constitutionally guaranteed freedom or right. In addition to those stated in the present (1958) Constitution, such freedoms and rights also have their source in the Declaration of Rights of August 26, 1789, the Preamble to the Constitution of October 24, 1946, and the fundamental principles recognized by the laws of the Republic.

615. PRIVATISATION — PRIVATIZATION: Decision taken by the Government or another public authority to transfer to private individuals the ownership or control of certain public sector enterprises (privatization of enterprises) or to allow the market to take over certain activities previously provided or controlled by a public administration (privatization of activities).

A wave of enterprise privatizations took place in France in 1986-1987; it involved about a dozen enterprises (and their subsidiaries), most of which had been earlier nationalized (see **nationalization**) in 1982.

616. PRIVILÈGE — PREFERENTIAL CLAIM: Legally recognized right of a creditor to be paid out of the sale price of one (specific preference) or all (general preference) of the debtor's assets in preference to other creditors. In cases where the employer becomes subject to compulsory administration (see **bankruptcy**), all employees have a right of general preference which guarantees them payment of any pay for the preceding six months still owing to them, and of any entitlements payable on termination of the employment contract (see **compensation for dismissal, compensation in lieu of notice**). Since the effectiveness of this right of general preference is very relative, the law has introduced a reinforced right of preference ("superprivilège") which is in fact an absolute priority for the payment, out of the first funds that become available, of recent pay outstanding, up to a maximum limit. This reinforced right of preference is combined with a compulsory insurance mechanism (see **wage guarantee insurance**).

617. PROCÉDURE — PROCEDURE:
1. In court proceedings, set of rules specifying the formal manner in which legal actions are conducted. Procedure before an **Industrial Tribunal** is oral, but the other major principles of civil procedure (including the principle of contentious parties) are applicable.
2. In a more general sense, sequence of acts that must be completed before a decision is made. A number of decisions relating to employment relationships and labour relations are subject to a preliminary procedure. Examples include a decision

to take disciplinary action (see **disciplinary sanction**) or to dismiss an employee (see **dismissal**), an economic, financial or technical decision which is likely to affect employees' circumstances (see **works council**), or a decision to take strike action in the **public services**. This "proceduralization" is a fundamental phenomenon.

618. **PROCÉDURE D'ALERTE — NOTIFICATION PROCEDURE**: See **notification**.

619. **PROCÉDURE DE NÉGOCIATION — BARGAINING PROCEDURE**: The collective bargaining process is in principle a forum for the expression of collective autonomy. In direct line with this principle, although it is difficult to apply, bargaining has increasingly been organized by collective agreement, in particular through **framework agreements**. A bolder example is to be found in the tendency of certain judges, when presiding over court proceedings during industrial disputes, to encourage bargaining and, to that end, to outline procedures.

However, in 1982 the law, in creating obligations relating to collective bargaining (see **duty to bargain**), laid down the outline of a bargaining procedure (including, in particular, the prohibition of unilateral measures while negotiations are in process). The purpose behind a law of collective bargaining is to ensure the effectiveness of the right to bargain collectively.

620. **PROCÈS-VERBAL DE CONCILIATION — MINUTE OF CONCILIATION**: Written document recording the total or partial agreement or disagreement of the parties, drawn up at the end of the meeting either of the conciliation board of an **Industrial Tribunal** or of a conciliation committee to which an industrial dispute is referred (see **conciliation**).

621. **PROCÈS-VERBAL DE DÉSACCORD — MINUTE OF FAILURE TO AGREE**: Document which must, by law, be drawn up when compulsory bargaining at enterprise level (see **duty to bargain**) fails to lead to an agreement. It must record the respective proposals put forward by the parties and the measures which the employer unilaterally intends to adopt. The employer is then bound by these measures as a unilateral commitment.

622. **PROCÈS-VERBAL DE FIN DE CONFLIT — MINUTE OF DISPUTE SETTLEMENT**: Document, often called a "protocole" (protocol) or "constat" (record), drawn up on the spot to record the principles and conditions for the ending of

a strike. In principle, it has the legal status of a **collective agreement** only if it is negotiated and signed by one or more representative unions. However, even when signed only by a **strike committee** or delegates it has been accorded a certain legal force, sometimes as a settlement by compromise ("transaction") and sometimes as a stipulation for another party.

623. **PRODUCTIVITÉ — PRODUCTIVITY**: Quantitative link established between a form of output and one or more of the factors of production used. Hence, defining labour productivity entails measuring output against the input of labour.

624. **PROFESSION — PROFESSION/OCCUPATION**: Concept covering three different (although historically intermingled) meanings:
1. Used in reference to guild corporations and the liberal professions, a "profession" is an occupation (in the sense of a **métier**) which carries prestige because of its intellectual or artistic nature and whose practice is governed by a set of rules, with its practitioners forming an organized body.
2. Trade unionism, in having originated from an occupation-based form of organization, is referred to as representing the interests of a "profession". In this case, the term has lost its connotation of a profession in the above sense; it denotes a form of activity in the overall context of the division of labour.
3. Lastly, a "profession" is a given occupation which provides a means of earning a living.

625. **PROFESSIONNALITÉ — PROFESSIONAL COMPETENCE AND STATUS**: A specialist term used mainly in two senses. It sometimes designates the relation established between a set of practical and theoretical qualities exhibited by an individual or group and the organization of work in the enterprise (see **skill**).

It is also sometimes used to describe a tendency to establish guarantees surrounding the recognition and valuation of abilities *i.e.* in the sense of "professionalism".

626. **PROGRAMMATION — PROGRAMMING**: Formulation and ordered presentation of a sequence of operations required to obtain a result: calculators, computers, etc., are programmed. The term "lois de programme" is also used in the sense of Government Plans setting out overall objectives.

627. **PROJET D'ENTREPRISE — ENTERPRISE PLAN**: Practice whereby the management of an enterprise draws up a document

outlining the enterprise's future, setting out its development objectives and defining the ways in which they are to be accomplished. The plan helps to give the enterprise a corporate identity and hence foster staff commitment (see **business plan**).

628. **PROMOTION — PROMOTION**: Term used in two different senses:
1. Advancement to a higher-ranking job.
2. Development, encouragement or stimulation. The term "promotion ouvrière" refers to measures intended to allow workers access to a better position in society. Also, the expression "législation promotionnelle" is used to emphasize that certain laws are directed at supporting collective bargaining, either in supplying means or resources to certain bargaining agents (see **representativeness**) or in stimulating bargaining activity itself (see **duty to bargain**).

629. **PRORATA — *PRO RATA***: Term used in French as a noun meaning a proportion or percentage, and in English as an adjective or adverb meaning proportional(ly). The recently coined expression *pro rata temporis* means being in proportion to the length of time involved. Calculating something on a *pro rata temporis* basis is referred to in French as "proratisation" (in English, to prorate).

630. **PROTECTION SOCIALE — SOCIAL PROTECTION**: A term which is broader in scope than **social security**, although the two are often used interchangeably. Social protection encompasses the entire range of provisions, whether or not compulsory and whether or not organized by law, by means of which individuals are protected against social risks. In particular, it includes **social welfare** arrangements, which extend beyond the coverage provided by social security.

631. **PROTOCOLE (D'ACCORD) — PROTOCOL OF AGREEMENT**: Document drawn up, without any special formalities, by the parties to an industrial dispute in order to record the terms of its settlement (see **minute of dispute settlement**). It does not always have the legal force of a collective agreement, in particular because the parties involved do not necessarily possess the legal capacity required to conclude one (*e.g.* a strike committee).

632. **PRUD'HOMME — INDUSTRIAL TRIBUNAL MEMBER**: Elected lay judge of an **Industrial Tribunal**, still also referred to under the former title of "conseiller prud'homme".

Q

633. **QUALIFICATION — SKILL/SKILL LEVEL/QUALIFICA-
TION**: In the language of educationalists and sociologists, this
term usually refers to an individual's level of education and
training, *i.e.* personal qualifications.

In labour law, it designates an employee's competence, as
agreed with the employer, to occupy the post to which they are
assigned (*i.e.* a level or grade). It is therefore the subject of an
agreement and constitutes an element of the contract of
employment. Hence, employees have a right to be employed in
a post which corresponds to the skill level or grade specified in
their contract of employment. In cases where the parties to the
contract of employment are in disagreement concerning the
employee's skill level or grade, employees are legally entitled to
assert their right to the skill level or grade corresponding to the
functions which they actually perform. But if the employer has
assigned them to a skill level or grade higher than that
corresponding to their actual functions (a situation referred to
as "surclassement"), they may still assert their right to it.

634. **QUALITÉ — QUALITY**: Recent years have seen developments
in the quest for quality, aimed at the detection and elimination
of defects. Traditionally focused on products and procedures,
the concept of quality has in many enterprises been broadened
to include relationships with suppliers and customers and relations
within the workforce as a collective group (see **quality circle**).
It is often stressed that, when ambitious, quality assurance
("gestion de la qualité") is incompatible with any immediate
lowering of costs or rapid penetration of certain sections of the
market.

635. **QUALITÉ DE LA VIE — QUALITY OF LIFE**: Expression
much favoured by those who challenge the idea that work can
be the principal or sole means of conferring social identities or
achieving personal fulfilment.

636. **QUESTIONNAIRE — QUESTIONNAIRE/APPLICATION
FORM**: In the recruitment of personnel, a document containing
a list of questions which every applicant is requested to answer.
The French courts hold that the questions must have a direct
bearing on the type of employment being sought.

637. **QUOTA — QUOTA**: Percentage which is fixed in advance or
decided in the light of existing conditions. A quota system was
applied in France under immigration policy for some time before
the Second World War. It has been proposed, without much
success, as a means of attaining **equality between men and
women**, both within the enterprise and in trade union and
political organizations.

177

R

638. RAPPORT (OFFICIEL) — OFFICIAL REPORT: Document stating the conclusions of an individual, group or commission to whom an authority has entrusted the task of studying an issue or problem, and suggesting appropriate action.

The practice of commissioning a report from one or more experts or specialists has become fundamental. It owes its success to the breathing-space given to the authority concerned during the preparation of the report, the objectivity that can be maintained in its analysis and conclusions, and the general esteem in which experts are held.

639. RAPPORT DE TRAVAIL — EMPLOYMENT RELATION-SHIP: Relationship in law which comes into being by virtue of a **contract of employment**.

640. RATIFICATION — RATIFICATION:
1. Formal acceptance or confirmation by one person of an act performed in their name by another person who did not originally possess the authority to commit them to it. The person who ratifies the act then holds the rights and is bound by the obligations deriving from the act in question. In general, such acceptance is a unilateral juristic act. Under French law, however, the conclusion of a **profit-sharing agreement** may come about via the ratification, by a two-thirds majority of the employees, of a proposal put forward by the head of an enterprise, *i.e.* by way of a **ballot**.
2. Act required to translate the provisions of an international treaty into national law. In France, this is a decree issued after authorization by a Law (see **international agreement**).

641. RECHERCHE D'EMPLOI — JOB-SEARCHING: Activity of looking for work that an individual must undertake in order to qualify for inclusion on the list of job-seekers (see **National Employment Agency**) and continue receiving unemployment benefits (see **unemployment**). Some people are, however, exempted from this condition on the grounds of their age.

642. RÉCLAMATION — GRIEVANCE: See **claim**.

643. RECLASSEMENT — REDEPLOYMENT: Measure whereby an alternative job may be found for an employee when their formerly existing job has been abolished or they are no longer able to perform it (*e.g.* because of **physical unfitness**) or when they have been made redundant (see **redundancy**).

Various obligations regarding redeployment have been imposed on French employers by law or case law: for employees who are

178

the victims of an **accident at work** or **occupational illness**, for **employee representatives** whose jobs are abolished, etc. In such cases, redeployment must be within the enterprise (or company group).

644. **RECOMMANDATION (MÉDIATION) — MEDIATION RECOMMENDATION**: Proposal for the settlement of an industrial dispute made by a mediator (see **mediation**), which is binding on the parties only if they both accept it.

645. **RECOMMANDATION SALARIALE — PAY RECOM-MENDATION**: Unilateral proposal emanating from an employers' organization which is issued in the absence of agreed terms laid down by a collective agreement. It may be binding on the organization's member enterprises.

646. **RECONDUCTION — RENEWAL (OF CONTRACT)**: Entry into force of a new contract when the previous one expires, in general under the same terms and conditions, for a specified period. In France, such renewal of fixed-term contracts of employment (see **fixed-term contract**) is strictly regulated.

647. **RECONVERSION — RE-TRAINING**: Synonym of **conversion**. See also **re-training agreement**.

648. **RECOURS — APPEAL/REMEDY**: Term used with several meanings:
    1. Sometimes designates, loosely, any procedure by which a decision or act may be challenged.
    2. Legal action whose aim is to secure the annulment, reversal or setting aside of a court judgment. Synonymous, in this sense, with "voie de recours" (appeal proceedings).
    3. Term traditionally reserved for particular procedures organized by law for contesting or referring to a higher authority an administrative act or court judgment. Thus, all actions for contesting an administrative act bear the name "recours".

649. **RECRUTEMENT — RECRUITMENT/HIRING**: Term used in two senses:
    1. Synonym for the conclusion of a contract of employment or **hiring**.
    2. Recruitment as an activity which precedes hiring, since this necessitates various operations which in some cases are compulsory (competitive examinations for the **civil service**) and in others are left to the discretion of enterprises. The latter sometimes entrust these preliminary recruitment activities to another specialist enterprise.

650. **REÇU POUR SOLDE DE TOUT COMPTE — RECEIPT ACKNOWLEDGING FULL SETTLEMENT**: Document which employees are asked to sign when their contract of employment comes to an end, to confirm what monies are due to them and what monies have been paid to them. Provided that the receipt complies with the rules laid down by law, the act of signing it prohibits employees (unless they cancel it, stating their reasons, within a time limit of two months) from subsequently claiming any pay or other entitlements whose payment was envisaged at the time when the receipt was drawn up.

651. **RÉCUPÉRATION — MAKE-UP**: Mechanism which enables hours of work not performed at the proper time to be made up at another time. Regulated by law, it means that hours of work lost collectively may be carried over during the 12 months following or preceding the interruption of work. It is optional for employers, but if they decide to use it employees must comply. The law defines what constitutes lost working time that may be made up in this way ("heures récupérables"): for the most part, the interruption of work must be due to exceptional circumstances. Before deciding to make use of the mechanism, an employer must consult the works council and inform the Labour Inspector. Lastly, the resultant extra hours of work, which do not attract an increased rate of pay, may not, in principle, be added to normal workloads at rates in excess of one hour per day or eight hours per week.

652. **REDRESSEMENT JUDICIAIRE — COMPULSORY ADMINISTRATION**: Since 1985, name given to the procedure that must be followed for any enterprise which becomes insolvent. It entered the terminology when the aims and techniques of the procedure were altered (see **bankruptcy**). The procedure now always begins with an observation phase, which leads either to a rescue plan (see **business plan**) or to compulsory **liquidation**.

653. **RÉDUCTION (DURÉE DU TRAVAIL) — REDUCTION OF WORKING HOURS**: Classic subject of union claims in which, in France, considerations regarding employee protection and concerns about work sharing have always played a part.

Three types of reduction may be distinguished. Firstly, statutory **working hours** ("durée légale") may be reduced by law; for instance, in 1982 they were reduced from 40 to 39 hours per week, with pay remaining virtually unaffected. Secondly, working hours may be reduced by collective agreement, giving rise to collectively agreed working hours ("durée conventionnelle") which are, necessarily, shorter than statutory working hours. Reductions of this type have been introduced in the context of integrative bargaining, or concession or "give-and-take" bargaining, whereby working hours are reduced as a counter-concession in return for new demands imposed on employees. Lastly, the employer may decide unilaterally to shorten working hours, with consequent loss of pay. In general, the reduction in this case is only temporary and presented as an economic measure. This unilateral step may encounter resistance from employees. If, in line with prevailing opinion, working hours are considered to be an integral part of the individual contract of employment, it is legitimate for employees to refuse to accept the reduction and they may succeed in securing, if not always the continuance of their original working hours, at least the retention of the corresponding pay. To overcome their resistance, in such cases the only real option open to the employer is to initiate the **redundancy** procedure.

654. **RÉFÉRÉ — PROCEDURE IN CHAMBERS**: Accelerated procedure whereby application is made to a judge sitting alone (except in the procedure in chambers for **Industrial Tribunals** ("référé prud'homal"), where there are two lay judges) to prescribe any measures which are not open to serious challenge or are justified by the existence of a disagreement, or any protective or restorative measures required to prevent imminent loss or harm or stop a manifestly unlawful disruption, or, also, where an obligation is not open to serious contestation, to order the obligor to meet it.

A judge presiding over procedure in chambers ("juge des référés") has considerable powers. The procedure plays an essential role both in individual labour disputes and in collective industrial disputes.

655. **RÉFÉRENDUM — BALLOT**: Process whereby a body of employees express their collective wish on a matter, as distinct from the channels of election or the internal decision-taking procedures of a trade union. French law does not assign any specific role to it in the event of conflict. The unions may, at their own discretion, organize a ballot before or during a strike, and this option is sometimes used. The same applies during collective bargaining. There are, however, two circumstances for which the law does make explicit provision for the permissible, and sometimes compulsory, use of the ballot: it is permissible as an alternative procedure for concluding profit-sharing agreements, and compulsory for making changes to welfare institutions.

Although not a ballot in the strict sense, the practice of organizing a formal consultation of the workforce to seek its views is being used increasingly by employers.

656. **RÉGIME COMPLÉMENTAIRE (DE RETRAITE) — SUPPLEMENTARY PENSION SCHEME**: System of protection, supplementing the statutory social security scheme, set up by the members of a group to create a retirement pension fund for the benefit of contributors.

Originally introduced under collective agreements, supplementary schemes have now been made compulsory in all enterprises. This means that there are compulsory supplementary schemes. Over and above these, there are voluntary supplementary schemes called "régimes surcomplémentaires".

657. **RÉGIME DE SOLIDARITÉ — GUARANTEE SUPPLEMENTARY SCHEME**: See **unemployment benefit**.

658. **RÈGLEMENT — REGULATION**: Universally applicable text issued by the executive authorities. It thus differs from a **law** (statute) in that the latter is promulgated by Parliament.

A Regulation may lay down provisions in areas that cannot be governed by a law. In such cases it is called a "règlement autonome". It may also supplement a law by laying down provisions necessary for its implementation.

659. **RÈGLEMENT DES CONFLITS — DISPUTE SETTLEMENT**: Resolution of, or process for resolving, disputes (see **industrial dispute**). A distinction is made between judicial settlement (*i.e.* by the courts) and extra-judicial settlement, and between processes organized by law (see **arbitration, conciliation, mediation**) and autonomous processes (*i.e.* negotiation; see **minute of dispute settlement, protocol of agreement**).

660. **RÈGLEMENT INTÉRIEUR — WORKS RULES**: Document setting down rules on health, safety and **discipline** within the enterprise which is a compulsory requirement in enterprises normally employing 20 or more employees.

Under French law, the authority to set these rules lies with the employer, after consultation with the works council. Only in exceptional cases are they contained in a collective agreement.

The legality of works rules is monitored by the Labour Inspector, who may at any time demand the withdrawal or amendment of an illegal provision. The law specifies, in outline, the manner in which works rules must accommodate the protection of individual and collective rights and freedoms. This is an area which gives rise to numerous matters of dispute.

661. **RÉGLEMENTATION — REGULATION(S):**
   1. The formulation or production of legal rules by the relevant authorities, or a set of rules thus produced. The term may be related to a particular sphere, such as "réglementation du travail" (labour regulations).
   2. In a pejorative sense (and so perhaps best translated as "rules and regulations"), a set of rules which governs matters down to the very last detail.

662. **RÉGULATION — REGULATION:**
   1. Term designating the function of a mechanism or set of mechanisms which keeps a system in equilibrium. In this sense, a rule or institution may be referred to as having a regulatory function. This is sometimes extended to the point of likening the law itself to a vast regulatory mechanism.
   2. A number of major works by economists, reasoning that general equilibrium theories do not satisfactorily take account of growth and recession, have proposed analyses in terms of regulation. In this sense, the term refers to all the formal or implicit processes which combine to adjust social production and demand and correspond to a given state of organizational forms and production structures.

663. **RÉINTÉGRATION — REINSTATEMENT:** Consequence of the pronouncement of a **dismissal** to be null and void, whereby the employee returns to the same job which he or she formerly occupied. Under French law, such a remedy is exceptional and occurs only in the following cases: dismissal may be ruled null and void when an employee representative has been dismissed without (due) authorization from the Labour Inspectorate; the same applies where the reason for dismissal is a contravention of public policy principles (dismissal on the grounds of ethnic origin, sex, nationality, legitimate exercise of the right to strike, etc.). However, since the law gives an actual list of such reasons the extension of this remedy to all dismissals that contravene public policy is controversial.

   In cases of unjustified dismissal (*i.e.* dismissal without genuine and serious cause), reinstatement is discretionary, both for the judge, who may or may not propose it, and also for the parties, including the employer, who may or may not accept a judge's proposal. Most cases in fact result in the payment of compensation.

664. RELATION(S) DE TRAVAIL — EMPLOYMENT RELATIONSHIP/LABOUR RELATIONS: Under French law, the employment relationship exists only by virtue of having its source in a contract of employment. There is no recognition of the employment relationship as a legal concept. The term is used as a synonym of **rapport de travail**.

It is also used in the plural in the sense of labour relations, *i.e.* as a synonym of **relations professionnelles**.

665. RELATIONS HUMAINES — HUMAN RELATIONS: See **work organization**.

666. RELATIONS INDUSTRIELLES — INDUSTRIAL RELATIONS: Term borrowed from the English-speaking countries and used in France to designate a field of study whose purpose is to describe the particular features of national **labour relations** systems and interpret the differences between them. The emphasis is on the actors (see **social actors**), the rules governing relations between them, and the economic and political, technological and also ideological context.

Approaching the subject in terms of a system tends to underline the role of dynamic interaction in labour relations.

667. RELATIONS PROFESSIONNELLES — LABOUR RELATIONS: Social relations which become established in connection with employment. Analysis of labour relations is mainly concerned with the actions to which they give rise (disputes, bargaining), the respective organizations formed by employers and employees and the pattern of resultant rules.

This indicates that within France the centre of interest lies at a level midway between the State and the enterprise, *i.e.* at industry or occupation level.

668. RELATIONS SOCIALES — SOCIAL RELATIONS (INDUSTRIAL RELATIONS): Term used by the central administration and certain major enterprises to refer to the relations which become established, in connection with employment, between employers' organizations or enterprises on the one hand and trade unions, employee representatives or groupings of employees on the other. In France, the term finds favour because of its peaceable connotation and because the expressions "**relations industrielles**" and "**relations professionnelles**" are very rarely used.

669. RENONCIATION — WAIVER: Act whereby a person relinquishes an existing right of which he or she is the holder

184

or forsakes the assertion of a means of action or defence. In France, waiver is not, in principle, possible during a contract of employment. However, by way of court decisions it is sometimes allowed, particularly in the matter of pay.

670. **RÉPARTITION — DISTRIBUTION**: In the sense used by economists, the distribution of income or wealth between social groups or between workers and capital providers.

671. **RÉPARTITION (DU TEMPS DE TRAVAIL) — PATTERN OF WORKING TIME**: Manner in which periods of work are distributed (see **annualization of working hours, scheduling of working hours, working hours**).

672. **REPOS — REST**: Period of suspension of the obligation to work to which all employees are entitled. It is treated as working time for the purposes of eligibility for and calculation of entitlements which are linked to length of service and attendance at the workplace.

673. **REPOS COMPENSATEUR — TIME OFF IN LIEU**: Period of rest prescribed by law to compensate for the performance of **overtime**, which is granted in addition to the payment of an overtime premium.

In enterprises with 11 or more employees, for overtime up to the limit of the annual overtime quota it amounts to 20 per cent. of the time worked over and above 42 hours per week. For hours of overtime worked in excess of this quota, time off in lieu amounts to either 50 per cent. or 100 per cent. of these hours, depending on whether the enterprise has fewer than 11 employees or 11 or more employees.

Time off in lieu may be taken as soon as the employee has accumulated a credit of eight hours and must be taken in the form of full days.

It is now possible for overtime premium pay to be replaced by time off in lieu under a collective agreement.

674. **REPOS DOMINICAL — SUNDAY REST**: The choice of Sunday as the day in the week on which employees may not be required to work is one of the elements of the principle of the **weekly rest day**. This choice, which is prompted partly by Christian tradition but also by the fact that a secular State must give proper consideration to religious beliefs and the needs of family life, is the target of criticism from certain quarters. Despite this, the most recent legislative intervention on the matter (1992) upheld the rule, while modifying the conditions under which

exceptions are permitted. In some instances exceptions to the rule are laid down by law; others require authorization from the Prefect of the département concerned, as the authority representing the State.

The rule that Sunday must be the weekly rest day raises the question of competition between enterprises. Hence, in order to avoid any distortion of competitiveness the law empowers a Prefect, after consultation with employers' organizations and trade unions, to issue a formal decision concerning the Sunday **closure of establishments** within a particular sphere of activity and a particular geographical area.

675. **REPOS HEBDOMADAIRE — WEEKLY REST DAY**: Two principles established by law must be combined: every employee is entitled to a weekly rest period of at least 24 consecutive hours, and this weekly rest day must fall on a Sunday.

A few exceptions are allowed to the principle of the weekly rest day (in particular, urgent work). The principle that this weekly rest day must fall on a Sunday is subject to three types of exemption. Firstly, automatic exemptions because of the nature of the activity concerned (hotels, restaurants, tobacconists, hospitals, performing arts enterprises and industries in which an interruption of work would cause loss of the product being manufactured); secondly, exemptions granted by the administrative authorities; and thirdly, exemptions provided for by collective agreement. In this last category, the use of relief shifts to work at weekends is conditional on the existence of a collective agreement that has been extended (see **extension of collective agreements**), plus a company-level or establishment-level agreement or, failing this, authorization from the **Labour Inspectorate**.

676. **REPRÉSENTANT DE COMMERCE — SALES REPRESENTATIVE**: An individual whose work consists in seeking out and visiting a clientele and taking orders for sales on behalf of the enterprise. Under French law, provided that they perform this activity as their permanent and sole occupation (on behalf of one or more enterprises) and do not conduct any commercial transactions on their own account, sales representatives are treated as similar to employees and enjoy a special status. This means that they are covered by the laws protecting employees but that their special status also guarantees them a degree of independence and accords them special rights, in particular entitlement, in the event of termination of their contract, to an "indemnité de clientèle" (goodwill indemnity, a form of compensation paid in consideration of the customers they have recruited for the enterprise).

677. **REPRÉSENTANTS DU PERSONNEL — EMPLOYEE REPRESENTATIVES**: Employees invested with the authority to represent the interests of the personnel of an enterprise or establishment. Some are elected by the employees (see **workforce delegate, workplace health and safety committee, works council**), while others are appointed by the representative unions (see **trade union delegate, union representative on the works council**).

They are all protected by a special status to enable them to perform their function as representatives. The elements of this status include a rule prohibiting their dismissal without prior administrative authorization (see **Labour Inspectorate**).

678. **REPRÉSENTANT SYNDICAL — UNION REPRESENTATIVE ON THE WORKS COUNCIL**: Additional **trade union delegate**, who sits on the **works council** in a consultative capacity. In enterprises with fewer than 300 employees, the same employee performs both functions.

679. **REPRÉSENTATION DU PERSONNEL — EMPLOYEE REPRESENTATION**: Action whereby a person, invested with due legal authority, voices the interests of an enterprise's employees. By extension, all institutions serving this function (see **trade union delegate, union representative on the works council, workforce delegate, workplace health and safety committee, works council**).

680. **REPRÉSENTATIVITÉ — REPRESENTATIVENESS**: Sociological quality of an agent which entitles them to be identified with a group and justifies their fitness to express the group's aspirations accurately. The agent may, consequently, claim eligibility to undertake representation of the group. Representation and representativeness are, therefore, closely interrelated.

With the advent of the legal requirement for a trade union to possess representative status, first introduced in France in 1936 as a criterion of the capacity to conclude collective agreements that may be extended (see **extension of collective agreements**) and subsequently widened to include large areas of union activity, representativeness has become not so much a sociological quality as a legal capacity. It now constitutes a trade union's legal capacity to represent the interests of a particular **occupation** in dealings with the public authorities and the employers. The concept of a group and its agent has been supplanted by formal recognition of a representative by third parties.

The legal concept of union representativeness implies a process of selection within the trade union movement; only certain unions that meet certain criteria are deemed capable of representation. This leaves the question of defining the logic on which this selection is based. The weight of legal doctrine in France has been towards basing it on a union's authenticity as an established counterweight to the employers, which means that priority is given to tradition and a strongly established presence. A different logic might have given priority to recognition of the representative by the social group itself.

The legal system governing representativeness adopts standard solutions applicable to all the circumstances in which representative status is a requirement (negotiation and conclusion of a collective agreement, formation of a union branch within the enterprise, workplace elections, organization of strikes in the public services and, sometimes, representativeness before the courts). It establishes two routes for attributing representative status: a representativeness which, if contested, can be proven principally on the basis of historical criteria (independence from employers, length of existence, experience, patriotic attitude during the Occupation) and secondarily on the basis of criteria concerning membership numbers and electoral support; and a legal presumption of representativeness by reason of a union's affiliation to one of the five **trade union confederations**. This latter method of attributing representative status on the basis of affiliation established the supremacy of the five confederations and, at the same time, the structural division of French trade unionism. It may be judged that this division produced a fragmentation of representation which, in turn, contributed to the weakness of the trade union movement and its integration into the political system.

681. RÉPRESSION DES COMPORTEMENTS ANTI-SYNDICAUX — REPRESSION OF ANTI-UNION BEHAVIOUR: See **interference**.

682. RÉPRESSION SYNDICALE — UNION REPRESSION:
Action directed at preventing or restricting the presence and activity of trade unions, in particular within the enterprise. The expression is often used to emphasize that the "fact of trade unionism" is far from being always accepted in enterprises, even though French law recognizes the right to unrestricted exercise of the right to organize (see **trade union freedom**) within the enterprise.

683. RÉPRIMANDE — REPRIMAND: Old-fashioned term denoting a disciplinary sanction of a purely moral nature. Nowadays, the synonym "blâme" or the term "avertissement" (**warning**) are used in preference.

684. RÉQUISITION — REQUISITION/CONSCRIPTION FOR PUBLIC SERVICES: Order whereby, in the interests of ensuring that the "nation's needs" are met, the public authorities require a person, under pain of penalty, to supply a good or a service (see **provision of services**) and to perform the work that he or she intended to interrupt.

This procedure, which is intended in particular to paralyse **strikes**, is subject to regulation. It has not been used against strikers for more than 20 years.

685. RÉSERVE DE PARTICIPATION — PROFIT-SHARING RESERVE: Combined amount of all the sums due to employees as a result of the operation of **profit-sharing** arrangements required by law. This reserve is entered in the employer's accounts. The money is in principle not available for employees' use until a five-year period has elapsed but there are exceptions in specific cases.

686. RÉSILIATION — TERMINATION (BY THE PARTIES): Name given to the ending of an employment contract of indefinite duration either by the decision of one of the parties ("résiliation unilatérale", *i.e.* unilateral termination) or by their mutual agreement ("résiliation conventionnelle", *i.e.* agreed termination). Where it is unilateral, it may refer to **dismissal**, **resignation** or **retirement**.

687. RÉSOLUTION (CONTRAT) — VOIDANCE OF CONTRACT (FOR NON-PERFORMANCE): Cancellation of a contract (or action with this end in view), in principle operating retrospectively, whereby one party is released from their obligations because the other party has failed to perform theirs.

It is relevant in labour law only where an application for voidance is made to the courts ("résolution judiciaire"). If imposed, however, it can never operate retrospectively here because the nature of the employment contract means that performance is successive, with performance by one party following performance by the other. It is prohibited to apply to the courts for voidance of the employment contract of an **employee representative**.

189

688. RÉSOLUTION (VIE SYNDICALE) — RESOLUTION (IN UNION AFFAIRS): Position formally adopted by all members of a union assembled at a meeting or congress empowered to make policy. It fixes the union's policy guidelines and thus dictates subsequent action by its members.

689. RESPONSABILITÉ DE L'EMPLOYEUR — EMPLOYER LIABILITY: Obligation to accept responsibility for damage and to bear its consequences (see **delegation of authority**). Liability may be criminal or civil and, in the latter case, with respect to third parties or to employees.

With respect to third parties an employer, as the principal (see **agent and servant**), is obliged to make good any damage caused by his or her employees. This is the principle of vicarious liability.

With respect to employees, employers are obliged to make good any damage deriving from failure to meet their own obligations as employers. The nature of such liability depends, in principle, on the source of these obligations.

Employers are not, in principle, obliged to pay the wages of striking employees, unless the strike is due to fault on their own part.

690. RESPONSABILITÉ DU SALARIÉ — EMPLOYEE LIABILITY: Under French law, liability of employees with respect to their employer can be invoked only in the event of gross **misconduct**. Otherwise, no compensation for loss or harm may be claimed by the employer from an employee.

This is not so with respect to third parties; here, the employee's liability is governed by the provisions of general law.

691. RESPONSABILITÉ EN CAS DE GRÈVE — LIABILITY IN THE EVENT OF A STRIKE: The idea of immunity for those taking part in a strike does not exist in French law. The general law of civil liability is applicable to them and tends to be strictly enforced. Consequently, a trade union (see **legal personality**) can be held liable only if it is itself responsible for the civil wrongs committed, which in principle is not the case if their perpetrators are the employees or trade union delegates (who are not organs of the union). Also, a relationship of cause and effect must exist between these wrongful acts and the harm or loss complained of by the aggrieved party (employer, third party or non-striking employee). Lastly, the employer may not claim compensation for harm or loss resulting from the strike itself if it is a lawful strike.

692. RESTRUCTURATION — RESTRUCTURING: Change made to an enterprise's structures. It may be legal in nature and result, for example, from a merger (see **company merger**) or transfer of a business as a going concern (see **change of ownership or control**). The principle whereby contracts of employment are transferred to the new employer (see **transfer of undertaking**) is applicable in such cases. Alternatively, restructuring may be purely technical, economic or administrative. In these circumstances the **works council** must, by law, be informed and consulted regarding the proposed restructuring. Its repercussions for individual employees fall within the legal system governing **variation of the contract of employment**.

693. RETENUE (SUR SALAIRE) — DEDUCTION FROM PAY: Part of pay which the employer is entitled to withhold from payment to the employee. A collective agreement may impose such a deduction (employee's contribution to a statutory or collectively agreed social protection scheme). Otherwise, the employer is justified in making a deduction from pay only if the employee has not performed work (performance that is considered defective does not justify a deduction). And the deduction must be strictly proportional to the duration of the employee's absence.

694. RETRAIT — WITHHOLDING OF LABOUR: See **right to withhold labour**.

695. RETRAITE — RETIREMENT: Concept that appeared with the introduction of social insurance providing cover for old age. It designates the situation of workers who have ceased to practise the occupation by virtue of which they have been registered members of a social protection institution and are now in receipt of a pension from that institution.

The retirement age ("âge de la retraite"), also called pensionable age, is the age from which it is possible to receive a full retirement pension without any age-related reduction. For a long time, attainment of the retirement age had no particular effect on the contract of employment (although occasioning the termination of employment in the special case of **established civil servants**): if employees decided to terminate their employment they resigned (see **resignation**), and if retirement originated from a decision by the employer it constituted **dismissal**. Since a Law of 1987, this latter case has been subject to special rules.

Since 1982, the retirement age has been lowered to 60 for employees covered by labour law. This social measure is contributing to the financial difficulties being experienced by pension schemes.

696. RÉUNION SYNDICALE — UNION MEETING: Meeting organized at the initiative of a union branch within the enterprise (see **workplace branch**). French law grants every union branch the right to do so, but the details of its exercise differ according to whether the meeting is open only to the union's members or to all of the enterprise's employees, and there are special provisions concerning the invitation of people from outside.

The **works council** also possesses the right to organize meetings in the context of its management of **company welfare and cultural facilities**.

697. REVENDICATION — CLAIM/DEMAND: Aim of collective action as cited by its originators. The term generally refers to the specific objectives of trade union action.

According to French case law, in order to be protected by law (see **right to strike**) a strike must be in support of employment-related claims. These must be known to the employer at the time when the strike begins.

In addition, the law introduces a distinction between a claim and a grievance ("réclamation"): the powers conferred by law on **worforce delegates** relate only to presenting grievances, which are interpreted as demands aimed at securing compliance with the law (deriving from statutes, collective agreements, custom, individual contracts of employment, etc.), and not as demands for a change to the law. This distinction is the target of much criticism and difficult to apply.

698. REVENU MINIMUM — MINIMUM INCOME: General term covering both the level of pay guaranteed to an employee by law or collective agreement (see **minimum wage**) and the level of resources which may be claimed by any person either involuntarily deprived of work ("allocation de garantie de ressources", *i.e.* income guarantee allowance) or without employment ("revenu minimum d'insertion", *i.e.* minimum work programme income). A major innovation in 1988 was the introduction of a minimum income level guaranteed to all persons aged 25 or over residing in France who do not possess the necessary means to maintain themselves and their family, provided that they participate in a state-funded scheme to improve their labour market prospects (see **absorption into employment**).

699. RÉVISION (CONTRAT) — REVISION (OF THE CONTRACT OF EMPLOYMENT): See **variation of the contract of employment**.

700. RÉVISION (CONVENTION COLLECTIVE) — REVISION (OF COLLECTIVE AGREEMENTS): Process for adjusting a collective agreement to economic or technological change or to the results of bargaining at a higher level. If it leads to an agreement, it constitutes a collectively agreed change to collectively agreed rules. The relevant procedure and conditions may be stated in the collective agreement itself, since the law is not specific on the matter.

The agreement which is the outcome of revision is often called an "avenant" (see **amendment**). According to most recent court decisions, it replaces the provisions it changes only if it has been signed by all the trade union organizations which were signatories to the original agreement.

701. RISQUE DE L'ENTREPRISE — ENTREPRENEURIAL RISK: Responsibility for business risks is undoubtedly the central issue of labour law. The employer assumes these risks and the employee bears no responsibility for them with respect to the employer. The absolute nature of this formula, which some see as a principle of public policy, does not tally with positive law. It is, however, the reasoning underlying the fact that the enterprise's economic difficulties can never constitute an instance of *force majeure* and that **employee liability** is possible only in the event of gross misconduct by employees themselves.

702. RISQUE PROFESSIONNEL — OCCUPATIONAL RISK/OCCUPATIONAL HAZARD: Term used in two senses:
1. Concept underlying the existence of certain obligations to make recompense for harm or loss even when no fault can be attributed to the person bound by them.
2. Event to which workers are exposed and which justifies the provision of social insurance (see **social insurance, social security**).

703. ROBOTIQUE (INDUSTRIEL) — INDUSTRIAL ROBOTICS: An industrial robot is a technological device capable of performing a variety of physical tasks.

The field of robotics covers the design, construction and use of robots.

704. ROTATION — LABOUR TURNOVER: Rate of replacement of personnel. Replacement in this sense refers to incoming employees from the external labour market. It must thus be distinguished from internal mobility (see **labour mobility**).

193

705. **ROULEMENT — ROTATION**: Term applied both to the organization of work and to the manner in which rest days are allotted. Hence, "travail par roulement" is a system under which the same job is successively performed by several employees in rotation, *i.e.* shiftwork. As a method of allotting the **weekly rest day** in rotation, "repos par roulement" is confined to certain sectors where it is used either for technical reasons (chemicals industry, refining industry) or for social reasons (activities performed on Sundays, such as hotels, cafés and restaurants).

706. **RUPTURE (CONTRAT) — TERMINATION OF THE CONTRACT OF EMPLOYMENT**: Generic term for the legal dissolving of the contract of employment. It may be effected by the parties themselves (*cf.* **résiliation**), *i.e.* by the unilateral decision of one party (see **resignation, dismissal**), except in the case of a **fixed-term contract**, or by their mutual agreement; by way of a court judgment pronouncing the contract to be null and void because of serious misconduct (see **voidance of contract**); or as a result of certain events that automatically end the contract (see *force majeure*).

707. **RUPTURE (NÉGOCIATION COLLECTIVE) — BREAKING-OFF OF NEGOTIATIONS**: Action of halting discussions whose purpose was to conclude a collective agreement. The situation is regulated in outline by the law for cases where collective bargaining is a legal obligation (see **duty to bargain**); in principle, negotiations may not be broken off until the timetable set at the start has expired, and the failure to reach an agreement must be recorded in a **minute of failure to agree**.

708. **RYTHME — WORK RATE**: Rate or speed at which an action is performed. An essential element in the analysis of **working conditions** and in ergonomic studies (see **ergonomics**). The term "cadence" (pace of work) is used when the movements required of the worker are regular and repetitive.

S

709. SABOTAGE — SABOTAGE: Wilful act intended to hinder the functioning of an enterprise, department or machine. It does not, as such, constitute a criminal offence in France, but may incur penalties on other grounds.

710. SAGE — SPECIALIST: See **official report**.

711. SAISIE — SEIZURE/ATTACHMENT:
1. Placing an asset under the authority of the courts to prevent its holder from using it for certain purposes. Certain assets are immune from seizure or attachment (see **immunity from seizure/immunity from attachment**).
2. Remedy at law available to creditors with respect to the assets of their debtor in order to preserve their entitlement or secure payment.

(In the case of pay, such procedures are referred to specifically in English as "attachment of earnings".)

712. SALAIRE — PAY/WAGE: In its most general sense, remuneration received by employees in return for their work performance.
1. The legal concept is a complex one, owing to the network of rules in which pay features. For instance, pay serves as the basis for calculating social security contributions; for this purpose all components of remuneration are taken into account, and the arrangements under which they are paid are of little importance. Also, guarantees concerning the payment of wages or pay have been instituted (see **wage guarantee insurance, immunity from seizure/immunity from attachment, preferential claim**) and have in part been extended to cover entitlements payable on termination of the employment contract (see **compensation for dismissal, compensation in lieu of notice**).

   In the contract of employment the concept is narrower, since it serves to determine the sum owed to the employee. Here, the systems and arrangements under which remuneration is paid assume considerable importance. There is, of course, no problem in the case of time-based pay ("salaire au temps"), which is due because the employee has worked the corresponding number of hours. But in the case of the various bonuses and special payments (see **bonus**) a distinction must be made: they must be paid by the employer in accordance with the conditions laid down in the contract of employment and, where no such contractual stipulation exists, they are due if **custom** imposes their continuance. This means that in certain circumstances there is scope for discretionary bonuses.

2. The amount of pay is in principle fixed by contract, but there are in fact a number of rules relating to this. Some set minimum levels, such as the rules on the national **minimum wage** and the rules deriving from collective agreements for particular industries (see **industry-wide agreement**). Others establish obligations to negotiate levels of actual pay (see **duty to bargain**). And others, lastly, restrict contractual freedom by laying down principles of non-discrimination or equality, as in the case of the principle of equal pay for men and women (see **equality between men and women**).

713. **SALAIRE DE SUBSTITUTION — "SUBSTITUTE PAY":** Various mechanisms impose an obligation on employers or social protection institutions to pay employees who are compelled to break off work an allowance such that their income is maintained.

The terms "salaire d'inactivité" (pay while not working), "garantie de ressources" (income guarantee) and "revenu de remplacement" (replacement income) are also used. See **early retirement, illness, monthly pay system, partial unemployment, sick leave, unemployment.**

714. **SALAIRE DIRECT ET INDIRECT — DIRECT AND INDIRECT PAY**: Direct pay refers to any form of remuneration paid by the employer because work has been performed. Indirect pay refers to any benefit paid to employees who are obliged to break off work, for income guarantee purposes. The term "salaire d'inactivité" (pay while not working) is also used.

715. **SALAIRE GARANTI — MINIMUM WAGE (GUARANTEED)**: Freedom in fixing pay is a fundamental principle of French labour law. It is, however, subject to limits and restraints.

The institution of a government-fixed minimum wage applicable to all employees dates back to 1950. The present statutory national minimum wage, which was introduced in 1970 ("salaire minimum interprofessionnel de croissance" or SMIC), is intended to guarantee the lowest-paid workers their purchasing power and a share in the nation's economic growth. To this end, the SMIC is not only pegged to one of the consumer price indices but may also, through the application of a review procedure, be raised by decree of the Council of Ministers.

The SMIC is an hourly rate of pay but since 1972 it has been complemented, for all employees whose working hours are at least equal to the statutory working week (39 hours), by a minimum monthly pay level.

In addition, it is the traditional role of collective agreements at industry level to fix minimum rates of pay for each occupational category.

716. **SALAIRE MONÉTAIRE OU EN NATURE — PAY IN MONEY OR IN KIND**: Remuneration in the form of the supply of goods or access to the use of property (housing, food, heating, clothing) is still common in certain sectors (see **payments in kind**). It is even permissible for remuneration to be made up entirely of payments in kind, provided that the value is not lower than the national minimum wage; *au pair* work is one such example.

717. **SALARIÉ — EMPLOYEE**: Synonym of "travailleur subordonné" (see **contract of employment**). The concept is therefore contrasted with that of the "travailleur indépendant" (self-employed person).

718. **SANCTION — SANCTION/PENALTY/REMEDY**: Term with three different meanings:
    1. In the narrowest sense, punishment imposed by an authority on a person who contravenes a rule. It may be penal, administrative or disciplinary (see **disciplinary sanction**).
    2. In a more comprehensive sense, any measure justified by the breach of an obligation.
    3. In its broadest sense, any method or procedure intended to enforce observance of a right or performance of an obligation. In this sense, legal proceedings are a remedy aimed at securing such enforcement.

719. **SANCTION CIVILE — CIVIL SANCTION**: Term reserved for measures justified by the breach of an obligation (see **sanction**, in its second sense) which derive from the techniques of the law of obligations or civil procedure. Examples include compensation of the injured party or nullity of a legal transaction.

720. **SANCTION DISCIPLINAIRE — DISCIPLINARY SANCTION**: Any action, other than verbal comment, which is taken by the employer consequent to misconduct on the part of the employee and which may or may not directly affect the employee's presence in the enterprise, job, career path or pay.
    It is, therefore, to be distinguished from the exercise of a contractual right or any action taken by the employer in the context of the **employer's managerial authority**.
    French law establishes a system governing disciplinary sanctions. A procedure must be followed before one may be imposed. Fines and discriminatory sanctions (see **discrimination**)

are prohibited. A permanent amnesty is provided for: the employer may not exercise a sanction which has been imposed for more than three years. The courts (see **Industrial Tribunal**) must, if applied to on the matter, check whether a sanction is proportionate to the degree of seriousness of the misconduct concerned.

This development of a set of rules regulating disciplinary sanctions moderates the employer's unilateral authority. In some enterprises joint committees have been set up; as a rule, their powers do not challenge ultimate managerial authority.

721. **SANCTION PÉNALE — PENAL SANCTION**: Punishment imposed by a criminal court on the perpetrator of an **offence**. Contrasted, traditionally, with the issue of a caution, which constitutes a measure imposed to prevent future offences ("mesure de sécurité").

722. **SCRUTIN — POLL/VOTING**: All the acts involved in an election (see **workplace elections**). The term is sometimes interpreted in the narrower sense of the process of voting: "scrutin public" (open vote), "scrutin majoritaire" (voting by absolute majority), "scrutin de liste" (voting for several members from a list).

723. **SECRÉTAIRE (COMITÉ D'ENTREPRISE) — SECRETARY OF THE WORKS COUNCIL**: Under French law, a secretary must be elected from among the employee members of the **works council** elected by the workforce. Although the secretary does not chair the council, he or she arranges the dates of meetings and the agenda in conjunction with the chairperson, and also takes the minutes of meetings and represents the council before the courts.

The works council is chaired either by the head of the enterprise or by his or her representative.

724. **SECTEUR ÉCONOMIQUE — ECONOMIC SECTOR**: Subdivision of economic activity. The classification criterion may be its position in the economic process (production, distribution, consumption), the end use of the goods or services produced, or their nature. As a bargaining level, the economic sector is virtually synonymous with the industry or branch (see **branch of economic activity**).

725. **SECTEUR PUBLIC — PUBLIC SECTOR**: All the assets, activities and enterprises owned and controlled by the public authorities. The connection between the public sector and a

public service is a complex one. A public sector enterprise is not necessarily responsible for administering a public service. This applies to a number of enterprises (insurance companies, banks, etc.) that were nationalized in 1982 (see **nationalization**). Conversely, however, an enterprise may be responsible for administering a public service without being part of the public sector. This is the case when its capital is not owned by the State or any other public authority.

726. **SECTION SYNDICALE — WORKPLACE BRANCH**: Institutionalized form of trade union presence in the enterprise, as provided for by a major Law of December 27, 1968 which ensured the unions a formal footing in the workplace for the first time. Since the law views it merely as an offshoot of the union, the workplace branch does not possess legal personality.

There are no formalities governing the creation of a workplace branch, but only a representative union (see **representativeness**) may create one and, hence, acquire access to the facilities accompanying it: a **union room**, the right to organize meetings within the enterprise (see **union meeting**), the right to invite individuals from outside to attend meetings (see **expert**), the right to display notices and distribute pamphlets and publications (see **display of notices, union communications**), and the right to time off (see **time-off rights**) to prepare for bargaining at enterprise level.

727. **SÉCURITÉ DU TRAVAIL — SAFETY AT WORK**: Preventive protection of employees against the risks of **accidents at work** and **occupational illnesses**. The past 20 years have seen French regulations develop in three main directions: a broadening of the range of factors taken into account as being likely to affect employees' physical and mental health (see **ergonomics, working conditions**); the gradual integration of safety requirements into the design of materials, machines and methods of operation; and the provision of channels for action by employee representatives within the enterprise (see **workplace health and safety committee**) and by employees themselves (see **right to notify, right to withhold labour**).

728. **SÉCURITÉ SOCIALE — SOCIAL SECURITY**: Set of mechanisms and institutions whose purpose is, on the basis of philosophies of shared risk (''solidarités'') of varying extent, to guarantee individuals protection against the consequences of various events classed as risks (see **occupational risk/occupational hazard**).

The outlines of the French system were laid down in 1945-46, combining the basic option of the **social insurance** approach with the philosophy of solidarity or shared risk within particular occupations. Since then, the system has developed and integrated various elements inspired by the idea of a solidarity or shared risk at national level.

729. **SEGMENTATION — SEGMENTATION (OF THE LABOUR MARKET)**: As a concept underlying labour market analyses based on an approach used by American economists, segmentation is a representation of the labour market in a number of different segments. The simplest formula, sometimes referred to as dualism, implies a "primary" segment grouping together the best-paid and most secure jobs and the employees with the highest status, and a "secondary" segment. The contribution made by such analyses lies in demonstrating the dispersion of labour demand and the active role played by enterprises in creating this.

730. **SEMAINE COMPRIMÉE — COMPRESSED WORKING WEEK**: Refers to the form of organization of the working time of employees who work at weekends to replace regular employees (see **relief (weekend) shift**).

731. **SENTENCE — AWARD**: Name traditionally given to certain formal rulings, in particular the decision of an arbitrator or arbitration tribunal.

732. **SÉQUESTRATION — FALSE IMPRISONMENT**: Offence consisting in the illegal deprivation of an individual's freedom of movement. Strikers who occupy the workplace (see **sit-in**) and exert pressure on the enterprise's managers are sometimes accused of this offence.

733. **SERVICE FAIT — SERVICE RENDERED**: Under the "service rendered" rule, applicable in all administrative authorities, establishments and enterprises that are publicly accountable (which is not so in the case of enterprises responsible for administering an industrial or commercial public service, see **public service**), public money may be paid over to creditors only when the latter have actually rendered their due performance. As a consequence, if an administrative authority or the management of a public establishment so requests, **established civil servants** or **public employees** are obliged to prove that they have worked during a strike if they wish to be paid.

734. **SERVICE MINIMUM — MINIMUM SERVICE**: Essential level of activity which, in the event of a strike, must be maintained by administrative authorities and enterprises responsible for administering a public service and is, therefore, imposed on established civil servants, public employees and other employees (see **public service**). It must be expressly specified by law, and outside the public administration exists in only rare instances (telecommunications, air traffic control, etc.).

735. **SERVICE NATIONAL — NATIONAL SERVICE**: All the obligations incumbent on male citizens aged 18-50 in order to meet the needs of the armed forces for protecting the civilian population or for co-operating with other countries. For the former purpose, there is a 12-month period of compulsory military service.

736. **SERVICE PUBLIC — PUBLIC SERVICE**: Term which designates both an activity directed at satisfying a need of the general community and the administrative body responsible for managing that activity. The term figures centrally in the creation, special principles and delimitation of administrative law. Of the two elements, the first (*i.e.* as applying to the activity pursued) has become preponderant. The fact of being a public service is not determined by the nature of the activity but derives from its recognition as such by the public authorities. There are administrative public services, and there are industrial and commercial public services which are exactly the same as private sector enterprises as regards their activities, organization and operation but differ from them purely in being labelled as public services. The establishments or enterprises which administer these services are, therefore, regulated partly by the rules of private law (for instance, personnel who do not participate directly in performing the public service in question are employed under a contract of employment) and partly by the rules of public law.

Special regulations on **strikes** apply in the public services, restricting the right to initiate strike action to the representative unions, requiring them to give advance notice of the intention to strike, and prohibiting the use of **rotating strikes**.

737. **SEUIL — THRESHOLD**: The stipulation of **workforce thresholds** is a technique whereby employees' rights, the facilities granted to the unions and institutions of employee representation and, more generally, the employer's obligations are adjusted according to the size of the collective labour unit, measured in terms of the number of employees (normally employed). This technique is one of the main factors in the differentiated

application of provisions under French labour law. Several hundred instances of its use are to be found in the **Labour Code**.

738. **SIDA — AIDS**: Acronym signifying acquired immune deficiency syndrome, *i.e.* infection by the human immune deficiency virus, HIV. The development of the disease has not prompted any special regulations under French labour law, other than the prohibition, since a Law of 1990, of all discrimination based on state of health. An intensive information campaign has, however, made it possible to prevent enterprises from imposing compulsory tests at the time of **recruitment** and to convince people of the effectiveness of existing regulations, provided they are scrupulously observed. The lack of adequate regulatory provisions is more apparent in social security law.

739. **SMIC**: Abbreviation for "salaire minimum interprofessionnel de croissance" (see **minimum wage**).

740. **SOCIOLOGIE DU TRAVAIL — SOCIOLOGY OF WORK**: Field of study concerned with the application of sociological approach(es) to productive activity and work. In contemporary France it encompasses numerous elements, some of them in continuation of the founding studies on the characterization and organization of work, and others which have moved towards the analysis of organizations, the composition of the collective actors, and the rules or principles and forms of co-ordination of actions.

741. **SOLIDARITÉ — SOLIDARITY**: Term used in several contexts:
   1. State of mutual dependence and obligation of mutual assistance between the members of a group, including the nation. The French Constitution proclaims a principle of solidarity in the face of national disasters.
   2. Support given to an individual or collective action, particularly in the form of a strike. The French courts accept its lawfulness when there is a commonality of interests between the original protagonist(s) and the employees expressing solidarity by striking in sympathy ("grève de solidarité").
   3. Name given to a generation, now past, of government aid schemes for enterprises which undertook to reduce general working hours or organize **early retirement** for certain employees and, concomitantly, to hire new employees (see **employment support**). The agreements concluded to this effect between the Government and these enterprises were called "contrats de solidarité" to emphasize their objective: in a period of high unemployment (1982-85), this was to give

general encouragement to work sharing, *i.e.* to redistribute the available jobs (see **job creation agreement**). In the case of such measures, the conception of solidarity is as a philosophy of shared sacrifices.

4. The term also refers to a special relationship between several creditors of the same debtor ("solidarité active") or between several debtors of the same creditor ("solidarité passive"), *i.e.* joint and several liability.

742. SOUS-ENTREPRISE — SUBCONTRACT (EXTERNAL): Secondary agreement, concluded by a party to a main agreement that makes them responsible for performing a task or supplying a service (see **provision of services**), whereby they contract out to a secondary contracting party ("sous-entrepreneur") responsibility for all or part of the performance of the main agreement. This contractual practice is dangerous for employees when the secondary entrepreneur does not observe the general obligations incumbent on any enterprise. The law has imposed, under certain conditions, a special responsibility on the commissioning party. (It is difficult to differentiate clearly in English between this form of contracting out and subcontracting as represented by **"sous-traitance"**.)

743. SOUS-TRAITANCE — SUBCONTRACT (INTERNAL): Contract whereby an entrepreneur (called the principal) entrusts, still under his or her own responsibility, to a person called the subcontractor ("sous-traitant"), all or part of the production of goods or supply of services required for his or her business activity. This may, in some certain cases, constitute unlawful **hiring-out of labour** or fall within the scope of the special rules on external subcontracting (see **subcontract (external)**).

744. STABILITÉ DE L'EMPLOI — JOB SECURITY: Tendency for the contract of employment to continue and employment to be maintained. Contrasted with **precariousness** of employment.

745. STAGE — TRAINING SCHEME/PERIOD OF TRAINING: Term which refers sometimes to a period of probation compulsory for persons preparing to enter a profession (*e.g.* a trainee lawyer); sometimes to a period of practical experience forming part of a course of education (*e.g.* students receiving training in an enterprise); and sometimes to a period of training organized for a worker who is either currently under a contract of employment or seeking employment.

It is this last meaning which has nowadays become the most widely used, since numerous schemes bearing this name have been set up to encourage enterprises to accept young job-seekers. Under an agreement between an enterprise and the Government, a young person is assigned production tasks, sometimes accompanied by job training given within the enterprise or in a specialized establishment. The pay under such a scheme, which is modest, is paid by the Government.

This formula has been very widely taken up but has provoked criticism, mainly because it excludes the "stagiaires" (**trainees**) from all or most of the protection of labour law and does not guarantee a real form of training. The latest generation of such schemes, called "stages d'initiation à la vie professionnelle" or SIVP (job-start schemes), do not in fact claim to be providing training. They are seen as an element of a policy not to provide training but to assist entry into active employment (see **absorption into employment**).

746. **STAGIAIRE — TRAINEE**: Worker undergoing training in the form of a "stage" (see **training scheme/period of training**). The legal status of the trainee is ill-defined.

The expansion of training within the enterprise which involves "stages", and of training schemes for young job-seekers which also bear this name, has prompted the inclusion in the Labour Code of outline regulations covering "stagiaires" undergoing further vocational training.

747. **STATUT — SERVICE REGULATIONS/STANDING RULES**: Coherent set of rules defining the position of a category of persons or the functioning of an institution. **Established civil servants** are covered by such special regulations, as are the employees of certain large enterprises, particularly in the public sector.

748. **STATUT (DES SYNDICATS) — UNION RULES**: All the standing rules of a trade union, or the document in which they are recorded. In principle, they lay down the obligations incumbent on members.

749. **STRUCTURE CONVENTIONNELLE — BARGAINING STRUCTURE**: Term sometimes used to refer to the characteristic elements of the collective bargaining system and the links between them. These elements usually include the **bargaining levels**, the issues covered (bargaining scope) and the bargaining agents.

750. **STRUCTURE DES SALAIRES — PAY/WAGE STRUCTURE**: The way in which total remuneration is made

up of a number of components whose relative weight and dynamic importance may be measured. For instance, the proportion of pay which is linked to working time is distinguished from that linked to performance. In this second proportion, further distinctions are made between components based respectively on individual performance, the collective performance of a work unit, and the overall results of the enterprise. Thus, the study of pay structure makes it possible to evaluate the role of **individualization** and the growing importance of pay based on productivity and company performance (see **pay related to company performance**).

751. **STRUCTURE SYNDICALE — UNION STRUCTURE**: Term used to denote the organizational basis of the form of worker collectivity or solidarity on which a trade union is built. It is said, for example, that French trade unionism has opted for an industry-based structure rather than an occupation-based structure.

752. **SUBORDINATION — "SUBORDINATION"**: Main distinguishing feature of the **contract of employment** which also determines compulsory membership of the general social security scheme (see **registered membership**).

753. **SUJETS COLLECTIFS — SOCIAL ACTORS**: Term used synonymously with **acteurs sociaux**.

754. **SUSPENSION (CONTRAT) — SUSPENSION OF THE CONTRACT OF EMPLOYMENT**: Interruption of performance of the contract of employment (or, more accurately, of its non-continuous obligations, *i.e.* the obligation to work and the obligation to pay wages) without any effect on its existence. The use of this procedure, which has shown a striking increase over the past 50 years, allows the exercise of certain rights (see **right to strike, educational leave**) and ensures the continuity of the contract (see **job security**) when the impossibility of performance is temporary (see **sick leave, maternity leave, partial unemployment**).

755. **SYNDICALISATION — UNIONIZATION**: The fact of belonging to a union. Measurements are made of union density ("taux de syndicalisation"), *i.e.* the proportion of employees who are members of a union. (Owing to the meaning of "syndicat", these same terms may also apply to employers and their organizations.)

Although it is difficult to arrive at accurate figures because of traditions of secrecy and the impossibility of defining actual membership of trade unions, there is general agreement that union density is declining in France: the estimated figure is 8-15 per cent. It is true that, other than during exceptional periods, membership has never been high, that the payment of union dues is not a reliable indicator of true commitment, that in workplace elections the unions demonstrate their ability to win votes, and that in France union membership does not bring any particular advantages. Nevertheless, the low level of union membership is a matter of great concern to union leaders, the public authorities and the heads of certain enterprises and employers' organizations.

756. SYNDICAT — TRADE UNION/COLLECTIVE INDUS-TRIAL ORGANIZATION/ EMPLOYERS' ORGANIZA-TION: As defined in French law, a group of persons practising the same occupation or similar or allied occupations, formed for the purpose of protecting their occupational interests (see **"association professionnelle"**). It acquires legal personality simply by declaring itself a "syndicat".

A special feature of French law is that the "syndicat" has this sense of a collective industrial organization, with no distinction in legal form between the "syndicat ouvrier", to which only employees belong (*i.e.* a trade union), and the "syndicat d'entreprises" or "syndicat patronal", *i.e.* an employers' organization. However, where the freedom to exercise the right to organize collectively ("droit syndical") is recognized within the context of the enterprise, the reference is specifically to trade unions.

French trade unions have complex structures, including both horizontal groupings (see **horizontal union**) and vertical groupings (see **vertical union**). If they possess representative status (see **representativeness**) they have the right to appoint **trade union delegates** within the enterprise and to form **workplace branches** there.

The employers' organizations are often referred to collectively as the **"patronat"**.

757. SYNDICAT AUTONOME — AUTONOMOUS UNION: Union which is not affiliated to any of the confederations recognized as representative at national level (see **trade union confederation, representativeness**).

758. SYNDICAT D'ENTREPRISE — COMPANY UNION: Trade union representing, and confining its recruitment to, the employees of a particular enterprise or group of companies.

This form of organization is common when the enterprise is a large one.

759. SYNDICAT D'ENTREPRISES — EMPLOYERS' ORGANIZATION: Synonym of **organisation d'employeurs**.

760. SYNDICAT HORIZONTAL — HORIZONTAL UNION: Union constituted on a geographical and multi-industry basis. This structure is found in all the major French unions, in the form of **area unions** at département level and sometimes local (town) or regional level.

761. SYNDICAT INDÉPENDANT — INDEPENDENT UNION: Term used to refer to a tendency in French trade unionism which has its origin in a rejection of the centralized structures of the union movement and vigorous denunciation of the ideology and confrontational practices of the confederated unions (see **trade union confederation**). The history of its most active supporters and leaders shows this tendency to be present in paramilitary groups and the private police forces of enterprises. (The term must not be confused with **syndicat autonome**, which is simply a non-confederated union.)

762. SYNDICAT NATIONAL — NATIONAL UNION: Union constituted on a national basis.

763. SYNDICAT RÉGIONAL — REGIONAL UNION: Union constituted on a regional basis. In the confederated union movement (see **trade union confederation**) it takes the form of the "union régionale" (**area union** at regional level), a structure which is important in some confederations but non-existent or weak in others.

764. SYNDICAT TERRITORIAL — TERRITORIAL UNION: See **horizontal union**.

765. SYNDICAT VERTICAL — VERTICAL UNION: Union constituted on the basis of form of activity, such as the **federations** grouping unions by industry ("fédérations d'industrie") or by occupation ("fédérations de métiers").

T

766. **TARIF — TARIFF/COLLECTIVELY AGREED WAGE**: Term formerly used to refer to the wage fixed by collective agreement.

Nowadays, it refers to the price of a product or service as set out in a list, or to the list itself.

767. **TAUX DE SYNDICALISATION — UNION DENSITY**: See **unionization**.

768. **TAXE — LEVY/TAX**: Term which designates either a fiscal deduction intended for financing a particular public service or, in most cases, a levy. Hence, in this latter sense, the "taxe d'apprentissage" (apprenticeship tax) and "taxe de formation professionnelle" (vocational training tax) levied on French employers.

769. **TAYLORISME — TAYLORISM**: See **work organization**.

770. **TECHNOLOGIE — TECHNOLOGY**: Term frequently used to refer to a technique, machine or process, whereas what it signifies, rather, is the knowledge required to use them. A technological innovation is a new way of conceiving the production process and the organization of work. Technology transfer is the transfer of know-how. Because it represents changes in production methods and work organization, technological change justifies, in the view of many, a new collective bargaining model. Bargaining must bear on fundamental choices and not merely on the consequences of choices; it must, therefore, take place upstream of decision-making and supervision rather than of substantive rules.

In fact, French law encourages the emergence of such a model, by stipulating that the **works council** must be consulted before new technologies are introduced, giving the council the opportunity to enlist the help of technology experts and obliging management to draw up a programme of updating training for the workforce. Various collective agreements at multi-industry, industry and enterprise level attempt to give substance to this bargaining model.

771. **TÉLÉTRAVAIL — TELEWORK**: Term coined in recent years to designate a form of remote working or **homeworking** using telecommunications and information technology techniques. Although expected to develop rapidly, it has taken hold to only a limited extent. The questions which it raises flow from these two characteristic features: as a form of remote working, it means

that methods of work supervision and employee guarantees have to be reviewed; and as a form of VDU work, it necessitates health protection measures.

772. **TEMPORAIRE — TEMPORARY PUBLIC EMPLOYEE**: Synonym of **vacataire**.

773. **TERME — EXPIRY DATE**: Date on which a fixed-term contract of employment ends. In principle, it must be fixed precisely, in advance. Some scope for flexibility is, however, permitted when there is a specific task to becompleted.

774. **TOLÉRANCE — TOLERANCE**: Acceptance of conduct by employers even though they could forbid it or require it to be modified. It is deemed not to imply the establishment of a **custom**. In principle, however, the conduct tolerated does not constitute misconduct until such time as the employee has been clearly informed by the employer that it will be tolerated no longer.

775. **TRACT (SYNDICAL) — UNION PAMPHLET**: Document in which a trade union makes its arguments and claims known to employees (or the general public). See **union communications**.

776. **TRAITEMENT (ÉGALITÉ DE) — EQUAL TREATMENT**: Legal treatment specified for certain categories of people (women, workers who are nationals of other EC Member States, etc.). Given that it must be equal to that applied to other categories (men, workers who are French nationals, etc.), the equal treatment rule has little effect on the employer's discretionary prerogatives.

777. **TRANSACTION — SETTLEMENT BY COMPROMISE**: Agreement whereby the parties (employer and employee) arrive at a definitive settlement *inter se* of a legal action which has already started or is about to start, by way of mutual concessions. Under the Civil Code, such a compromise settlement has the same validity as a court judgment. In practice it can be contested only on the grounds of duress or deception; consequently, it is generally the very nature of the agreement which is contested. The courts examine the existence of mutual concessions and, in cases of **dismissal**, recognize a compromise settlement only where dismissal has already been decided.

778. **TRANSFERT D'ENTREPRISE — TRANSFER OF UNDERTAKING**: Transaction which concerns the legal person

209

of the employer but entails, through the operation of the law, the transfer of contracts of employment from the former employer to the new employer.

Nowadays, the French courts define it as any transfer of an economic entity which retains its identity and whose activity is continued or resumed, attaching little importance to the fact that there is no legal tie between successive employers. This definition owes much to the interpretation given by the European Court of Justice to the Directive of February 14, 1977, known as the "Transfer Directive". The rule that contracts of employment must be maintained prohibits **dismissal** on the grounds of the transfer of an undertaking. It does not prohibit the new employer from reorganizing the enterprise and dismissing employees as a result of this. Contracts of employment are continued and the law establishes a relationship of joint and several liability between the two successive employers as regards the payment of wages and entitlements owed by the former employer.

779. **TRANSFERT DE SALARIÉ — CHANGE OF EMPLOYER THROUGH LEGAL TRANSFER**: Expression specifically denoting transfer in the sense of an operation whereby employees are transferred, at their employer's invitation, to another employer. In principle, it requires the agreement of all three parties. Its consequences are regulated by collective agreement and the agreement concluded at the time of transfer, particularly as regards the maintenance of acquired rights based on length of service.

780. **TRAVAIL — WORK/LABOUR/EMPLOYMENT**:
   1. Up to the end of the eighteenth century, a term which essentially designated the effort required to create a piece of work. Its emphasis shifted in the early nineteenth century as work began to be seen as the source of all wealth and happiness.
   2. Nowadays, it designates a human activity performed to achieve a useful purpose and tends to be identified with a gainful **occupation**.
   Sometimes also used specifically to refer to gainful employment as an employee (see **contract of employment**).

781. **TRAVAIL À DISTANCE — REMOTE WORKING**: See **externalization of employment, homeworking**.

782. **TRAVAIL À DOMICILE — HOMEWORKING**: Work performed in or near the worker's home at the behest of a commissioning party, which in French law is treated as equivalent to work under a **contract of employment** when remuneration is calculated on a fixed-rate basis. (May also be referred to in English as "outwork".)

783. **TRAVAIL À TEMPS PARTIEL — PART-TIME WORK**: Part-time work, which is both encouraged and controlled, is defined in French law as work for which the working hours are at least one fifth less than the statutory working week (39 hours) or the collectively agreed working hours. It must, according to the law, constitute a free choice on the part of the employee. Various measures have encouraged the increase in its use, which has in fact been considerable over the past 20 years. Nowadays, it is becoming more widespread in retail and distribution but appears to be on the decline in services such as banking and insurance.

784. **TRAVAIL AUTONOME — SELF-EMPLOYMENT**: Work which is performed for third parties without there being any relationship of "subordination" to them (see **contract of employment**). Also referred to as "travail indépendant".

785. **TRAVAIL CLANDESTIN — CLANDESTINE EMPLOYMENT**: Despite its name, the form of work which as such incurs special restriction under the Labour Code is in fact an entrepreneurial activity (as distinct, therefore, from "travail noir"; see **undeclared employment**). It is deemed to be clandestine on the grounds of failure to comply with the proper formalities which every entrepreneur must complete with respect to the tax authorities, social security institutions and employees (issuing itemized pay statements, keeping personnel records, keeping a paybook).

786. **TRAVAIL DE NUIT — NIGHT WORK**: Night work is still prohibited in France for young people under the age of 18 and for apprentices. The rule has been made more flexible in the case of women. In 1979 the ban was lifted, in particular, for women occupying what are referred to as positions of responsibility. Subsequently, the possibility of collectively agreed exemption was made available (see **derogation agreement**). It is subject to the conclusion of an extended collective agreement (see **extension of collective agreements**) and its detailed organization must be fixed by a company-level agreement (or, in exceptional cases, in accordance with authorization from the Labour Inspectorate). The unions adopt strongly conflicting views on the matter.

787. **TRAVAIL D'INTERÊT GENERAL — COMMUNITY SERVICE**: Penalty (replacing any other form of punishment) which may be imposed on an offender (see **offence**) and which consists in the performance of unpaid work, for a limited period, for the benefit of a public authority, public establishment or

association. Introduced into French law in 1983, this penalty, whose merits are stressed, has been little used by the criminal courts.

788. **TRAVAIL D'UTILITÉ COLLECTIVE — YOUTH EMPLOYMENT SCHEME**: Type of youth training and employment scheme (see **training scheme**), also referred to as TUC, intended to encourage half-time work for young people who are without employment. This formula, which was introduced in 1984, was used very widely before being recently discontinued (see **job creation contract**).

789. **TRAVAIL EN ÉQUIPES SUCCESSIVES — SHIFTWORK**: See **rotation, shifts**.

790. **TRAVAIL EN GROUPE — GROUP WORK/TEAM-BASED WORK**: See **autonomous work group, relief (weekend) shift, shifts**.

791. **TRAVAIL FAMILIAL — WORK PERFORMED WITHIN THE FAMILY**: The compatibility of a **contract of employment** with a matrimonial or parental relationship is nowadays largely accepted. The recognition of spouses and children who work in family business as possessing employee status is even encouraged. Only "entraide" ("helping out" informally) is still deemed not to constitute an employment relationship.

792. **TRAVAIL FÉMININ — FEMALE EMPLOYMENT/ EMPLOYMENT OF WOMEN**: The growth in female employment has been one of the dominant features of recent years. However, closer analysis reveals that this has done little to break up patterns of job segregation (see **equality in employment**).

793. **TRAVAIL INTELLECTUEL — "INTELLECTUAL WORK"/NON-MANUAL WORK**: Term traditionally used to indicate work demanding mental rather than physical activity (see **manual work**).

794. **TRAVAIL INTERMITTENT — INTERMITTENT WORK**: Work in which periods of activity alternate with periods of inactivity. It gives rise either to a succession of **fixed-term contracts** whose lawfulness is sometimes contested, or to a single contract, fixed-term or of indefinite duration, in which provision is made for the intermittent nature of the work.

This latter formula has led to an intervention by the law creating special regulations on intermittent work, which is treated as a form of part-time work organized on an annual basis. The law makes provision for the possibility of organizing an alternation of periods worked and periods not worked within a single contract of indefinite duration, but makes it subject to certain conditions, including the conclusion of a collective agreement.

795. **TRAVAIL MANUEL — MANUAL WORK**: Characteristic traditionally attributed to the activity of an "ouvrier" (see **manual worker**). Contrasted with "intellectual" or non-manual work, which demands mental rather than physical effort.

796. **TRAVAIL NOIR/TRAVAIL AU NOIR — UNDECLARED EMPLOYMENT**: Work performed for a third party in breach of the conditions of declaration laid down by tax and social laws (see **registered membership, itemized pay statement**) in order to ensure that the obligations they institute will be observed. (Also called "moonlighting" in English if it relates to a second job, *i.e.* dual jobholding.)

When such work is performed on a self-employed basis (see **self-employment**), undeclared employment constitutes **clandestine employment**.

797. **TRAVAIL OCCASIONNEL — CASUAL WORK**: Occasional, short-term work which, even if repeated, does not recur at regular intervals. It lends itself to the conclusion of a **fixed-term contract**.

798. **TRAVAIL POSTÉ — SHIFTWORK**: Name often used synonymously with **travail en équipes successives**.

799. **TRAVAIL PRÉCAIRE — PRECARIOUS EMPLOYMENT**: See **precariousness**.

800. **TRAVAIL SAISONNIER — SEASONAL WORK**: Work which has the nature of a regular activity but is subject, over the course of the year, to interruption(s) imposed by the discontinuity of demand for the products or services concerned. It is traditionally covered by a **fixed-term contract** known as a seasonal employment contract. If contracts are repeated for several successive seasons, they may sometimes be deemed to constitute, together, a single contract of indefinite duration.

801. **TRAVAIL SUBORDONNÉ — WORK UNDER AN EMPLOYMENT CONTRACT**: See **contract of employment**.

213

802. TRAVAIL TEMPORAIRE — TEMPORARY-EMPLOYMENT AGENCY WORK: Work performed by employees hired by an employer and placed temporarily at the disposal of another user enterprise. In France this form of work has been formally regulated since 1972. The employer must practise the hiring-out of labour as his or her sole occupation and must hire employees under **fixed-term contracts** covering the period during which they will be assigned to work in the user enterprise. Hence, only temporary-employment agencies are authorized to hire out labour on a profit-making basis (see **hiring-out of labour**).

The use of this form of work has shown remarkable growth. And the enterprises operating as agencies of this kind have endeavoured to forestall criticism by concluding major collective agreements relating, in particular, to the vocational training and trade union freedom of the temporary workers concerned (called "intérimaires").

803. TRAVAILLEUR ÉTRANGER — FOREIGN WORKER: See **alien, immigration**.

804. TRIPARTISME — TRIPARTISM: Structural element of **concerted consultation** when it has a macrosocial dimension and involves the State (in France, the Government), the employers and the unions. It thus constitutes an instrumental manifestation of **neo-corporatism**.

In some instances it is not formally organized; in others it is inherent in the composition of certain institutions (see, for example, **National Employment Agency**) administered jointly by the State, the employers and the unions.

805. TUTELLE — GUARDIANSHIP/SUPERVISION/PROTECTION: In the private sphere, system of protection created by law to guarantee the personal and financial protection of individuals who are incapable of looking after their own interests.

In the administrative sphere, all the controls to which decentralized structures are subject.

In the context of employment relationships and labour relations the term is little used; it designates a form of protection or set of guarantees.

U

806. **UNEDIC**: Abbreviation denoting the National Union for Employment in Industry and Commerce (Union nationale pour l'emploi dans l'industrie et le commerce), which serves as an umbrella organization for all the **ASSEDIC**s. Like them, it is administered on a joint basis (as a consequence of the fact that the unemployment insurance scheme is based on collective agreement, see **unemployment benefit**), and oversees the running of the scheme, by issuing directives, and manages a compensation fund.

807. **UNION — AREA UNION/AREA EMPLOYERS' ORGANIZATION**: A grouping of "syndicats" (which, in France, may be either **trade unions** or **employers' organizations**). The name is reserved for groupings with territorial coverage, which may be of varying extent: local or district level, département level or regional level.

808. **UNITÉ DE PRODUCTION — WORK/PRODUCTION UNIT**: Basic element of the production system. In labour law and industrial relations it is, in principle, the **establishment**. Nowadays, however, there is a tendency to use smaller units such as a workshop, department or group of workers as the context for analysis. The formation of **quality circles** and "groupes d'expression" (see **right of expression**) are examples of this.

809. **UNITÉ ÉCONOMIQUE ET SOCIALE — UNIT OF ECONOMIC AND EMPLOYEE INTEREST**: Subdivision invented by the courts, and given recognized identity by law in 1982, defining eligibility for the establishment of the institutions of employee representation (see **works council, workforce delegate, trade union delegate**) when several separate companies are deemed to constitute a single enterprise. The criteria for recognition vary for different institutions of employee representation but always include unified direction and control, combined or complementary activities and an identifiable collectivity of employee interests.

810. **UNITÉ SYNDICALE — UNION UNITY**: The profound divergences between the major **trade union confederations** preclude any realistic chance of organizational unity in French trade unionism. On the other hand, evidence does exist of unity of action. At confederation level, the most outstanding recent example is the "unity of action" agreement which was concluded in 1966 between CGT and CFDT and broken off in 1977. And numerous forms of alliance are practised between federations,

industrial unions and company unions belonging to different confederations.

811. **URGENCE — EMERGENCY/URGENCY**: In a general sense, pressing circumstances which justify the adoption of juristic acts or forms of conduct that are normally illegal or unwarranted.

In a more technical sense, nature of a situation which justifies temporary measures, ordered by a judge under **procedure in chambers**, without which irreparable harm or loss would ensue.

812. **USAGE — CUSTOM**: Practice followed within one or more industries (see **branch of economic activity**), a locality or an enterprise, which comes to be imposed on the parties to contracts of employment or on management in its relations with the unions or institutions of employee representation. To acquire this compulsory force within an enterprise, the practice must be applied generally, be fixed in nature and be followed persistently.

Custom is, therefore, a source of law. However, its status is not firmly established. There is little likelihood of a custom that prevails at multi-industry or industry level ever being discontinued. But at enterprise level the courts do recognize that, under certain conditions, a custom may cease.

V

813. **VACATAIRE — TEMPORARY PUBLIC EMPLOYEE**: Term used in the public administration which designates any employee who is hired to perform a task for a specified amount of time, and paid on the basis of the task or hours of work performed. Also called a "temporaire". See **public employee**.

814. **VETO — VETO**: Right granted by law to the **works council** to oppose the introduction by the employer of **individualized working hours**. This right enables the works council to block an initiative, but not to modify the employer's proposal.

   The individualization of working hours is the only matter on which French law grants the works council this power.

815. **VIE PRIVÉE — PRIVATE LIFE OF THE EMPLOYEE**: The right to respect for individual privacy may be invoked against employers. This means, in particular, that employers may not allow their decisions to be influenced by an employee's personal or family way of life and must refrain, when using data processing systems, from collecting certain data (see **personal data**).

816. **VIEILLESSE — OLD AGE**: There is no legal definition of old age. Although the medical profession traditionally places the emphasis on physiological deterioration, the law uses various social categories to define the extent and form of protection available to the elderly. The main categories are based on the retirement age (see **retirement**).

817. **VISITE MÉDICALE — MEDICAL EXAMINATION**: Examination of an employee's state of health by a doctor. It is compulsory for the company doctor (see **company medical service**) to carry out such an examination when an employee is being recruited (see **hiring**) or when an employee becomes incapable of continuing to perform his or her job for reasons of health (see **physical unfitness**).

   Most of the collective agreements which first instituted the **monthly pay system** stipulated that, when an employee was absent from work because of illness, the employer was entitled to arrange for a medical examination to be carried out at the employee's home. These provisions, which were intended to discourage **absenteeism**, aroused critical reactions.

818. **VOIE DE FAIT — BLATANTLY UNLAWFUL CONDUCT**: Irregular act which is so overt that it justifies, on application from the aggrieved party, immediate measures ordered by a judge (see **procedure in chambers**) to ensure that the disruption ceases.

819. VOL — THEFT: The dishonest appropriation of property belonging to someone else.

If committed by an employee against the employer, it was at one time held to justify termination of the contract of employment on the grounds of serious or gross **misconduct**. Nowadays, the courts adopt a more moderate attitude and take account of the context, the significance of the deed and the extent of the harm or loss suffered by the enterprise.

820. VOTE — VOTE/VOTING: Term which designates, according to circumstance, the action of an elector taking part in a **poll**, the result of this expression of choice, or the **election** itself.

Voting is a regular feature of life in the labour sphere, since there are numerous elections in which employees are invited to participate, both within and beyond the context of the enterprise (see, for example, **ballot, workplace-level elections**).

TABLES

1. Employment, unemployment and proportion of numbers in employment since the end of the 19th century

2. Economically active population by age group

3. Employment over the age of 55

4. Female employment

5. Labour turnover in 1990 (by sector and size of establishment)

6. Enterprises
   A. Number
   B. Distribution by major sector
   C. Size and structure (enterprises in industry, commerce and services)

7. Union membership

8. Works council elections and union support

9. Union presence in enterprises
   A. Analysis by enterprise
   B. Analysis by union

10. Industrial disputes

TABLE 1

EMPLOYMENT, UNEMPLOYMENT AND PROPORTION
OF NUMBERS IN EMPLOYMENT
SINCE THE END OF THE 19th CENTURY

(in thousands)

Year	Total economically active population	Unemployed	Economically active population in employment	Economically active population in employment as % of total population
1896*	19,490	270	19,220	49.9
1913*	20,100	200	19,900	50.1
1929	20,540	240	20,300	49.0
1938	19,490	730	18,760	44.8
1954	19,494	327	19,167	44.8
1962	19,742	196	19,547	42.0
1968	20,683	436	20,247	40.7
1975	22,043	831	21,212	40.3
1982	23,776	2059	21,717	40.0
1987	24,366	2567	21,799	39.2

* Excluding Alsace-Lorraine

Sources: J.J. Carré, P. Dubois and E. Malinvaud, *La croissance française. Un essai d'analyse économique causale de l'après-guerre*, Paris, Ed. du Seuil 1972 (for 1896-1938 figures); population censuses 1954-1987; employment survey 1987

Table appearing in "Histoire économique de la France au XXème siècle", *Les Cahiers français* No. 255, La Documentation française 1992

221

TABLE 2

ECONOMICALLY ACTIVE POPULATION
BY AGE GROUP
(%)

Age group	Year 1911	1936	1968	1989
15-24	26.3	20.9	20.9	13.3
25-39	31.4	35.6	32.2	43.8
40-54	25.3	25.2	28.3	32.5
55-59	6.3	7.0	8.4	7.2
60-64	5.0	5.3	6.2	2.4
65 and over	6.0	5.9	4.0	0.8

Source: O. Marchand and C. Thelot, *Deux siècles de travail en France*, INSEE, Collection Etudes, 1991

TABLE 3

EMPLOYMENT OVER THE AGE OF 55

Activity rate of the over-55s

Year	Age 55-59	60-64	65 and over
1911	67.1	58.4	35.5
1921	67.6	59.8	36.1
1931	63.5	55.2	31.8
1936	58.8	50.9	28.2
1954	61.4	50.1	22.2
1962	63.3	51.4	17.5
1968	61.6	48.0	12.4
1975	61.6	40.4	7.1
1982	60.3	30.2	3.3
1989	57.4	20.5	2.4

Source: O. Marchand and C. Thelot, *Deux siècles de travail en France,* INSEE, Collection Etudes, 1991

TABLE 4

FEMALE EMPLOYMENT

Activity rate of women by age group

Year	Age* 15-24	25-39	40-54	25-54	55 and over
1911	67.4	46.5	48.4	47.3	34.3
1921	62.7	42.5	45.2	43.8	34.1
1931	60.9	41.5	40.9	41.2	29.8
1936	60.2	41.8	39.5	40.8	27.4
1954	50.6	40.1	45.8	43.1	24.8
1962	47.2	41.5	44.1	42.7	23.2
1968	46.0	44.4	44.8	44.6	20.3
1975	44.0	57.6	50.4	54.0	15.0
1982	41.8	68.0	58.1	63.7	14.8
1989	35.1	74.0	65.9	70.5	13.2

* For 1911-1936, age as at January 1; for 1954-1989, age attained during the year.
Source: O. Marchand and C. Thelot, *Deux siècles de travail en France*, INSEE, Collection Etudes, 1991

Table 5

LABOUR TURNOVER IN 1990

(by sector and size of establishment*)

As % of employees present on January 1	Sector			Size of establishment			Overall total
	Industry	Construction Civil and agricultural engineering	Tertiary	50-199 employees	200-499 employees	500 or more employees	
New entries	22.3	28.0	44.7	41.2	33.1	17.0	32.2
of which							
• fixed-term contracts	15.0	13.1	29.5	27.0	22.6	10.1	21.1
• contracts of indefinite duration	5.5	12.7	12.2	11.5	8.1	5.0	8.8
Fixed-term contracts as proportion of new entries	67.2	46.8	65.8	65.6	68.3	59.8	65.4
Departures	22.9	26.5	43.3	39.9	33.3	17.6	31.8
of which**							
• end of fixed-term contract	11.1	6.6	23.0	19.6	17.9	8.1	15.9
• resignation	4.9	11.0	11.2	11.1	7.4	3.5	8.0
• redundancy	1.5	0.8	0.6	1.1	1.0	1.1	1.1

* Including only establishments with 50 or more employees in the public and private trading sector.

** In addition to the categories indicated, the figures also include other dismissals, transfers from one establishment to another within the same enterprise, retirement and other cases such as death or illness.

Source: *Economie et statistique* No. 249, December 1991 based on surveys by INSEE and the Ministry of Labour

Note: The table is interpreted as follows: employees entering establishments with 50 or more employees in 1990 represented 32.2% of the workforce present on January 1; 21.1% were hired under fixed-term contracts and 8.8% under contracts of indefinite duration. Of the employees present on January 1, 31.8% left their establishment during 1990: 15.9% were at the end of their fixed-term contract, 8% resigned and 1.1% were made redundant.

TABLE 6

ENTERPRISES

A. *Number*

	1987	1991	Distribution in 1991
	(in thousands)		(%)
Enterprises in industry, commerce and services	2028	2187	63
Agricultural enterprises	1059	994	29
Financial enterprises	36	40	1
All enterprises	3123	3221	93
Public bodies	116	116	3
Private bodies	117	133	4
TOTAL	3356	3470	100

Source: INSEE, SIRENE series
Table appearing in "La France des entreprises", special issue of the journal *L'Entreprise*, in collaboration with INSEE

TABLE 6 (continued)

ENTERPRISES

B. *Distribution by major sector*

	1987	1991	Distribution in 1991
	(in thousands)		(%)
Agri-foodstuffs	60	57	3
Manufacturing industry	200	199	9
Construction-Public works	309	328	15
Commerce	537	543	25
Transport	73	85	4
Services	849	975	44
All enterprises in industry, commerce and services	2028	2187	100

Source: INSEE, SIRENE series
Table appearing in "La France des entreprises", special issue of the journal *L'Entreprise*, in collaboration with INSEE

TABLE 6 (continued)

ENTERPRISES

C. Size and structure
(enterprises in industry, commerce and services)

	1987	1991	Distribution in 1991
	(in thousands)		(%)
"Micro" enterprises (0 employees)	972	1078	49
Very small enterprises (1-9 employees)	911	955	44
Small and medium-sized enterprises (10-499 employees)	143	152	7
Large enterprises (500 or more employees)	2	2	—
Enterprises with a single establishment	1878	2046	94
Enterprises with multiple establishments	150	141	6
Enterprises operating in a single region	2007	2165	99
Enterprises operating in multiple regions	21	22	1
All enterprises	2028	2187	100

Source: INSEE, SIRENE series
Table appearing in "La France des entreprises", special issue of the journal *L'Entreprise*, in collaboration with INSEE

TABLE 7

UNION MEMBERSHIP

(estimated number of members, in thousands)

Unions	Years Start of 1950s	Start of 1970s	Start of 1990s
CGT	1500	2000	850
CFTC	400	250	200
CFDT	—	950	500
CGT-FO	400	800	500
CGC	100	250	200
FEN	200	550	300
Total	2600	4800	2550

Source: J.L. Robert, "Le syndicalisme des salariés", in "L'Histoire économique de la France au XXème siècle", *Les Cahiers français* No. 255, La Documentation française 1992

TABLE 8

WORKS COUNCIL ELECTIONS AND UNION SUPPORT*

Analysis of votes recorded by branch of activity (1989+1990 combined)   (%)

Branch of economic activity	Total votes recorded (1989+1990)	Percentage of votes recorded obtained by:						
		CGT 89+90	CFDT 8+90	CFTC 89+90	CGT-FO 89+90	CFE-CGC 89+90	Other unions 89+90	Non-union 89+90
01. Agriculture, fishing	10,977	19.3	20.0	3.2	4.6	5.0	10.8	37.1
02. Agri-foodstuffs	159,126	25.4	20.9	2.1	9.7	5.2	3.8	32.9
03. Energy	28,885	25.1	28.0	2.6	19.9	14.0	3.5	6.8
04. Intermediate goods	444,244	36.4	19.3	3.1	8.0	5.8	3.6	23.7
05. Machinery and equipment	655,630	31.4	21.3	3.7	12.4	8.7	5.7	16.9
06. Household goods	322,954	25.7	15.8	3.1	8.5	4.8	3.5	38.7
07. Construction, Civil and agricultural engineering	158,803	25.6	9.4	1.6	12.3	3.9	3.2	43.9
08. Distributive trades	338,604	13.2	11.4	4.2	14.3	4.4	4.3	48.2
09. Transport, telecommunications	345,419	34.0	21.6	4.5	11.1	2.6	13.8	12.4
10. Market services	416,646	14.2	21.0	3.9	10.8	5.5	4.6	40.0
11. Renting, leasing of real estate	9,078	11.4	17.4	2.9	13.2	4.1	13.7	37.2
12. Insurance	62,497	20.2	31.2	2.3	14.4	8.0	7.3	16.5
13. Financial institutions	189,840	10.7	32.0	7.2	16.9	13.9	13.3	6.1
14. Non-market services	250,545	20.7	30.8	8.9	18.7	3.0	4.9	13.1
Unidentified	60	—	—	—	—	—	—	—
TOTAL	3,393,308	25.0	20.5	4.1	12.0	6.0	6.0	26.5

* The elections take place every two years. Thus, combining two years' results makes it possible to include all enterprises in which elections are held. In 1990, the percentage of employees who voted was 64.90%.
Source: Dossiers statistiques du travail et de l'emploi, No. 77, January 1992

TABLE 9

UNION PRESENCE IN ENTERPRISES

A. Analysis by enterprise

Size of enterprise	1989			1987		
	Number of enterprises	Number of enterprises with trade union delegates	Percentage	Number of enterprises	Number of enterprises with trade union delegates	Percentage
50-99 employees	13,202	4,101	31.1	12,343	4,286	34.7
100-199 employees	6,704	3,638	54.3	6,498	3,699	56.9
200-499 employees	3,765	2,835	75.3	3,728	2,968	79.6
500-999 employees	1,171	1,061	90.6	1,169	1,093	93.5
1000 or more employees	791	759	96.0	791	768	97.1
Total	25,633	12,394	48.4	24,529	12,814	52.2

B. Analysis by union

Union	Year	Number of enterprises where at least 1 union is present	Percentage as related to all enterprises	Percentage as related to enterprises with at least 1 trade union delegate
CGT	1985	8,633	34.4	62.5
	1987	7,842	32.0	61.2
	1989	7,415	28.9	59.8
CFDT	1985	7,132	28.5	51.6
	1987	6,740	27.5	52.6
	1989	6,525	25.5	52.6
CGT-FO	1985	5,206	20.8	37.7
	1987	5,079	20.7	39.6
	1989	4,829	18.8	39.0
CFE-CGC	1985	3,888	15.5	28.1
	1987	3,736	15.2	29.2
	1989	3,454	13.5	27.9
CFTC	1985	2,093	8.4	15.1
	1987	2,130	8.7	16.6
	1989	2,018	7.9	16.3
Other unions	1985	1,654	6.6	12.0
	1987	1,637	6.7	12.8
	1989	1,855	7.2	15.0
All	1985	25,062	55.1	100.0
	1987	24,529	52.2	100.0
	1989	25,633	48.4	100.0

Source: Dossiers statistiques du travail et de l'emploi, No. 68, April 1991, based on a survey of labour inspectors

TABLE 10

INDUSTRIAL DISPUTES*

	Disputes settled			Number of individual days not worked
	Disputes settled	Establishments affected	Number of employees who stopped work	
	units	units	thousands	thousands
1977	3,302	20,287	1,919.9	3,665.9
1978	3,206	12,178	704.8	2,200.4
1979	3,104	22,010	967.2	3,636.6
1980	2,107	4,829	500.8	1,674.3
1981	2,504	3,875	329.0	1,495.6
1982	3,240	4,086	467.9	2,327.2
1983	2,929	3,308	617.2	1,483.6
1984	2,612	3,014	555.0	1,357.0
1985	1,957	7,278	549.1	884.9
1986	1,469	2,681	455.7	1,041.6
1987	1,457	2,857	359.7	969.1
1988	1,898	2,744	403.2	1,242.1
1989	1,781	2,301	298.5	904.2
1990	1,558	1,876	277.8	693.7
1991	1,320	3,292	408.2	665.5

Source: Ministry of Labour (Service des études et de la statistique), *Premières informations* No. 302, October 1992
Table reproduced in *Liaisons sociales*, Document No. 112/92 of November 13, 1992
* These statistics are based on records kept by the labour inspectors. The disputes concerned are in the form of strikes, since the quantity measured is the number of days on which work stops because of strike action.

BIBLIOGRAPHY

SELECTED BIBLIOGRAPHY

1. *Books*

a) There are numerous published works which describe and analyse French labour law. In accordance with a long-established tradition, which is partly due to the abundance of statutory rules and the variety of the topics they cover, these works contain detailed expositions on trade unionism, collective bargaining and disputes. Examples include:

G. Lyon-Caen and J. Pélissier, *Droit du travail [Labour Law]* (16th edn), Dalloz 1992.

J. Rivero and J. Savatier, *Droit du travail [Labour Law]* (12th edn), P.U.F., Coll. Themis 1991.

G. Couturier, *Droit du travail [Labour Law]*, P.U.F., Coll. Droit fondamental: Vol. 1 Les relations individuelles de travail (Individual Employment Relationships), 1990; Vol. 2 Les relations collectives de travail (Collective Labour Relations), 1991.

b) There are also indexes which are updated continuously or re-issued annually. For example:

Répertoire Dalloz de droit du travail [Dalloz Index of Labour Law] (in three volumes), grouped under headings arranged in alphabetical order (Dalloz).

Jurisclasseur de droit du travail [Index-Book of Labour Law], published in sections (Litec).

Lamy-Social [Lamy-Social Law], re-issued annually (Société Lamy).

An employers' organization, the Union des industries métallurgiques et minières or UIMM (Federation of Metal and Mining Industries), publishes a *Manuel de législation sociale [Handbook of Social Legislation]* which is updated regularly (currently in its 18th edition).

c) A major *Treatise on Labour Law* is published under the chief editorship of G.H. Camerlynck (Dalloz); it comprises nine volumes:

Vol. I   *Le contrat de travail [The Contract of Employment]* by G.H. Camerlynck (2nd edn) 1982, updated in 1988 in collaboration with M.A. Moreau-Bourlès.

235

Vol. II   *Le salaire [Pay]* by G. Lyon-Caen (2nd edn), 1991.

Vol. III   *La réglementation du travail et de l'emploi [The regulation of labour and employment]* by J. Blaise (1st edn), 1966.

Vol. IV   *L'entreprise [The Enterprise]* by N. Catala (1st edn), 1980.

Vol. V   *Syndicats et droit syndical [Trade Unions and Trade Union Law]* by J.M. Verdier (2nd edn), in two parts: Part 1 Freedom, structures and activities, 1987; Part 2 The right to unionize within the enterprise, 1984.

Vol. VI   *La grève [The Strike]* by H. Sinay and J.C. Javillier (2nd edn), 1984.

Vol. VII   *Négociations, conventions et accords collectifs [Collective bargaining and collective agreements]* by M. Despax (2nd edn), 1989.

Vol. VIII *Droit international du travail [International Labour Law]* by N. Valticos (2nd edn), 1983.

Vol. IX   *Les juridictions du travail [The Labour Courts System]* by A. Supiot (1st edn), 1987.

d) For a view of French society, labour relations, the role of the State and social policies, the most comprehensive general work is J. Fournier, N. Questiaux and M. Delarue, *Traité du Social [Treatise on Social Matters]* (2nd edn), Sirey.

A good overview of industrial relations and their history is provided by F. Sellier, *La confrontation sociale 1936-1981 [Social Confrontation 1936-1981]*, P.U.F. 1984.

On the subject of trade unionism, the following may usefully be consulted: R. Mouriaux, *Les syndicats dans la société française [The trade unions in French society]*, Presses de la Fondation nationale des sciences politiques 1983; by the same author, *Le syndicalisme face à la crise [Trade Unionism in Crisis]*, La Découverte, Coll. Repères 1986; and P. Rosenvallon, *La question syndicale [The Trade Union Issue]*, Calmann-Lévy 1988.

2. *Labour Codes*

Several publishers, including Dalloz and Litec, publish annual editions of the Labour Code incorporating references to court decisions and studies of legal theory.

Also, an annotated Labour Code is published by Les Editions La Villéguerin.

3. *Periodicals and official publications relevant to labour law and industrial relations*

a) In France, the Ministry responsible for Labour issues numerous publications. These include, notably:

- *Bulletin mensuel des statistiques du travail* (BMST), a monthly bulletin which provides the latest detailed figures on the labour market.

- *Dossiers statistiques du travail et de l'emploi* (DSTE), with ten issues per year, which summarizes information on topics relating to employment and industrial relations.

- *Revue Travail et Emploi,* issued quarterly, which publishes more detailed studies on unemployment, employment policies, employment and working conditions, pay, collective bargaining, etc.

- *Documents Travail-Emploi,* which contains substantial studies on varied topics. One issue per year is devoted to an overall survey of collective bargaining.

b) The principal journal is *Droit Social* (monthly), which publishes studies and commentaries on labour law and industrial relations and also on social protection law.

The major employers' and trade union organizations have their own journals; these include reviews on labour law, such as *Droit ouvrier and Revue pratique de droit social* (published by CGT), *Action juridique* (published by CFDT) and *Jurisprudence sociale* (published by UIMM, see above), and reviews on topical issues and thinking such as *Aujourd'hui* (published by CFDT) and *Actualité économique et sociale* (published by UIMM).

A major publishing group (Liaisons) publishes handbooks, reviews and, in particular, a daily bulletin called *Liaisons sociales* which presents up-to-date legal information, the main collective agreements, a review of the press, summaries of research and official documents, etc.

LIST OF USEFUL ADDRESSES

Agence nationale pour l'amélioration des conditions de travail (ANACT)
(National Agency for the Improvement of Working Conditions)
7, Bd Romain-Rolland
92120 Montrouge

Agence nationale pour la création d'entreprise (ANCE)
(National Enterprise Creation Agency)
142, rue du Bac
75007 Paris

Agence nationale pour l'Emploi (ANPE)
(National Employment Agency)
Le Galilée, 4 rue Galilée
93198 Noisy-le-Grand

Association pour la formation professionnelle des adultes (AFPA)
(Association for Adult Vocational Training)
88, rue Robespierre
93100 Montreuil Cedex

Centre INFFO
(Information on Training)
Tour Europe, 33 place Corolles
92049 Paris-La Défense

Confédération Française démocratique du travail (CFDT)
(French Democratic Confederation of Labour)
4, Bd de la Villette
75019 Paris

Confédération Française de l'Encadrement-Confédération Générale des Cadres
(CFE-CGC)
(French Confederation of Professional and Managerial Staff-General
Confederation of Professional and Managerial Staff)
30, rue Grammont
75002 Paris

Confédération Française des Travailleurs Chrétiens (CFTC)·
(French Christian Workers' Confederation)
13, rue des Ecluses Saint Martin
75483 Paris Cedex 10

Confédération Générale du Travail (CGT)
(General Confederation of Labour)
263, rue de Paris
93516 Montreuil

Confédération Générale du Travail-Force Ouvrière (CGT-FO)
(General Confederation of Labour-"Force ouvrière")
198, avenue du Maine
75014 Paris

Conseil National du Patronat français (CNPF)
(National Council of French Employers)
31, avenue Pierre Ier de Serbie
75784 Paris Cedex 16

Documentation française
(publisher and distributor of government publications and documentation)
29, Quai Voltaire
75007 Paris

Institut national de la statistique et des études économiques (INSEE)
(National Statistical and Economic Research Institute)
195, rue de Bercy
75012 Paris

Journal officiel
(Official Gazette)
26, rue Desaix
75727 Paris Cedex 15

Ministère du travail, de l'emploi et de la formation professionnelle
(Ministry of Labour, Employment and Vocational Training)
127, rue de Grenelle
75700 Paris
    (main departments:
    1, place de Fontenoy
    75007 Paris)

UNEDIC (Union nationale interprofessionnelle pour l'Emploi dans l'Industrie
    et le Commerce)
(National Union of Associations for Employment in Industry and Commerce)
77, rue de Miromesnil
75008 Paris

ENGLISH INDEX

References are to entry numbers. This index is to be used in conjunction with the list of main entries at the front of this volume.

preferential claim 616
Benefit
  see also **Allowance; Social Security**
  disability 461
  family 49
  guarantee supplementary 46
  means-test limit 582
  social 606
  unemployment 46
Blacklisting *see* **Boycott**
Bonus 611
  anti-strike 612
  discretionary 401
  length of service 53
Boycott 102
  see also **Industrial Action**
Branch of Economic Activity 103
  economic sector 724
  industry 444
  industry-wide agreement 7
Break 574
Business Cycle 252
Business Plan 583
  enterprise plan 627
  training plan 585

Career 113
  see also **Length of Service;**
    Promotion (at Work)
  staff appraisal 350
Casual Work 797
  fixed-term contract 215
Certificate of Employment 122
Change of Employer 132
  see also **Change of Ownership or**
    Control; Transfer of Undertaking
  through legal transfer 779
Change of Ownership or Control 124
  see also **Enterprise**
  bankruptcy 356
  change of employer 132
Charter of Amiens 136
Child Employment 330
  see also **Minor**
Civil and Political Rights
  see also **Constitution; Economic and**
    Social Rights
  freedom of association 65
  freedom of the individual 475
  right of expression 304
  right to information 306
Civil Law
  civil sanction 719
Civil Service 374
  see also **Established Civil Servant**
  Joint Technical Committee 159
Clandestine Employment 785

  see also **Undeclared Employment**
Closed Shop 148
Co-Determination 152
  see also **Employee Representation;**
    Workers' Participation
Co-Operative 238
Collective Action *see* **Industrial Action**
Collective Agreement 6, 218, 234
  see also **Collective Bargaining**
  acquired rights 90
  acquired rights clause 146
  adjustable hours agreement 54
  amendment 93
  annualization of working hours 54
  approval 40
  collectively agreed wage 766
  company-level agreement 9
  concession agreement 524
  derogation agreement 15
  erga omnes 344
  extension of 354
  favourability to the employee 358
  framework agreement 5
  freedom of labour 474
  general multi-industry agreement 18
  "give-and-take" agreement 524
  group agreement 10
  industry-wide agreement 7
  joint collective agreement committee
    166
  joint committee 163
  minute of dispute settlement 622
  National Collective Bargaining
    Commission 165
  night work 786
  no-strike clause 147
  notice of termination 273
  peace obligation 281
  profit-sharing agreement 14
  re-training agreement 235
  representativeness 680
  revision 700
  right of objection 545
  union membership (closed shop)
    clause 148
  wage 712
  "win-win" agreement 524
Collective Bargaining 523
  see also **Collective Agreement**
  articulated 522
  bargaining level 532
  bargaining procedure 619
  bargaining structure 749
  branch of economic activity 103
  breaking-off of negotiations 707
  centralization 119
  collective autonomy 81

242

243

leave for education in economic, social and union affairs 190
workers' education 316
workers' educational leave 188
Election 322
ballot 655
poll 722
vote 820
workplace-level elections 323
Electronic Identity Card 95
see also **National Commission for Information Technology and Civil Liberties**
remote surveillance 95
Employee 717
see also **Employee Liability**
Employee Communication 167
see also **Information**
Employee Liability 690
gross misconduct 357
Employee Representation 679
see also **Co-Determination; Employee Representatives**
Employee Representatives 677
see also **Employee Representation; Workplace Health and Safety Committee; Works Council**
absence from work 1
election 322
electronic identity card 95
miners' delegate 268
redeployment 643
"shop steward" 264
time-off rights 250
trade union delegate 264
union representative on the works council 678
voidance of contract (for non-performance) 687
voting 722
workforce delegate 262
workplace delegate 260
workplace-level elections 323
Employer 328
see also **Change of Employer; Employer Liability**
Employer Liability 689
agent and servant 601
delegation of authority 258
Employers' Organization 549
area 807
freedom of collective industrial organization 476
General Confederation of Small and Medium-Sized Enterprises 179
membership 28

National Council of French Employers 208
"patronat" 573
pay recommendation 645
Employment 325, 780
see also **Work**
Employment Contract see **Contract of Employment**
Employment Division see **Ministry of Labour**
Employment Policy 591
see also **Employment Support; National Employment Fund**
Employment Relationship see **Contract of Employment**
Employment Support 42
see also **Job Creation**
Employment Division 259
government aid 43
incentive 431
solidarity 741
Employment and Training Contract see **Combined Training and Work**
Employment of Women see **Female Employment**
Engineer 451
Enterprise 333
see also **Craft Trades Enterprise; Enterprise Creation; Family Enterprise; Head of an Enterprise; Ideologically Oriented Enterprise; Intermediary Enterprise; Public Enterprise; Restructuring**
business plan 583
change of employer 132
change of ownership or control 124
discipline 290
employee communication 167
employment-related costs 135
government aid 43
hierarchy 422
individualization 443
modernization 514
organization chart 548
plan 627
politics within 590
retention of civil liberties in employment 142
scheduling of working hours 423
service memorandum 537
shop-floor and departmental committee 203
social balance sheet 97
sponsorship 572
training plan 585
union presence 680

245

246

251

252

election 322
faction 389
federation 361
freedom 476
freedom of collective industrial
  organization 476
full-time official 110
group(ing) 552
immunity from seizure 452
information 168
institution of legal proceedings 24
interference 332
label 497
Labour Centre 101
law 309
legal personality 578
liability in the event of a strike 691
mark 497
meeting 696
membership 28
merger 394
organization 552
pamphlet 775
"platform" 587
pluralism 589
power 597
rank and file 96
representative on the works council
  678
repression 682
resolution (in union affairs) 688
right to organize 309
room 484
rules 748
"shop steward" 264
strike 402
structure 751
training in union affairs 386
union employee 577
unionization 755
unity 810
workers' control over investment 231
workers' education 366
workplace branch 726
Trade Union Confederation 175
see also **Trade Union**
centralism 120
executive committee 162
French Christian Workers'
  Confederation 175
French Democratic Confederation of
  Labour 175
General Confederation of Labour 175
General Confederation of Labour-
  "Force ouvrière" 175
representativeness 680
senior full-time official 289

union power 597
union unity 810
Trade Union Movement 517
see also **Trade Union**
egalitarianism 320
Trade Unionism *see* **Trade Union
Movement**
Training *see* **Combined Training and
Work; Further Vocational Training;
Vocational Training**
Transfer of Undertaking 778
see also **Company; Enterprise**
restructuring 692
Tripartism 804
concerted consultation 171

Undeclared Employment 796
see also **Clandestine Employment**
Unemployment 138
see also **Partial Unemployment**
Associations for Employment in
  Industry and Commerce 60
bad-weather unemployment insurance
  scheme 456
benefit 46
enterprise creation 249
guarantee supplementary benefit 46
guarantee supplementary scheme 46
National Union for Employment in
  Industry and Commerce 806
technological unemployment 141
**Unit of Economic and Employee
Interest** 809
employee representation 679
Unjustified Dismissal *see* **Genuine and
Serious Cause; Reinstatement**

**Variation of the Contract of
Employment** *see* **Contract of
Employment**
Vertical Union 765
see also **Trade Union**
Veto *see* **Works Council**
Vocational Guidance 553
Vocational Training
see also **Combined Training and
Work; Further Vocational
Training; Young Worker**
tax 768
trainee 746
training scheme 745
Vote *see* **Election**

Wage 712
see also **Minimum Wage
(Guaranteed); Pay**
collectively agreed wage 766

255

256

FRENCH INDEX

References are to entry numbers. This index is to be used in conjunction with the list of main entries at the front of this volume.